THE TREE OF LIFE

The Tree of Life

◆

An Exploration of
Biblical Wisdom Literature

SECOND EDITION

Roland E. Murphy, O.Carm.

William B. Eerdmans Publishing Company
Grand Rapids, Michigan / Cambridge, U.K.

First published 1990 by Doubleday
a division of Bantam Doubleday Dell
Publishing Group, Inc.
666 Fifth Avenue, New York, New York 10103

This edition published 1996
by Wm. B. Eerdmans Publishing Co.
255 Jefferson Ave. S.E., Grand Rapids, Michigan 49503

Printed in the United States of America

02 01 00 99 98 97 96   7 6 5 4 3 2 1

Library of Congress Cataloging-in-Publication Data

Murphy, Roland Edmund, 1917-
The tree of life: an exploration of biblical wisdom literature /
Roland E. Murphy. — 2nd ed.
p.   cm.
Includes bibliographical references and index.
ISBN 0-8028-4192-9 (pbk.: alk. paper)
1. Wisdom literature — Criticism, interpretation, etc.
2. Wisdom (Biblical personification).   I. Title.
BS1455.M83   1996
223'.06 — dc20   96-28479
CIP

Matri decorique Carmeli
sapientiae sedi
dedicatum

Qui me invenerit inveniet vitam
(Prov 8:35)

CONTENTS

◆

FOREWORD

♦

The "discovery" of biblical wisdom literature in the last couple of decades is in fact a rediscovery. The popularity of these books (Proverbs, Job, Ecclesiastes, Ecclesiasticus, and Wisdom of Solomon [some would include also the Song of Songs]) in the medieval period has been brilliantly researched in the studies of Jean Leclerq and Beryl Smalley. In the twelfth century more than thirty works were given over to an analysis of the Song of Songs—a faint indication of how reading tastes have fluctuated. The modern reawakening can be symbolized by the life of an outstanding German Old Testament scholar, Gerhard von Rad (1901-71). His early work broke new paths in form-critical studies, the early history of Israel, Deuteronomy, and the Deuteronomistic history. These studies were climaxed by his *Old Testament Theology* (1957-60, Eng. 1962-65), which gave his audience an inkling of the bold and attractive thoughts he was already entertaining about biblical wisdom; such thoughts eventually appeared in *Wisdom in Israel* (1970, Eng. 1972). Especially since von Rad, Israel's wisdom has become an exciting area of research.

Within the Hebrew Bible itself, the wisdom literature is exciting, because it deals directly with *life*. The sages of Israel did not share the same interest in the saving interventions of the Lord as did the Deuteronomistic historians. Their concern was the present, and how to cope with the challenges provoked by one's immediate experience. Their intensity often equalled that of the Deuteronomists (cf. Deut 4–11, esp. texts like 4:1, 6:1–9). The choice between life and death which Moses dramatically places before Israel in Deut 30:15–30 is reechoed in the sages' emphasis on *life*. The life-death situation is expressed positively in the image of "the tree of life."

Wisdom "is a tree of life to those who lay hold of her; fortunate are they who embrace her" (Prov 3:18). This image was well known from its appearance in Genesis: the first dwellers in the garden were kept from that tree lest they live forever (Gen 2:9, 3:22–24). In a vivid turn of metaphor, wisdom has become the tree of life and is personified as a woman: "Long life is in her right hand—in her left, riches and honor" (Prov 3:16). She can boast that the one who finds her finds life (Prov 8:35), and the one who fails is ultimately in love with . . . death (8:36).

It is perhaps inevitable that the patriarchs and Moses, Exodus and Sinai, David and Jeremiah are better known to modern readers than Lady Wisdom. Even within the Bible she remains an elusive and allusive figure, despite the considerable attention given to ḥokmāh, or "wisdom." She is the object of a quest in the first recorded petition for wisdom (Solomon in 1 Kgs 3) and in the last wisdom book to be written (the Wisdom of Solomon in the first century B.C.E., where Solomon is once more represented as praying for Lady Wisdom, Wis 9:1–17). The "Sayings of the Fathers," a later product of Jewish thought collected ca. 200 C.E., testifies that the quest for Lady Wisdom has continued in the Judaic tradition.

This book aims at describing the biblical quest. It is not possible to do this in any neat line of historical development. One must let the five major books speak for themselves; a chapter is devoted to each of them so that Israel's journey is clearly presented. Like ancient Israel, the modern reader is also in quest of Wisdom, and this book has been written to aid in the search. It is written for those who need an orientation to Lady Wisdom, but also for those who have already explored her paths and continue to ponder over her astounding claims. I am indebted to students and colleagues who have stimulated my teaching and research in wisdom literature over many years. The many references in the notes and bibliography demonstrate this, and I hope that they will serve also to further the personal efforts of all who call wisdom "Sister!" (Prov 7:4). I am beholden to the kind and graceful women of the Duke Divinity School secretarial pool for processing the typescript. Let their works bring them praise "at the city gates" (Prov 31:31). I am grateful also to David N. Freedman for suggesting this volume for the Anchor Bible Reference Library, and for the careful editorial scrutiny that is one of his many talents. An earlier form of the first few chapters formed the basis of the Rockwell Lectures given at Rice University in 1983.

Israel's quest extended through centuries, and ours lasts but a lifetime. Hence the Bible exposes us to more wisdom than we can truly appropriate. Moreover, Wisdom is described in so many various ways, as we shall see. She is "fear of the Lord," instruction for moral formation, human experience, the mysteries of creation, Law or Torah, a mysterious divine call, and even a spouse. These are some of the "appearances" or guises she adopts in the course of a long career. And as for the one who pursues Wisdom? The advice is twofold: One must *hear* Wisdom obediently, on the one hand. But on the other, one must pray for the gift that she is. Both application and supplication are indispensable. And even then, the embracing of Wisdom (Prov 3:18; 4:8) is precarious, because there is more hope for a fool than for those who are wise in their own eyes (Prov 26:12). And wise old Ben Sira said it all:

> The first human never finished comprehending wisdom,
> nor will the last succeed in fathoming her.

(Sir 24:28)

CHAPTER 1

INTRODUCTION

◆

THE BOOKS

It has been suggested that "wisdom literature" is something of a misnomer, at least as it is applied to the comparable literature of ancient Egypt and Mesopotamia.[1] It is true that the term seems to have been borrowed from biblical scholarship and then applied to similar literary works that were discovered in the twentieth century. But the phrase is at least appropriate for certain biblical books. The point is not simply that they frequently employ the term "wisdom" (ḥokmāh). As we shall see, much more important are the typical approach to reality and the specific literary forms that can be found in this literature, setting it off from other biblical books.

Within the Hebrew Bible, three books deserve the title "wisdom literature": Proverbs, Job, and Ecclesiastes. Among the so-called Apocrypha, two more are in the same area and have to be considered in any treatment of biblical wisdom: Ecclesiasticus (or Sirach) and the Wisdom of Solomon. In recent times scholarship has turned to the investigation of wisdom in other books. Most would agree that one can speak of a few "wisdom psalms," but there is considerable uncertainty about the degree of wisdom "influence" on the other books (see chap. 7). The aforementioned five works stand out as preeminent examples of biblical wisdom.

The most striking characteristic of this literature is the absence of what one normally considers as typically Israelite and Jewish. There is no mention of the promises to the patriarchs, the Exodus and Moses, the covenant and Sinai, the promise to David (2 Sam 7), and so forth. The exceptions to this statement, Sir 44–50 and Wis 11–19, are very late, and they only prove the rule. Wisdom does not re-present the actions of God in Israel's history; it deals with daily human experience in the good world created by God. There are hidden connections between Yahwism and wisdom. The Lord of Israel is also the God who gives wisdom to humans (Prov 2:6). We will return to this issue in chap. 8.

Despite the lack of concern for the "history of salvation," the wisdom

1

books and movement are closely associated with one of Israel's national heroes, Solomon. His wisdom is celebrated in detail in 1 Kgs 3–10, and both Proverbs and Ecclesiastes, as well as the Wisdom of Solomon (written in Greek!), are attributed to him as "author."

In 1 Kgs 3:9 Solomon is portrayed as asking the Lord for a "listening heart" that he may be able to judge the people of God and "distinguish right from wrong." He receives the gift of wisdom, and immediately the famous episode of the two harlots is narrated. The detailed description of his wisdom in 1 Kgs 5:9–14 (Eng. 4:29–34) deserves to be quoted:

> God gave Solomon wisdom and understanding beyond measure, and breadth of mind like the sand on the seashore, so that Solomon's wisdom surpassed the wisdom of all the people of the East and all the wisdom of Egypt. For he was wiser than all others: than Ethan the Ezrahite and Heman, Chalcol and Darda, the sons of Mahol; his fame was in all the surrounding nations. He also spoke three thousand proverbs and his songs were a thousand and five. He spoke of trees, from the cedar in Lebanon to the hyssop that grows out of the wall; he spoke also of beasts and birds, reptiles and fish. Men came from all peoples to hear the wisdom of Solomon, and from all the kings of the earth who had heard of his wisdom.

It is noteworthy that his wisdom is compared with that of Egypt, whose reputation for wisdom was well known in the ancient Near East (see the reaction of the prince of Byblos to Wen-Amon, 2:20ff., *ANET*, 27). "People of the East" seems to be a vague reference to the tribes in the Syro-Arabian Desert (cf. Job 1:3) and to their clan wisdom; it can hardly refer to Mesopotamia, although considerable wisdom writings have been found there (see Appendix). We know nothing about the four specific characters who are mentioned. There is reference not to Solomon's writing, but to his "speaking" proverbs. And the royal concern is not human conduct, but "nature" wisdom, such as one finds in Job 38–41 or in Prov 31. The story of the queen of Sheba (1 Kgs 10:1ff.) exemplifies the worldwide reputation indicated in v 14.

It is doubtless this reputation of Solomon that is behind the ascription of three wisdom books to him. Today no serious scholar accepts Solomonic authorship for these works or for the Song of Songs (known also as the Song of Solomon, or the Canticle). But the tradition exercised a fascinating grip on readers of the past. Beryl Smalley has summarized the Christian tradition from Origen and Jerome to the medieval period: "Solomon wrote his three books, Proverbs, Ecclesiastes and the Canticle, in order to instruct mankind in the three stages of the spiritual life. Proverbs taught men how to live virtuously in the world and was meant for beginners. Ecclesiastes taught them to despise the things of the world as vain and fleeting and was meant for *proficientes* [those who were making progress]. The Canticle told initiates of the love of God. These three grades, it was held, had their parallel in the schools of philosophy, where the student began with ethics, went on to physics and thence to logic."[2]

THE SAGES—WHO WERE THEY?

We can answer this question only in a limited way.[3] We know that Qoheleth was a sage, for in Eccl 12:9 he is called a *ḥākām*, who "taught the people knowledge, and weighed, scrutinized and arranged many proverbs [*mĕšālîm*]." But the precise circumstances of his activity are unknown to us. Ben Sira invited his readers who needed instruction to come to his "school" or "teaching" (*bêt midrāš*, Sir 51:23), and he singled out the profession of the scribe (*sōpēr*) as excelling all others (38:24–39:11; "the scribe's profession increases wisdom," 38:24). By this time, ca. 180 B.C.E., the activity of the sage was concentrated particularly on the study of the Law (Sir 39:1). We know nothing about the author of the Wisdom of Solomon.

The author of Job is likewise an unknown figure, but the portraits that he has drawn of Eliphaz, Bildad, and Zophar are portraits of wise men. They are steeped in wisdom lore, as their "lectures" to Job make clear. In the Book of Proverbs "the sayings of the wise" is a clear title in 24:23 and probably in 22:17. The use of the term "the wise" (see also 1:6) suggests that they constitute a professional class, but they are left undefined. The "words" in 30:1–4 are credited to a certain Agur, who is otherwise unknown. "The words of Lemuel" (31:1–9) are described as the teaching that the king received from the queen mother. Thus, the explicit data provided by wisdom books provides relatively little information about the sages. We can only say that they are associated with royalty and with teaching.

However, several references to father and mother suggest that certain wisdom lore was communicated in the family: Prov 10:1; 15:20; 20:20; 23:22, 25; 30:11, 17. The teaching of parents, even if they are not described as official "sages," is clearly part of the wisdom program. This is vividly portrayed in the appeal to hear a father's *mûsar* (discipline) and *tôrâ* (teaching) in Prov 4:5. Another indication of the role of the parent is the frequent address "my son," in Prov 1:8, 10, 15; 2:1; 3:1, 11, 21; 4:10, 20; 5:1, 20; 6:1, 3, 20; 7:1; 19:27; 23:19, 26; 24:13, 21; 27:11. It is true that "son" can be understood in the metaphorical sense to indicate a teacher-pupil relationship. Even if this may explain the frequent appearance in Prov 1–9, it stands to reason that parents would have played a role in the training of their children.

3

The home may be regarded as perhaps the original site of wisdom teaching, before and after such teaching became professionalized among the sages.

This opens up the perspective of the oral or preliterary stage of the wisdom writings, before they ever received literary form and permanency. It is obviously impossible today to recover any evidence of this stage in ancient Israel, but analogies with modern "primitive" societies make this oral stage plausible.[4] Before the rise of complicated social stratification, the wisdom of a family or tribe—a certain ethos—would have been formed, based upon the house, the farm, and the town. The values of the group would receive expression governing work, speech, and the basics of daily life. Here the contrasts between poor and rich, lazy and diligent, appearance and reality would have been noted, and they would have entered into the basic formation of the individuals in the society. It is reasonable to think that what later became "wisdom" and "law" was at first an undifferentiated mass of commands, prohibitions, and observations concerning life. At this level there is a preurban and preschool stage of instruction where the family and tribe are at the center of society. Only later did instruction become differentiated into the scholastic and legal areas.[5] Indeed, the Decalogue itself is a reflection of the ethos of early Israel.

The implication of all this is that the origins of wisdom thought are to be sought in the family and tribe rather than in any kind of school associated with court and temple. This does not deny the likely role of trained scribes (such as the "men of Hezekiah," Prov 25:1) in the transmission and the formation of the wisdom sayings. But the sayings are not the creation of a study desk; they grew out of human situations and needs. Skill in literary expression is not to be found only with the formally educated. Centuries before Israel existed, Ptah-hotep the Egyptian sage wrote, "Good speech is more hidden than the emerald, but it may be found with maidservants at the grindstones" (*ANET*, 412). One may well admit that further refinement in speech was cultivated in various circles of Israelite society, but no argument can be based on the content of the sayings, as though aphorisms about the king and courtiers would necessarily have arisen in a court school. As one saying puts it, "A cat may look at a king."[6] One may not simply transfer the known setting of the Egyptian wisdom literature—that is, scribal schools of the court—to Israel.

It will be recalled that Solomon asked for "wisdom" that he might be a successful ruler of God's people (1 Kgs 3:6–14). Associated with royal wisdom are the counselors (*yôʿeṣîm*) who are to provide *ʿeṣâ* or "advice" to the ruler.[7] Thus Ahitophel, David's counselor, gave advice to Absalom, and it was regarded practically as a divine oracle (2 Sam 16:20–23), although Absalom rejected his advice. Similarly, Rehoboam takes counsel with advisers (1 Kgs 12:6). In a famous passage, counsel is associated with the wise (*ḥākām*), just as the word belongs to the prophet and Torah to the priest (Jer 18:18). In Jer

8:8 the "wise" seem to be identified as scribes (sōpĕrîm). In the context of the royal court, the counseling role of the sage is clearly indicated. Whether or not he was also engaged as an educator of a sort (training future courtiers, scribes, etc.) is not clear but is plausible.

The mention of education raises another problem.[8] What was the nature of educational institutions in Israel? There is no firsthand evidence of the existence of schools in ancient Israel. On the analogy of the various schools that are known to have existed in Egypt and Mesopotamia, it is logical to infer that there must have been similar institutions in Israel.[9] With Israel's ascendancy during the Davidic and Solomonic periods, some kind of training would have been necessary to support the bureaucratic government system (see the list of officials in 2 Sam 8:15–18; 20:23–26; 1 Kgs 4:1–6). The role of the "men of Hezekiah" in Prov 25:1 suggests the existence of a court school. The clear influence of Egyptian wisdom (Amenemope; see the Appendix) in Prov 22:17–24:22 and elsewhere is construed as another link in the Egyptian connection that would have involved scribal training. These considerations, certainly suggestive and advanced by many scholars, remain hypothetical. By and large, there is only modest royal coloring in the Book of Proverbs. This clearly does not reflect the relatively narrow class ethic of its Egyptian counterparts. The picture is certainly more complex than a court school; if such a school did exist, how did it compare with the education and training in the home by parents, or within the tribe by the elders? After the exile, was there a temple school to replace the court school, if such existed? One need recall here the sparse and vague indications about Qoheleth and Ben Sira mentioned earlier. There is reason to think that the Pentateuch in its final form issued from the postexilic community; was there a school for this?

If we shift the question from "schools" to training, perhaps we are on more secure ground. Obviously training for chancellery work is different from training for liturgical service, such as the Levites received. The ambiguous term "scribe" (sōpēr) could have served to designate the writer of various genres: legal, liturgical, political, literary (in the sense of Qoheleth and Ben Sira), and the official transcription of the documents that became the Law the Prophets, and the Writings. At least we can describe these literary activities, although we do not know the precise institutions that nourished them.

THE LANGUAGE
AND LITERARY FORMS

It has been said that a proverb in a collection is dead.[10] Those who read for the first time the various collections of sayings in the Book of Proverbs might firmly agree. After a while the sayings seem to blend together; the wise/

virtuous prevail over fools/wicked. Even what seemed to be perceptive at first becomes dull and trite because of repetition. However, the proverbs are far from dead, if they are read with alertness and awareness of their literary power and forms. Robert Alter was correct in entitling his chapter on Proverbs "the poetry of wit."[11] Some basic observations about wisdom sayings and forms can make the Book of Proverbs come alive.

Parallelism

Parallelism is a well-known phenomenon in the Bible and indeed throughout many literatures.[12] It refers to the grouping of lines or half lines in such a way that the full thought of the writer is presented. There are various degrees of association between the two (sometimes three) units. Even when the lines seem to repeat one another (often termed synonymous parallelism), they are not quite synonymous. The relationship can be one of intensification or sharper focusing. Thus, if A, then more so B. "He who finds a wife finds good and he obtains the favor of the Lord" (Prov 18:22). In the case of antithetic parallelism, a certain opposition is evident, even though the same general idea is expressed:

> One who fills granaries in the summer—a wise son;
> one who sleeps during the harvest—a shameful son. (Prov 10:5)

Sometimes the second line goes on to complete the first: "Entrust your works to the Lord/and your plans will succeed" (Prov 16:3). Some combinations are so frequent that they are called "word-pairs," such as "wise/fool," or "mouth/tongue."

Paronomasia

It is almost impossible to bring out this characteristic in a receptor language. But in the Hebrew the plays on words and sounds are unmistakable. Eccl 7:1, "A good name is better than good oil," does not do justice to the original, *ṭôb šēm miššemen ṭôb*, which is marked by alliteration, assonance, and chiasm in a taut line of four words. Neither does "When pride comes, disgrace comes" equal the original *bāʾ zādôn wayyābōʾ qālôn* (Prov 11:2).

The sages had a flair for literary art. When they wrote about "pleasing speech" (Prov 16:21), and "pleasant words" (16:24; cf. Eccl 12:10), they had in mind an aesthetic of words, not a content that would suit the pleasure of all. This seems to be the meaning of the obscure verse in Prov 25:11, "Like golden apples in silver showpieces is a phrase well turned" (*NJV*; literally, a phrase "on its [two?] wheels"). Timing was another important feature: "A joy to a man is the response of his mouth/and a word at the right time, how good it is!" (Prov 15:23).

The importance of paronomasia in the English language is equally obvious. Thus, one says "Look before you leap" (notice the *l*, *p*), not "before you jump." "He who hesitates is lost" (note the *h*, *s*, *t* repetitions) would suffer if the ending were "will lose."

Another characteristic that is lost in translation is the Hebrew style of juxtaposition. Thus, Prov 15:32 consists of the juxtaposition of participial phrases:

Spurner of discipline—despiser of his soul
and hearer of reproof—acquirer of heart.

The sharpness of this classification is lost when a copula or other verb is inserted in English translation; one fails to capture the (analogous, but not identical) associations between objects and phenomena.

Forms

Oddly enough, the Hebrew *māšāl*, commonly translated as "proverb," is far too general in meaning to provide much insight into the wisdom proverbs. Even the etymology is disputed; it can be associated with a root meaning "rule" (the power of the word?) and also with the idea of "comparison." But the term is used far too widely in the Bible (e.g., the poem in Isa 14:4–20) to be serviceable as a literary term. Of course, the English word "proverb" is not itself very helpful; everyone despairs of giving a definition of it. In the words of Archer Taylor, "The definition of a proverb is too difficult to repay the undertaking. . . . An incommunicable quality tells us this sentence is proverbial and that one is not. . . . Let us be content with recognizing that a proverb is a saying current among the folk."[13] His last statement is particularly apt. For a saying to be a proverb, it has to gain currency among the people. The people are not properly the author, although they may have played a role in the formation of the saying. It is not helpful to pursue distinctions between proverb, maxim, and aphorism; no unity can be obtained.

The two most frequent literary genres in wisdom literature are the saying and the admonition.[14] The saying is a sentence usually expressed in the indicative mood and based upon experience. It can be found in one line, but more commonly in two parallel lines. There are a few traditional sayings preserved in ancient Israel (1 Kgs 20:11, "Let not him that girds on his armor boast as he that puts it off"). In the wisdom books, the saying is usually couched in two-line parallelism. While all the wisdom sayings are supposedly the fruit of experience and traditional observation, it is helpful to distinguish between those that are almost purely observational or experiential and those that are openly didactic. The experiential saying does not counsel one how to act. It tells the reader "the way it is," and is thus open-ended and subject to verification. Thus,

> Hope deferred makes the heart sick
> but a wish fulfilled is a tree of life. (Prov 13:12)

This is a psychological observation. It does not attempt to teach a lesson or make a judgment about life-style. It informs the reader about reality. Any use or application of this statement is a second move. Of course, the context of the Book of Proverbs, where such observations are mixed in with overtly didactic sayings, opens up the applicability of even the most neutral observations to moral formation.

The didactic saying is not open-ended; it aims to promote a given ideal or value, a course of action. The intensity with which the lesson is inculcated may vary. It can be conveyed simply by indicating a relationship with God:

> The one who oppresses the poor insults his Maker,
> but one who is kind to the needy honors him. (Prov 14:3)

Or a value judgment, based on the common standard of righteousness or wickedness, is pronounced: "The just one will never be disturbed, but the wicked will not dwell in the land" (Prov 10:30). There is no choice left for the reader, since it is presumed that one would not follow the path of wickedness. Wisdom is practical above all, urging proper moral (wise/righteous) conduct.

The second general form is the admonition, which can be either positive or negative. The positive admonition, or command, is usually in the form of an imperative or some volitive mood, as when the student is urged to trust in the Lord in order that his plans may succeed (Prov 16:3). It is worth noting that a direct command can make explicit what is made only indirectly in a didactic saying; thus Prov 16:3 and 16:20. The negative admonition, or prohibition, can be expressed with varying degrees of emphasis, and often motive clauses are added:

> Do not rob the poor because they are poor,
> nor crush the needy at the gate;
> For the Lord will defend their cause,
> and will plunder the lives of those who plunder them.
> (Prov 22:22–23)

Within these two literary genres of saying and admonition there is a range of expressions that should be noted:[15]

1. The "good" saying. In fact, this is used more often in the phrase "not good." Thus, "Without knowledge, zeal is not good" (Prov 19:2).

2. The "better" saying. Qoheleth writes, "It is better to listen to the wise man's rebuke/ than to listen to the song of fools" (Eccl 7:5). This form can be built up into a binary opposition: "Better a little with fear of the Lord/than great wealth with anxiety" (Prov 15:16).

3. The numerical saying.[16] This consists of a title line with number, and a list of items. The line mentions the features that the items listed have in common (Prov 30:24, four things small but wise). Although two is a common number, three and seven are frequently mentioned in the title line; the pattern is *x* and *x* plus 1 (e.g., three and four). There is a cluster of these sayings in Prov 30.

4. The "abomination" saying. The term "abomination" (*tô'ēbâ*) suggests liturgical language, and it is used in Proverbs to designate wickedness and perversity as "abominations" to the Lord. Three times it is also used to describe sharp business practice:

False scales are an abomination to the Lord,
   but a full weight is his delight. (Prov 11:1; cf. 20:10, 23)

5. The "blessed" saying. This is the formula preserved in the New Testament beatitudes as "Blessed is the one [or, "Happy the one"] who . . .":

Happy the one who is always on guard;
   but the one who hardens his heart will fall into evil.
   (Prov 28:14)

6. The *a fortiori* saying. A conclusion is drawn on the basis of an assertion that is accepted by all:

The nether world and the abyss lie open before the Lord,
   but much more the hearts of men! (Prov 15:11)

9

Honored in poverty, how much more so in wealth!

Dishonored in wealth, in poverty how much the more!

(Sir 10:30)

A third general form may be called the wisdom poem, for lack of a better term. It is a consecutive piece of poetry, not simply a few lines; but sayings and admonitions (cf. Job 6:5–6; Prov 3:19) can appear within these poems. They are exemplified particularly in Prov 1–9, in the speeches in Job, and also throughout Sirach and the Wisdom of Solomon. They partake of the nature of "Instruction," of which we have many examples from Egypt (see Appendix). They also show a tendency toward alphabetizing. Thus Prov 2:1–22 has twenty-two lines corresponding to the number of letters of the Hebrew alphabet. This alphabetizing practice is related to the acrostic pattern, in which each unit or half unit begins with the next successive letter of the Hebrew alphabet (Prov 30:1–31; Ps 34). Ps 34, a wisdom psalm, illustrates the manner in which the sages played with the alphabet.[17] It consists of twenty-two verses, the number of letters in the Hebrew alphabet. These are in strict acrostic sequence, except that the *waw* verse is (deliberately?) omitted and a *pe* verse is added after the *taw* (or final) verse. The result is that the consonants beginning the first, middle, and end verses spell out *ʾlp*, the first letter of the alphabet, and also a verb meaning "to learn," or "to teach" *(Piʿel)*. The middle *lamed* verse (v 12) emphasizes *lmd*, which is also a verb "to teach." One may compare Ps 33, a nonalphabetic acrostic, but with twenty-two lines.

The Book of Job contains several genres, some taken from legal processes and others from wisdom. The general tone of lament (Job 3) is present, but the main type is the disputation speech that marks the dialogue between Job and the three friends (chaps. 4–26).[18]

Although Qoheleth makes use of the saying and admonition, the most characteristic form is what may be termed "reflection."[19] In such passages as 2:12–17 and 2:18–26, Qoheleth proposes as points for reflection the topics of the value of wisdom and the value of toil. The development of thought is rather loose, but there is frequent reference to his personal observations and insights.

Before the discussion of the literary forms preferred by the sages is terminated, attention should be paid to the truth claim of a saying. Because a proverb gains currency among a broad group, there is a tendency to overestimate its power. But in fact a proverb presents only a narrow slice of reality; much depends upon its context. An example can be found in sayings current in our own culture, which were mentioned earlier. On the one hand, "Look before you leap." On the other hand, "He who hesitates is lost." These sayings go in opposite directions, even if each retains its truth. They are not to be pitted against each other. What is needed is the proper context in which they are pertinent. This relationship to context is called "proverb performance."[20] The proverb "performs" when it is in line with the context from which it arises. The saying is not an absolute; it is relative. Moreover, a shift of context can provide another level of meaning: "Look before you leap" has specific nuances when it is directed to one about to engage in the stock market.

Hence, one must pay close attention to the comparisons and analogies that abound in the wisdom writings. "As the crucible tests silver and the furnace gold, so one is tested by the praise he receives" (Prov 27:21). "The north wind brings rain, and a backbiting tongue an angry face" (Prov 25:23). These sayings are generalizations. The north wind usually brings rain; the hot fire of the kiln will doubtless purify precious metals. In the sphere of human conduct there is a correspondingly specific result to backbiting, or to the effect of praise upon an individual. But the possibility of exception is always present in any generalization. The comparison points to similarity, not identity.

If one fails to attend to limitations that are intrinsic to a saying, an injustice is done to the sages. They were sensitive to the ambiguities in human affairs. Silence was an ideal for them when it proceeded from a person who was careful in speech, but not when it was a sign of stupidity (Prov 17:27-28). The ambiguity of poverty is particularly clear. The warnings against laziness often carry the threat of poverty (6:6-11; 10:4; 28:19), but there was also the awareness that poverty might not be the result of laziness (10:22; 12:9; 15:19).

The sages, then, were aware of the uncertainties that experience and observation yielded. There were limits built into the human situation that they attempted to analyze. But there was another limit situation, far more profound: the mystery of God.

> There is no wisdom, no understanding,
>> no counsel, against the Lord.
> The horse is equipped for the day of battle,
>> but victory comes from the Lord. (Prov 21:30-31)

The Lord was the completely unpredictable factor. This view, of course, was not peculiar to the sages. The laments of the psalmists and the "confessions" of Jeremiah are evidence of Israel's long-standing "why?" and dialogue with the Almighty. True wisdom never lost sight of its own limitations:

> In his mind one plans the way,
>> but the Lord directs the steps. (Prov 16:9)

> One's steps are from the Lord;
>   how, then, can one understand his way? (Prov 20:24)

Human conduct ("steps") cannot escape the control of the Lord. Despite the thoughts and care given to a course of action, there is always an unknown, the role of God. God alone knows how things will turn out; he has the last word. The ultimate mystery is the Lord's own mysterious activity, as Qoheleth emphasized very clearly in his teachings about the "work of God" (Eccl 7:13; 8:17; 11:5).

This sense of limitation is a warning that the proverbs are not to be interpreted in a dogmatic fashion. The temptation to inflexibility is clearly exemplified by the three friends of Job, who read Job's affliction as a pointer to his sinfulness. Individual sages were critical of the tradition (Qoheleth); others turned up new insights that sprang from the wisdom that had been handed down. Collections of sayings as found in Proverbs and Sirach are quite deliberately conceived and presented as teachings to be understood and obeyed. Despite the limit areas that the sages failed to penetrate, there was a large field of practical conduct that could be transmitted. Moreover, the sages of Israel were teachers, not searchers. We must not romanticize about them as if they were Greek philosophers. They were tradents—that is, those handing down the wisdom of the past, which had been verified by age and experience. Even the author of Job respected this emphasis. The three friends give strenuous lectures according to approved wisdom teaching. Bildad appeals to the teaching of "former generations," "the experience of the fathers" (8:8). Zophar appeals to a belief "from time immemorial" that the triumph of the wicked must be brief (20:4). Whoever the coiner of an original proverb might have been, his saying, not his name, was deemed worthy of retention, because it constituted a tried and true observation. Eliphaz credits a particular revelation that he received (Job 5:12–16), but he declares that his message is what wise men have received from their fathers (15:18).

The sages were more subtle than their collected sayings testify.[21] Wisdom itself is fragile, vulnerable. As Qoheleth pointed out, "More weighty than wisdom or wealth is a little folly!" (Eccl 10:1). Wisdom even carries danger with it. The one who is dedicated to the pursuit of wisdom can too easily deem oneself truly wise. The sages warned how perilous the pursuit of wisdom is:

> You see one who is wise in his own eyes?
>   There is more hope for a fool than for him. (Prov 26:12)

What a tenuous grasp one has on wisdom! The indefatigable pursuit of wisdom may result in losing it; one must beware of thinking one has attained it. The reason for this is not merely human weakness and the uncertainty of human judgment, but the Lord. In the last resort, the mystery of divine wisdom confronted Israel. Hence one is warned to trust in the Lord: "Trust in the Lord with all your heart; on your own intelligence rely not" (Prov 3:5; cf. 3:7; Sir 2:6–10). This caution against self-glorification is shared by the prophetic tradition as well (Jer 9:23–24).

NOTES TO INTRODUCTION

1. *BWL*, 1.

2. Cf. Roland E. Murphy (ed.), *Medieval Exegesis of Wisdom Literature: Essays by Beryl Smalley* (Atlanta: Scholars Press, 1986) 40–41.

3. For details, see J. G. Gammie and L. Perdue (eds.), *The Sage in Israel and the Ancient Near East* (Winona Lake: Eisenbrauns, 1990).

4. See the interesting observations of C. Westermann, "Weisheit im Sprichwort," in *Schalom: Studien zu Glaube und Geschichte Israels* (A. Jepsen Festschrift; ed. K.-H. Bernardt; Stuttgart: Calwer, 1971) 73–85; F. W. Golka, "Die Königs- und Hofsprüche und der Ursprung der israelitischen Weisheit," *VT* 36 (1986) 13–36.

5. This obvious inference was strengthened by the arguments of J.-P. Audet, "Origines comparées de la double tradition de la loi et de la sagesse dans la proche-orient ancien," *Acts of the International Orientalists' Congress* (Moscow, 1960) I, 352–57; see also Guy Couturier, "La vie familiale comme source de la sagesse et de la loi," *Science et Esprit* 32 (1980) 177–92.

6. Quoted in Carole R. Fontaine, *Traditional Sayings in the Old Testament* (BLS 5; Sheffield: Almond Press, 1982) 270.

7. See P. de Boer, "The Counsellor," in *Wisdom in Israel and in the Ancient Near East* (VTSup 3; H. H. Rowley Festschrift; ed. M. Noth and D. Thomas; Leiden: Brill, 1955) 42–71.

8. The differences of opinion on this topic only continue to mount. The bottom line is the nature of the evidence for the existence of schools in Israel; it remains inferential only. For a summary point of view, with complete bibliography (especially the debate between A. Lemaire and F. W. Golka), see J. L. Crenshaw, "Education in Ancient Israel," *JBL* 104 (1985) 601–15.

9. See, for example, H.-J. Hermisson, *Studien zur israelitischen Spruchweisheit* (WMANT 28; Neukirchen-Vluyn: Neukirchener, 1968) 113–36; B. Lang, *Die weisheitliche Lehrrede* (SBS 54; Stuttgart: KBW, 1972) 36ff.

10. W. Mieder, quoted in Fontaine, *Traditional Sayings*, 54.

11. Cf. Robert Alter, *The Art of Biblical Poetry* (New York: Basic Books, 1985) 163–84.

12. The basic study now is James L. Kugel, *The Idea of Biblical Poetry* (New Haven: Yale University, 1981).

13. Archer Taylor, *The Proverb and an Index to the Proverb* (2nd ed.; Copenhagen and Hatboro: Rosenkilde & Baggers, 1962) 3.

14. Cf. Roland E. Murphy, *Wisdom Literature* (FOTL 13; Grand Rapids: Eerdmans, 1981) 4–6.

15. On the following observations see Murphy, *Wisdom Literature*, 65–67.

16. See W. Roth, *Numerical Sayings in the Old Testament* (VTSup 13; Leiden: Brill, 1965).

17. Cf. A. Ceresko, "The ABCs of Wisdom in Psalm XXXIV," *VT* 35 (1985) 99–104.

18. Contra the idea of the "dramatization of a lament" favored by C. Westermann, *Der Aufbau des Buches Hiob* (CTM 6; 2nd ed.; Stuttgart: Calwer, 1977) 27–39.

19. Cf. Murphy, *Wisdom Literature*, 130 and 181.

20. Cf. Fontaine, *Traditional Sayings*, esp. 57–60.

21. This is confirmed by the study of Elizabeth Huwiler, "Control of Reality in Israelite Wisdom" (Duke University dissertation, 1988, forthcoming in a JSOT series), and see the discussion in chap. 8.

CHAPTER 2

PROVERBS—THE WISDOM OF WORDS

◆

It is too facile, although quite traditional, to characterize the Book of Proverbs as a compendium of ethics, of Israelite morality. This view is strengthened by the optimistic note that sounds frequently in the work: wisdom (justice) prospers, while folly (wickedness) self-destructs. As a result, the book has been very popular in Western culture, both for the picturesque language and for the timely truths it is seen to convey. It is quoted freely, and many times not exactly, and it has received greater authority than many another book of Holy Writ. But the true subtlety of the book is seldom recognized in its popular usage. A moral code undergirds it, but the real intent is to train a person, to form character, to show what life is really like and how best to cope with it. The favored approach is to seek out comparisons or analogies between the human situation and all else (animals and the rest of creation). It does not command so much as it seeks to persuade, to tease the reader into a way of life (although it must be admitted that chaps. 1–9 are much more dogmatic in style than the rest of the work).

Perhaps no other book of the Bible is as neatly laid out as this one. It has titles that mark off the main parts: 1:1, "the proverbs of Solomon" (this serves as a title to the entire thirty-one chapters, as well as to chaps. 1–9); 10:1, "the proverbs of Solomon" (but chaps. 10–22 are quite different in style from chaps. 1–9); 22:17, "the sayings of the wise" (an emended text; see later); 24:23, "these also [belong] to the wise"; 25:1, "the proverbs of Solomon" (the work of the men of King Hezekiah); 30:1, "the words of Agur"; 31:1, "the words of Lemuel"; 31:10–31, there is no title, but this is the acrostic poem about the ideal wife.

It is almost impossible to treat of this book without writing a commentary. Since that is out of the question here, it seems best to convey the sense of the various collections that comprise the work.

THE VISION OF PROV 1–9

The majestic introduction to the book (1:1–6) sweeps the reader up into the goal of wisdom instruction. The hermeneutical key to the entire work is given; all that follows is to provide guidance (or "steering," *taḥbulôt*, 1:5) and training in virtue (1:3). Obviously, the writer of these lines did not distinguish between the secular and the religious in the way we do. All the so-called "secular" advice that is given in the course of the thirty-one chapters belongs to training in a wisdom that is essentially religious. The vocabulary in 1:1–6 is overwhelming: learning, understanding, righteousness, discernment, knowledge, and so forth. All combine to spell out the riches of wisdom. These are not abstract, merely intellectual characteristics; they are tied to the practical aspects of human conduct.

Verse 7, about the fear of the Lord as the beginning of knowledge, serves as a motto after the introductory sentence (vv 1–6). The positioning of this verse (echoed in 9:10; 15:33; Job 28:28; Ps 111:10) is important. It is the seventh verse, following upon the introduction, and it is repeated in 9:10, at the end of the first collection. Fear of the Lord also appears in 31:30, as a kind of inclusion to the book. The notion itself is used frequently in the Bible with various nuances (awe before the divinity, worship, observance of the Law).[1] It is the equivalent of biblical religion and piety, and in the context of Proverbs, of proper moral behavior. For Gerhard von Rad this verse "contains in a nutshell the whole Israelite theory of knowledge."[2] It is surely remarkable that a commitment to God lies at the basis of the wisdom enterprise.

In the context of this book, "my son" (v 8) is the reader who is willing to follow the discipline of wisdom. The parental instruction (father *and* mother) would then be metaphorical for the wisdom teachers. If the father's advice is understood to be vv 8–19, it is a warning against being seduced by the proposals of sinners. Perhaps the mother's advice can be seen in the striking speech of Lady Wisdom in vv 20–33.[3] She speaks publicly and vehemently like a biblical prophet threatening with doom and destruction those who reject her message.[4] Two ways are laid out for the reader to choose—the way of the foolish and obedience to Wisdom (vv 32–33).

Chapter 2 is an astonishing literary composition.[5] In Hebrew it is one long sentence: an alphabetizing poem, in twenty-two lines according to the letters of the Hebrew alphabet. The first three strophes (vv 1–4, 5–8, 9–11) begin with the first letter, *'aleph,* and contain an "if-then" message. The strophes in part two (vv 12–15, 16–19, 20–22) all begin with *lamed,* the middle letter of the alphabet, and they stress how Wisdom "saves" (vv 12,

16

16) those who follow her. A program is announced that will be followed rather closely in the ensuing chapters. Fear of the Lord, knowledge of God, and wisdom are inseparably twined (vv 5–6). Even though wisdom is something to be pursued by individual effort, it is essentially a gift from God (2:6) —one of the many paradoxes in this book. The contrast between the good and the bad (vv 20–22) is reminiscent of Ps 1.

Chapter 3 begins with six admonitions accompanied by motivating clauses (vv 1–12). Typical wisdom concerns are touched upon: the need to "hear," the promise of "life," and a "trust in the Lord" that will eliminate the danger of being "wise in one's own eyes" (cf. 26:12). Finally, in a daring move the teacher anticipates an objection (vv 11–12; cf. Heb 12:5–6): if the promise of a full and prosperous life is not realized, one should consider it, paradoxically, as a sign of divine favor, for the Lord disciplines those who are the objects of divine love.

Verses 13–18 are held together by an inclusion, the repetition of "happy" (an ʾašrê saying, or beatitude). Traditional symbolism is employed in a eulogy of wisdom as precious beyond gold and silver, granting life and peace, indeed a "tree of life" (cf. 11:30). The recognition of the role of wisdom in the creative activity of the Lord is introduced rather suddenly (v 19), although it is a common theme (Ps 104:24; 147:5; Prov 8:22–31). A very simple picture is drawn: no one builds a house without wisdom (Prov 24:3–4); so also wisdom was at work in the making of creation, especially in the production of water so beneficent to the inhabitants of Palestine (v 20). The chapter ends as it began, with a series of admonitions in vv 25ff.

Chapter 4 contains a touching description of the teacher's reminiscence of parental training (vv 1–5). The teacher continues with an intensity (cf. also 7:1–4) that reminds one of the Deuteronomic preaching: get wisdom! The metaphor of diadem and crown recalls 1:9 and 3:3. "Way" and "life" are catchwords that form an inclusion for vv 10–27; the way of wisdom is the path of the just (v 18), which leads to life; the way of the wicked (v 14) is not to be entered. The two "ways" develop 1:32–33.[6]

The theme of 2:16, the "strange woman," is taken up in chaps. 5–7. The emphasis is puzzling. Granted that sexual conduct is a legitimate topic for wisdom teaching (22:14; 23:27–28), why is the treatment so detailed?[7] Perhaps it has something to do with the Lady Wisdom–Dame Folly antithesis (explicitly developed in chap. 9). The counterpart to the pursuit of Wisdom as woman is the seduction by Folly as woman. The use of sexual imagery in the Bible to express fidelity or infidelity to God is well known (Hosea). And Israel's unhappy history of "whoring" after other gods, the Baals and Asherahs, is attested to many times. It has been suggested that the "stranger" is a devotee of the Canaanite fertility cult that seduced so many Israelites.[8] This identification is hard to establish. The woman may simply be another Israelite, and the warning is strictly one of marital fidelity. At the same time, there

17

may be another level of meaning here, suggesting religious fidelity and pursuit of fear of the Lord. The figure of Lady Wisdom seems to have provided the model for the figure of Dame Folly (9:13–18). In any case it should be noted that the advice is one-sided. The young man is warned against enticement by the woman, but his own responsibility is not mentioned; he is never instructed about his own sexual desires or about enslavement to his sexual passion.

The warning in 5:1–14 is quite straightforward: the feet of the "stranger" lead to Death/Sheol (v 5), and only recrimination awaits the unfortunate man (vv 12–14). The youth is given positive recommendation to be faithful to his wife ("Drink water from your own cistern," v 15), whose love will be a source of life to him (vv 18–19). The theme of adultery is interrupted in 6:1–19 by advice concerning several topics: becoming surety for one's neighbor, diligence, a judgment on the evildoer. There is a numerical saying about things that are an abomination to the Lord (vv 1–5, 7–11, 12–14, 16–19). But the urgent warning against the smooth-talking adulteress is picked up again in 6:20–35. The youth is confronted with the negative results he can expect: "impossible questions" in vv 27–28, and the folly of adultery that ends up with physical beating (vv 32–35).

The sage's description of the seduction of a young man is vividly related in chap. 7. The smooth-talking lady speaks at length in vv 14–20. A striking feature about the scene is the emphasis upon speech, almost as if the seduction were verbal ("smooth-talking," 7:5; 6:24), not sexual. The power of the word to persuade, even to seduce, is highlighted as much as sexual indulgence itself.[9]

In chaps. 8–9 the author returns to the explicit personification of Wisdom as a woman (cf. 1:20–33). The structure of chap. 8 has been variously interpreted, but the general meaning is clear.[10] Wisdom is introduced, prophetlike and calling for an audience. She emphasizes the truth of her message, her royal connections ("By me kings reign"), and the wealth and honor she brings to those who love her. Then in a remarkable passage (vv 22–31) she describes her divine origin as the very first act of God's creation. She was present not only to God (as an "artisan," or "darling," v 30) but also to human beings in whom she delighted. Her speech ends with another appeal for attention ("listen" occurs three times in vv 32–34), and with the astounding promise of life as opposed to death (vv 35–36). The significance of Prov 8 is explained later in the treatment of the personification of Wisdom (chap. 9). Lady Wisdom is matched by Dame Folly in Prov 9 (where the sayings in vv 7–12 separate these two figures). Both issue an invitation to a meal that is characterized by life (for Wisdom, v 6) and by death (for Folly, whose guests end up in Sheol, v 18).

It will be easily recognized that chaps. 1–9 stand out from the rest of the book in regard to both form (long poems) and content (exhortatory tone, strong emphasis on moral right and wrong). Except for the few sayings (such as in chap. 3 and 6:1–19), the concern of these chapters is to persuade the reader to the path of wisdom/justice.

Because this section is noticeably different from the following chapters, various hypotheses have arisen concerning the setting and date of this material. Although these efforts have ended in a disappointing uncertainty, they have the value of stimulating the reader's imagination. Two views may be presented as typical. Bernhard Lang[11] begins with a dominant presupposition: the influence of Egyptian wisdom literature (see Appendix). Prov 1–9 consists of ten wisdom speeches addressed by a teacher to a student ("my son"). They were practice texts for the students who were trained to be court officials (as also happened in Egypt)—although their teaching was less class-oriented, perhaps an effect of the influence of tribal ethos in Israel. This Egyptian influence fits in with an early dating of the materials, even from the Solomonic era. Otto Plöger[12] is much more cautious about the pertinence of these chapters to a school. He suggests that they are a kind of enchiridion or handbook that was destined for a wider audience than students. The dating is left rather wide open. Some seven centuries (900–200 B.C.E.) witnessed a compilation of the admonitions (the style of chaps. 1–9) and sayings (the style of chaps. 10ff.). Common opinion dates chaps. 1–9 in the postexilic period, but it is obvious that there is a great deal of uncertainty. Compared to chaps. 10ff., chaps. 1–9 reveal a concentration on wisdom, what Gerhard von Rad termed "theological wisdom,"[13] but this offers little information about dating.

THE TWO SOLOMONIC COLLECTIONS
(10:1–22:16; 25:1–29:27)

The transition from chaps. 1–9 to chaps. 10ff. is a rocky one for the average reader. The long poems yield to short, staccato, two-line sayings that have little context to illuminate them. The intensive, persuasive speech of the teacher yields to dry aphorisms. There is no logical unity to the collections, although the sayings were not put together in a haphazard way. Catchwords (e.g., *lēb*, "heart," "mind," in 15:13–15) and common topics ("fool" in 26:1–12) can be recognized, but no specific context is provided. However, in some cases there is a clear relativizing of a saying by means of juxtaposition. The meaning of 18:11 (riches are the strength of a person—cf. also 10:15a) is relativized by the saying in 18:10 that the name of the Lord is a strong tower. This impression is strengthened when one examines 18:12 (pride goes before a fall). Many sayings throughout the book are in a certain tension with one another, but rarely in such a striking context as this (cf. also 26:4–5).

How can one best read collections of sayings? In the experience of many, the proverbs seem to blur all together when they are read at one sitting. The obvious move is to settle for a limited number—for example, to read a chapter at a time—and to select from the (roughly thirty) sayings in each chapter two or three verses that catch the reader's fancy. Perhaps none will appeal, but that may say more about the reader than about the sayings. The point is that one must concentrate on a limited number and sift out those sayings that, for whatever reason, stand out among the rest. Such an attentive reading can yield pleasant surprises, as the author can testify from teaching this book over the years.

Certain basic observations can be made about approaching a biblical proverb. We will not repeat here the remarks about parallelism and literary forms (and especially juxtapositional style) that have been discussed in chap. 1. J. G. Williams has given a helpful list of characteristics of aphoristic speech.[14] First, it is assertive; it looks a priori, but it is not that. The reader is left to qualify it by other contexts, by exceptions, by experiences that run contrary to it. Second, it provides insight, not only by what is said, but by the process: the reader can be startled, and thus invited to go beyond the proverb itself. For example, there is the caution not to be "wise in one's own eyes" (26:12). What is the proper attitude then? This seems to be answered in Prov 3:5–7 and 28:25–26. Third, the proverb often registers a reversal of one's expectation and provokes surprise. Here one may instance such sayings as a soft tongue breaking a bone (25:15b), or the bitter turning out to be sweet (27:7). This is the process of defamiliarization, looking at a thing afresh, from another perspective. Fourth, the proverb is marked by brevity and conciseness: "The point is a maximum of meaning in a minimum of words." Williams comments on the words of Hippocrates (*"vita brevis—ars longa"*): "How ironically interesting to be told by the briefest of art forms that art is long (enduring? immortal?) and life is brief!"

Certain tensions within the claims of the proverbs should be noticed. From one point of view, they are rooted in experience; one is to hear them carefully and recognize their empirical truth. On the other hand, they bear the authority of tradition; they are handed down as the teaching of parents and elders. Sometimes the conflict between authority and experience breaks out into the open. Thus, the teaching supports the thesis that wise conduct will be rewarded by prosperity and the good life; wisdom brings success. But reality often has it otherwise. The poor are not always to be blamed; indeed they are to be objects of particular concern, under penalty of blaspheming the creator of all (Prov 14:31; 17:5).[15] There are many ambiguities in life that cannot be solved by the deceptive simplicity of an aphorism. That is why there are so many sayings relative to such variables as wealth and poverty, or speech and silence. Complete wisdom will depend upon keeping in view the outward reach of all these sayings. A particular word at a given time may be out of order (cf. 26:4–5 on answering a fool).

Proverbs can have several levels of meaning. It has already been remarked that the original context of a given saying is usually irrecoverable. Hence the reader creates a certain context in which the saying is understood. Sometimes this is on target, but at other times the saying may be bent to support one's own prejudice or preunderstanding. Worse than faulty interpretation would be the failure to recognize further levels of meaning. In our own culture we recognize the saying that you can lead a horse to water but it cannot be made to drink. This undoubtedly arose from experience. Then it becomes an image for human activity, and the hermeneutical possibilities emerge: stubbornness? satiety? self-reliance? This open-ended character of proverbs will strike every reader.

Finally, some proverbs are simply obscure. This may be due to textual corruption, or to the density of expression. It is important, in any case, to try to find the point that is being scored. Usually there is a *tertium comparationis*, the point (or points?) of the comparison. Williams[16] illustrates this with the New Testament comparison in Matt 13:44: "The kingdom of heaven is like treasure hidden in a field which a man found and covered up, then in his joy he goes and sells all that he has and buys that field." Many points of comparison emerge. The kingdom is precious; it is hidden. But is that the point? Williams indicates the hidden comparison expressed in the second half of the verse: namely, the valuer and his action. But even here the focus of the comparison is manifold: the treasure? the burying and buying? joy? The story seems straightforward, but it is not at all clear. Is it wise to sell all one has? Or is the point to enlarge our concept of the kingdom—we should not count the cost, but change our lives radically? Parables like this one, and the comparisons with which the proverbs abound, make them exciting comments on the human scene. It would be a mistake to allow triteness and repetition to overpower the reach of the sayings.

The collection in 10:1–22:16 contains 375 sayings, the numerical equivalent of the proper name *šlmh* (1:1; 10:1), as P. Skehan has pointed out (see "Concluding Reflections" later in this chapter).[17] Many commentators favor a division between 10–15 (antithetic parallelism primarily) and 16:1–22:16 (synonymous and synthetic parallelism primarily). The frequency of the "Yahweh sayings" from 14:26 on has suggested to Skehan that they were deliberately inserted in 14:26–16:15 by the editor in order to suture the two parts and thus attain the number 375.[18]

The range of topics covered in this collection is too broad to be described in a meaningful way.[19] The theme of the just (wise) and wicked (fool) is dominant in chaps. 10–15. These chapters all deal with conduct and the corresponding fate. They are so general that they seem to lose their proverbial character. C. Westermann claims that they are the development of one basic idea, comparable to the monotonous elaboration of the same ideas in the speeches of Job's friends.[20] Here the aim of the teacher seems to be the emphasis of a lesson, and not experience. At the same time, various virtues (such as humility or generosity) as well as vices (such as dishonesty or pride) can be given due recognition.

The topic of speech deserves special mention. After all, words are the coin of the wisdom realm. In a world without our mass media, the power of the word reigned supreme. The concern in Proverbs is for both the proper and the improper use of speech. W. Bühlmann found in the Solomonic collections some 60 sayings dealing with proper speech; a study of improper speech (lies, calumny, prattling, etc.) would have been material for another book.[21] He found several judgments about proper speech: (1) it is precious, comparable to silver and gold (10:20; 20:15); (2) it is expressed graciously and eloquently (25:11; 15:2; 16:21, 23; 22:11); (3) it is beneficent (16:24; 15:26; 12:25); (4) it is gentle (15:1; 25:15); (5) it is "just" or open, even to giving reprimand (16:13; 10:10; 25:12); (6) it is honest and reliable (12:19, 22; 14:5, 25); (7) it is appropriate to its time (15:23); (8) it brings good to others, as a fountain of life (10:11; 13:14) or as a means of deliverance (11:9).

By and large, words will be wise because they are few (almost imitating the terse style of the saying!)—because the fewer the words, presumably the more intelligent the observation, and the more the speaker is in control of thinking and less prone to error. This mentality is reflected in many proverbs: be stingy with words for whatever reason (17:27; 10:19); think before you speak (15:28; 29:20); listen before you speak (18:13); watch your tongue (13:3; 21:23). This all implies that one knows how to observe silence, again for whatever reason: you stand to gain more (12:16, 23), and you may even be considered wise (17:28)! The importance of silence is underscored in the Egyptian teachings also, especially by Ptah-hotep (see Appendix).

The collection in chaps. 25–29 is introduced (25:1) as "also the proverbs of Solomon" and was transmitted (the word he'tîqû is unusual, ordinarily meaning "remove") by the men of Hezekiah (king of Judah in the time of Isaiah at the end of the eighth century). This points to the activity of the court in the wisdom enterprise and gives some support to the idea that the collection is designed for the training of courtiers. Many claim that there are two major collections here because of differences between chaps. 25–27 and 28–29. The former contain many striking comparisons and metaphors, and relatively little antithetic parallelism. In chaps. 28–29 these features are reversed, and in addition, the old just-unjust antithesis is more frequent. A more sophisticated analysis of chaps. 25–27 has been proposed by R. Van Leeuwen:[22] (1) 25:2–27, a "proverb poem" addressed primarily to courtiers, dealing with social rank and social conflict; (2) 26:1–12, a proverb poem dealing especially with the fool (ksyl), and the various life situations that call for a wisdom approach; (3) 26:13–16, a proverb poem dealing with the sluggard (*'ṣl*); (4) 26:17–28, a poem that develops themes taken from chap. 25; (5) 27:1–22, a collection of miscellaneous proverbs set out in couplets (vv 1–2, 3–4, etc.); (6) 27:23–27, an admonitory poem that can be read as advice to a farmer but in a metaphorical sense can be taken as addressed to the king, as "shepherd" of his people. Chapters 28–29 lack the bite of 25–27; the vivid language and comparisons are absent, and familiar contrasts are drawn between the just and the wicked, and the rich and the poor.

AMENEMOPE AND PROV 22:17–24:22

Most textual critics grant that there should be a title before 22:17, "the words of the wise" (see 24:23). It is found at the beginning in the Septuagint version, but it is swallowed up into v 17 in the Masoretic text. In any case, a new section clearly begins at this point. It is marked by admonitions, rather than sayings, usually in couplets (e.g., 22:22–23, 24–25, 26–27, etc.), in which reasons for the admonition are given (cf. Prov 3:1–12).

The "Egyptian connection" (see Appendix) of Israelite wisdom first came to light with the publication of the Instruction of *Amenemope* in 1922.[23] The ensuing studies established an indubitable relationship in favor of the dependence of the Hebrew upon the Egyptian sage. The connection was particularly clear for the section beginning with Prov 22:17, although similarities could be detected in verses scattered elsewhere (e.g., Amenemope 8:9–10 and Prov 16:1 about human plans and divine activity—or Amenemope 9:7–8 [= 16:13–14] and Prov 15:17, a "better" saying in favor of the repast of the poor accompanied by love). Prov 22:17–24:22 shows remarkable affinity to Amenemope's teaching. Perhaps the most striking instance is the enigmatic *šlšwm* in Prov 22:20. In the Masoretic tradition this has been translated as "formerly" and as "noble things." Neither is very satisfactory, and the ancient versions went in a different direction, reading the word as a number "three times" (Greek, and Latin Vulgate). The emendation that is now generally favored is the reading "thirty." This would be a clear reference to the "thirty chapters" (or "houses") found in Amenemope's work (27:7; *ANET*, 424). This hint of a relationship does not stand alone. It is bolstered by many other considerations. The introduction of Prov 22:17–18 is remarkably like the introduction to Amenemope's instruction (3:9–16; see *ANET*, 421–22). G. Bryce[24] has made a list of the parallels in the same sequence as they occur in both introductions.

Amenemope	*Proverbs*
your ears	your ear
hear	hear
what one says	words of

Amenemope	Proverbs
your heart	your heart
it is beneficial	it is pleasant
in the casket of your belly	in your belly
on your tongue	on your lips

Bryce goes on to point out that "of the nine sections dealing with different subjects in Prov 22:22–23:11, six begin with a word or phrase that corresponds exactly to its counterpart in Amenemope," and he provides the key words:

Amenemope	Proverbs
4:4 robbing a poor man	22:22 rob the poor
11:13 befriend a hot man	22:24 befriend a man of heat
27:16 skillful in his occupation	22:29 skillful in his occupation
23:13 eat . . . ruler	23:1 eat . . . ruler
9:14 labor to seek to gain wealth	23:4 labor to gain wealth
7:12 remove . . . landmark	23:10 remove . . . landmark

There is no need here to note other similarities (see *ANET*, 424, n. 46).

What is the nature of the relationship between the two works? It is not likely that both depend upon a third work, and the dependence of the biblical chapters on the Egyptian seems settled by the early dating of Amenemope's writing (in the Ramesside period, ca. 1200). But close comparison shows that the Israelite writer was quite independent; he adapted the Egyptian admonitions rather freely to suit his own purpose. His reference to the "thirty" in 22:20 is a general reference to the Egyptian work and does not indicate that he is offering thirty corresponding sayings. Efforts to identify precisely thirty sayings in 22:17–24:22 have not been successful, and in fact it seems as if the Egyptian connection ceases at 23:11.

One might not claim dependence if examples were scattered widely and were less striking. After all, it is conceivable that a given saying acquired currency on its own strength and became common coin. Bryce points to the thought in Ptah-hotep (lines 115–16) about the contrast between divine and human activity.[25] This also appears in the Instruction of Ani (8:9–10) and in Amenemope (19:16–17). The biblical equivalent is in Prov 16:1, the contrast between human plans and divine action. The point is that many ideas become common currency, and there is no need to speak of literary dependence in these instances.

Egyptologists have noted the religious tone of the work of Amenemope. Miriam Lichtheim has remarked on its "quality of inwardness," a shift to contemplation and humility.[26] This may explain the particular openness of

Hebrew wisdom to this work. Another correspondence may be pointed out: the contrast between the silent person and the "heated man," which is frequent in Amenemope and in other Egyptian writings. This theme is to be found also in Prov 15:18; 22:24; 29:22. In Prov 17:27 the expressive phrase "cool of spirit" is used to indicate self-control in speaking. For further details on Egyptian wisdom, see the Appendix.

THE OTHER COLLECTIONS

The collections that remain to be considered are somewhat unusual.

1. The least surprising is 24:23–34, whose title (v 23, "also these [belong] to the wise men") associates it with the previous sayings of the wise (22:17), perhaps as an appendix. It is a mixture of sayings and admonitions in traditional wisdom style. An "example story" is related in vv 30–32 concerning the sluggard, followed by a reprise of 6:10–11.

2. "Words of Agur, son of Yakeh the Massaite" is the title in 30:1, but there is no agreement about where his words end (vv 4? 6? 14?). We can be certain that vv 1–4 are his. They are called a nĕʾum, "oracle" or "pronouncement," and are best interpreted as a riddle. We know nothing about Agur, son of Yakeh. His place of origin (?), Massa, which also identifies Lemuel in 31:1, may be a region in Arabia. His opening words about Ithiel seem to be textually corrupt.[27] They are generally emended to a statement about his impotence before God, which is further developed in the statements of ignorance in vv 2–3. The questions in v 4 seem to announce a riddle, and to challenge the reader for an answer: "What is his name, what is his son's name . . . ?"[28] The clue to the names is the description in v 4 of one who went up to heaven and came down, and one who bound up the waters in a cloak. We might guess that the latter refers to God the creator (Gen 1:6–10; Ps 104:5–9). But who has gone up and come down? Skehan associates this with the Jacob of Gen 18:12–13 (Jacob's "ladder"). Now Jacob describes himself as a "sojourner" to Pharaoh in Gen 47:9. This brings us back to the name of Agur, which means "I am a sojourner." Agur, then, would be the "son's name" (v 4). The name of the one who is described as binding up the water can only be the Lord. Now the subtlety of the riddle emerges. If Agur is son of Yakeh, then Yqh must be some kind of acronym for yhwh qādôš hûʾ (the Lord, holy is he). On this interpretation, we have the answer to the riddle, and Agur must be understood as a reference, not to a non-Israelite, but to Jacob/Israel, God's "son" (Exod 4:22; cf. also Wis 10:10).

It is possible to construe vv 5–6 as a reply to Agur's statement of ignorance (v 2; for an "ignorant" man, he turns out to be adept at riddles!). The verses are an instruction about the reliability of the word of God (based upon

Ps 18:30 and Deut 4:2) and its sufficiency—nothing is to be added to it. Because the prayer in vv 7–9 is in the first person singular, like Agur's pronouncement, it is possible to see it as a continuation of his "words." The form anticipates the numerical proverbs that dominate the rest of the chapter. Two things are asked for in vv 7–9: honesty and the means to steer a middle way between riches and poverty. Verse 10 has the appearance of an errant saying that may have been inserted here because of the catchword "curse" beginning v 11. Verses 11–14 are a kind of numerical saying, in that four generations (the word *dôr* begins each verse), or groups, of wicked people are characterized.

   3.   The pattern of the numerical proverb is unmistakable in the rest of the chapter. Verses 15–16 associate, by way of contrast, the saying about the two daughters of the leech with things that do not "give" but are inexhaustible in taking. Verse 17 about the punishment for those who reject their parents is interruptive. The numerical proverb in 18–19 is typical of nature wisdom.[29] In each saying a "way" is admired. Does this refer to the fact that no trace is left by the items that are mentioned? Or is the marvel admired by the sage the mystery of movement (the bird's flight, the serpent's progress without legs, the ship's ability to stay afloat and to go forward)? It seems better to say that the point of the comparison lies in the term "way," which occurs four times. Then one can see that in every case the way is irrecoverable. One cannot recover the ways of the eagle or serpent or ship. In the culminating line the sage wonders how a particular human situation or way between man and woman came about, the marvelous attraction that brings them together; this, too, is a mystery that can never be recovered. In v 20 another "way" has been added, which goes beyond the three-four pattern enunciated in v 18: it is the "way" of a particular woman, the adulteress, and one that is in conflict with the fourth marvel of sexual attraction. The next numerical proverb (21–23) deals with the general topos of the "world upside down" and gives four examples of proper societal hierarchy.[30] Verses 24–28 single out four of the smallest animals and praise their "wisdom." Although the text of the next numerical saying is uncertain, it clearly exalts royal power. The string of numerical proverbs closes with an admonition against pride: be silent, for persistence ("pressure" three times in v 33) will not work.

   4.   The "words of Lemuel" (31:1–9) are really those of his mother. We know nothing about either of them. In contrast to the identity of Agur in 30:1, this man seems to be real, and his name can be understood to mean "(belonging) to God." Advice to a prince is in the tradition of international wisdom, as exemplified in the Instruction of Merikare (*ANET*, 414–19) and the Babylonian *Advice to a Prince* (*BWL*, 110–15). Verses 1–9 are unusual in that they are ascribed to a queen mother. The prohibitions are directed against sexual excess and intoxication, and they urge the king to justice. This

bit of royal wisdom can be understood to have been "democratized" within the biblical tradition: what is fit for a king is fit for all.

5. The ideal of the worthy wife (31:10–31). An *ʾēšet ḥayil* (31:10, literally, "a woman of strength") was already celebrated in 12:4 as the "crown" of her husband. The book now ends with an acrostic poem describing such a woman. One is reminded of 18:22, which implies that one who finds a wife finds happiness and the favor of the Lord. The capabilities of this woman are simply astonishing, so much so that one must ask if this ideal is really proposed for imitation. O. Plöger claims that this figure is real, but the problem is to find her.[31] He correlates her with the question of Job 28:12, 20 about the location of Wisdom: where is she to be found? Indeed, this woman is described in a manner reminiscent of Wisdom herself: she is described as more precious than corals (v 10; cf. 3:15; 8:11). "Happy the man who finds wisdom" proclaims the sage in 3:13. Ben Sira says almost the same thing— "Happy the husband of a good wife" (*ʾiššâ ṭôbâ*)—in Sir 26:1, and a good wife is a gift to one who fears the Lord (Sir 26:3). Wisdom and the good wife seem intertwined.

Considerations such as these have led many scholars to take a second look at the acrostic poem, and to ponder its role in the book. As T. McCreesh has noted, it serves as a summary, or "coda," which concludes the book in a significant way (as in Sirach, where the acrostic in 51:13–30 is the conclusion).[32] Rather than being a model for performing the everyday tasks of marital life (who could perform all the things this woman does?), she is a symbol of wisdom, or to quote A. Barucq, "a form of wisdom."[33] The poem is a pendant to the picture of Lady Wisdom presented in 9:4–6. One may even find here a subtle riddle. McCreesh correlates the opening line, "Who can find . . . ?" with the answer of Samson to his opponents, "You would not have found my riddle" (Judg 14:18): "Could the poet of Prov 31:10a be suggesting that the woman is not only incomparable, but a riddle whose identity is to be solved, discovered?" This is a delicate allusion, but support for it can be found in reference to the riddles of the sages in 1:6 and in 30:1–4, the riddle of the "words of Agur." It would seem that the last two chapters contain riddles; 30 begins with that of Agur, and 31 concludes the words of Lemuel with the riddle in vv 10–31.

CONCLUDING REFLECTIONS

1. Structure. Is this book merely a somewhat haphazard collection of ancient Israelite wisdom? Looked at solely from a structural point of view, it seems more than that. P. Skehan has claimed that the author laid out the columns of text in the design of a house (which is called "wisdom's house" in

9:1), and it is modeled on Solomon's Temple.[34] Whether or not one is prepared to accept all the architectural details in this reconstruction, Skehan's remarks about the numerical values of the names (and the term *ḥkmym*, or "wise") in the titles deserve serious consideration.

First, 1:1 has three names, *šlmh*, *dwd*, and *ysrʾl*, which have the numerical value of 375, 14, and 541, for a total of 930. We shall see that this hint in the title of the book is verified by the total number of lines in the book, 930. Second, the title of 10:1 has *šlmh*, equivalent to 375, and this is the number of single-line proverbs in this Solomonic collection (10:1–22:16). Third, the "Hezekian" collection (chaps. 25–29) has 140 lines or sayings. In the title at 25:1, Hezekiah is the operative word. Depending on the spelling, it could yield the numerical equivalent of 130 (so the MT spelling), 136, 140, or 146. The correct choice, in view of the entire book, is 140 (*yḥzqyh*). Fourth, the term *ḥkmym* (title in 22:17, 24:23) or "wise" has a numerical value of 118, and this is the number of lines in 22:17–24:32 and 30:7–33. Fifth, one can now add to all of this the rest of the sayings: 16 (for Lemuel and Agur) and 22 (the acrostic poem about the woman in 31:10ff.) for a total of 38, and 259 lines in chaps. 1–9.

The yield now is: 259 (chaps. 1–9); 375 (10:1–22:16); 118 (for the *ḥkmym* sayings in 22:17–24:32 and 30:7–33); 140 (chaps. 25–29); 38 (Lemuel, Agur, and the acrostic). Sum total: 930 lines in the entire book, as was hinted at in 1:1 (see previous paragraph). This count does not include the harmonizing glosses at 1:16; 8:11; 24:33–34, which have been questioned by many scholars for various reasons.[35] Needless to say, this outcome can hardly be coincidental. And it leads to the plausible conclusion that the hand of one person is responsible for the book as author-editor.

2. Theology. Chapter 8 has had a distinguished history in theology, serving as a source in the Arian controversies of the early Church. The personification of Wisdom in chaps. 1, 8, 9 is important, as we shall see in chap. 9. But theologians hardly advert to the book as a whole as a theological source.[36] It is not the kind of work that finds commentators, except for the great reformer Melanchthon, who wrote two commentaries on it! By and large it is viewed as a kind of source for moral guidance, and here it rates behind the Torah itself. It is no small contribution, and one can easily imagine the importance of the collections as means of moral formation among the Israelites. The range of the sayings, along with a content that aims at persuasion rather than enforcement, must have made it an attractive source for establishing the group ethos.

This somewhat utilitarian approach to the book is still not adequate. It flattens it out to the status of a moral handbook. One should attend to the mysterious blend of chaps. 1–9, to the manner in which this introduction to the book (a continuation of the program set down in 1:1–6) shapes a theological vision. The vision can be stated sharply: the book purports to offer "life" or "salvation" to the reader. When the psalmists pray to be "saved," they seek restoration to a full life in the here and now. Such is also the understanding in Proverbs. Personified Wisdom has a kerygma; she announces "security" (1:33) and "life" (8:35). The teaching of the wise is "a fountain of life" (13:14); this is also applied to "fear of the Lord" (14:27), which is also the beginning of wisdom. The symbols of fountain and tree of life are frequent: 10:11; 16:22; 3:18; 11:30; 13:12. Concretely "life" means riches and honor (22:4), a good name (10:7; 22:1), a long existence of many years (3:16; 28:16). The kerygma of the sages is found also in other books. Amos urged Israel to seek good and not evil, "that you may live" (5:14). In Isa 55:1–3 Israel is invited by the Lord to a banquet: "Listen, that you may have life." The Deuteronomic preaching offered Israel a choice between life and death (Deut 30:15–20; cf. Sir 15–17). Caution is in order here. Life is more than merely material goods; these are seen as sacramentals, signs of the Lord's blessings (Prov 10:22). For many readers the concept of life is an ever expanding one (even within the Old Testament; cf. Wis 1:15; 2:23–3:3; etc.). But the perspective of Proverbs is life in the here and now.

This offering of life is a gift, because Wisdom herself is a gift of God (Prov 2:16). Paradoxically, however, wisdom cannot be attained without human endeavor. The need for discipline and obedience to the teachings is also asserted. Wisdom has at least two faces in this book: she calls (chaps. 1–9), but humans must respond (chaps. 10–31).[37]

It may be objected to this understanding of Proverbs that its optimistic teaching is in conflict with the Books of Job and Qoheleth. The conflict is not to be denied: the suffering of the just person is not adequately handled in Proverbs (see Prov 3:11–12), and Qoheleth takes a harsh stand against traditional wisdom, as it does not provide the answers to the questions he is asking. But tension between various parts of the Bible (the description of the conquest in Joshua compared to chap. 1 of Judges) or within a single book (Qoheleth) is nothing new. It would be a mistake to underrate the achievements of the sages whose heritage is gathered up in Proverbs. One may say that they share in the weakness of Deuteronomy (on the problem of retribution), but in the strength of many psalmists (e.g., Pss 16:11; 23:6).

NOTES TO "PROVERBS—
THE WISDOM OF WORDS"

1. Cf. J. Becker, *Gottesfurcht im Alten Testament* (AnBib 25; Rome: Biblical Institute, 1965) esp. 210ff.; J. Marböck, "Im Horizont der Gottesfurcht: Stellungnahme zu Welt und Leben in der alttestamentlichen Weisheit," *BN* 26 (1985) 47–70.

2. Gerhard von Rad, *Wisdom in Israel* (Nashville: Abingdon, 1972) 67.

3. Cf. Carole R. Fontaine, "Proverbs," in *HBC*, 503.

4. On Prov 1:20–33 as a threat, see Roland E. Murphy, "Wisdom's Song: Proverbs 1:20–33," *CBQ* 49 (1986) 456–60.

5. The analysis of this book by P. Skehan is found in his *Studies in Israelite Poetry and Wisdom* (CBQMS 1; Washington: Catholic Biblical Association, 1971) 1–45, esp. 9–10 for chap. 2.

6. On the theme of "way," see N. Habel, "The Symbolism of Wisdom in Proverbs 1–9," *Int* 26 (1972) 131–57.

7. Cf. Roland E. Murphy, "Wisdom and Eros in Prov. 1–9," *CBQ* 50 (1988) 600–3.

8. This was first proposed by G. Boström, *Proverbiastudien: Die Weisheit und das fremde Weib in Sir 1–9* (LUA n. f. A 1, vol. 30:3; Lund: Gleerup, 1935).

9. See J.-N. Aletti, "Séduction et parole en Proverbes I–IX," *VT* 27 (1977) 129–44.

10. Skehan detects seven units of five lines (with 8:11 being a gloss based on 3:15), guided by the emphatic *'ănî* ("I") in vv 12 and 17, the origins of Wisdom in vv 22–31 (with *'ănî* in v 27), and the conclusion "now then" (*we'attâ*) in 32; cf. Skehan, *Studies*, 14. M. Gilbert describes 8:1–3 as an introduction and claims that "all authors" distinguish four sections: 8:4–11, 12–21, 22–31 (a unity), 32–36 (the ending). He regards these sections as a collection that motivates the audience to listen: the teaching of Wisdom (contained in chaps. 10–31). Cf. "Le discours de la sagesse en Proverbes 8," in *La Sagesse de l'Ancien Testament* (BETL 51; ed. M. Gilbert; Leuven: Leuven University Press, 1979) 202–18, esp. 218.

11. Bernhard Lang, *Die weisheitliche Lehrrede* (SBS 54; Stuttgart: KBW, 1972).

12. Otto Plöger, *Sprüche Salomos* (*Proverbia*) (BKAT 13; Neukirchen-Vluyn: Neukirchener, 1984) 111–12.

13. In his *Old Testament Theology* (New York: Harper & Row, 1962) I, 441–53, Gerhard von Rad treats Prov 1–9 under "Israel's theological wisdom." Although it is hazardous to attempt a description of the historical development of wisdom, one can agree that Prov 1–9, especially with Lady Wisdom (see chap. 9), represents a theologizing, a deeper reflection on the data that composed the wisdom tradition.

14. Cf. J. G. Williams, "The Power of Form: A Study of Biblical Proverbs," in *Gnomic Wisdom* (Semeia 17; ed. J. D. Crossan; Chico: Scholars Press, 1980) 35–58, esp. 37–40; the quotation is taken from p. 39.

15. See the careful treatment of the theme of material prosperity by Elizabeth Huwiler, "Control of Reality in Israelite Wisdom" (Duke University dissertation, 1988) chap. 3.

16. Williams, "The Power of Form," 39–40.

17. Cf. Skehan, *Studies*, 43–45. *Šlmh* in "proverbs of Solomon" (10:1) is the numerical equivalent of 375, and there are 375 single-line proverbs in the Solomonic collection of 10:1–22:16.

18. Skehan, *Studies*, 18–20, 35–36.

19. For a general summary, see U. Skladny, *Die ältesten Spruchsammlungen in Israel* (Berlin: Vandenhoeck & Ruprecht, 1961). The commentary of A. Barucq is built upon a topical treatment; *Le Livre des Proverbes* (SB; Paris: Gabalda, 1964).

20. Cf. C. Westermann, "Weisheit im Sprichwort," in *Schalom: Studien zu Glaube und Geschichte Israels* (A. Jepsen Festschrift; ed. K.-H. Bernhardt; Stuttgart: Calwer, 1971) 73–85, esp. 84–85, n. 7.

21. Cf. W. Bühlmann, *Vom Rechten Reden und Schweigen* (OBO 12; Fribourg: Universitätsverlag, 1976). See also Huwiler, "Control of Reality," chap. 4.

22. R. Van Leeuwen, *Context and Meaning in Proverbs 25–27* (SBLDS 96; Atlanta: Scholars Press, 1988).

23. The most recent history of the question can be found in G. Bryce, *A Legacy of Wisdom* (Lewisburg: Bucknell, 1979). The appearance of Amenemope in the *NAB* translation of Proverbs 22:19 is due to an emendation of a seemingly corrupt text, rendered in the *NJV* as "I let you know today—yes, you—. . . ."

24. Bryce, *Legacy*, 101–11.

25. Bryce, *Legacy*, 154–59.

26. *AEL*, II, 146.

27. The translation of the MT in the *NJV* is "The speech of the man to Ithiel, to Ithiel and Ucal."

28. This interpretation of Agur's statement as a riddle is found in Skehan, *Studies*, 42–43.

29. Cf. Roland E. Murphy, "The Interpretation of Old Testament Wisdom Literature," *Int* 23 (1969) 289–301.

30. Cf. R. Van Leeuwen, "Proverbs 30:21–23 and the Biblical World Upside Down," *JBL* 105 (1986) 599–610.

31. Cf. Plöger, *Sprüche*, 376.

32. See T. McCreesh, "Wisdom as Wife: Proverbs 31:10–31," *RB* 92 (1985) 25–46; the quotation about Samson is from p. 38. See also Claudia Camp, *Wisdom and the Feminine in the Book of Proverbs* (BLS 11; Sheffield: Almond Press, 1985) 90–93, 251–52.

In a letter to the writer, David N. Freedman has further observed that "it is possible to connect the description of the virtuous woman with the alphabetic scheme. The description encompasses all the virtues and attributes of such a woman, as we would say in English idiom, from A to Z; so here one runs through the whole alphabet from *alef* to *tav*, running the gamut of her qualities and accomplishments, and thereby providing a fitting conclusion to the book (as also in Ben Sira, where the book closes with an alphabetic acrostic, after beginning with a non-alphabetic acrostic, similar to Proverbs)."

33.   Barucq, *Le Livre des Proverbes*, 230.

34.   Cf. Skehan, *Studies*, 27–45, with the numerical details indicated esp. on pp. 43–45.

35.   Objections can be made against this numerical calculation for the Book of Proverbs. Thus, is the elimination of 1:16 and 8:11 dictated by a desire to reach a certain number (in chaps. 1–9, 259 lines are the count)? These two lines have been questioned independently and legitimately by commentators in the past. Two important LXX mss. do not have 1:16, which is a reflection of Isa 59:7. In Wisdom's speech of chap. 8, the first person is interrupted by a statement in the third person, namely 8:11, which reflects Prov 3:15. The case of 24:33–34 is more delicate. These verses repeat Prov 6:10–11, which are addressed to the sluggard in the second person. In the context of 24:30–32, in which an "I" is reflecting about the overgrown field of a sluggard, an address in the second person is at least strange and could possibly be a borrowing of 6:10–11. There is no intentional skewing of the text merely to arrive at preconceived numbers. It may be that verses other than these should be recognized as insertions. The strength of the argument comes from an overall analysis of the manner in which the numerical equivalent of the names in the titles has indicated the extent of the book (930 lines), and the improbability of sheer coincidence. At the present time there is no way of determining when the equation of letters and numbers came into use in this fashion. But the sages undeniably do betray a preoccupation with the letters of the alphabet (acrostics, and poems of 22–23 lines).

36.   Cf. Roland E. Murphy, "Proverbs and Theological Exegesis," in *The Hermeneutical Quest* (J. L. Mays Festschrift; ed. D. G. Miller; Allison Park: Pickwick, 1986) 87–95. See also the treatment of theology in chap. 8.

37.   Cf. Roland E. Murphy, "The Faces of Wisdom in the Book of Proverbs," in *Mélanges bibliques et orientaux en l'honneur de M. Mathias Delcor*, AOAT 212; (ed. A. Caquot et al.; Neukirchen-Vluyn: Neukirchener, 1985) 337–45.

CHAPTER 3

JOB THE STEADFAST

♦

The well-known phrase "the patience of Job" comes from the New Testament, not the Old. The Epistle of James (5:11) points to the *hypomonē* of Job as an example to the community. The word was rendered "patience" in the King James Version, but modern translations usually and correctly render it as "steadfastness." That is exact; Job is steadfast, not patient.

The book is rightly placed in the category of wisdom literature. The main protagonists, Job and his three friends, are not Israelites. Their origins outside Israel are carefully noted. With the exception of 12:9 (in the mouth of Job), the sacred name of the Lord (*yhwh*) is never mentioned by them in the great debate (chaps. 3–31). The events of Israel's history are not referred to, in contrast to the type of motif sounded in Ps 89:50 ("Where are your ancient favors?"). Job never has recourse to the sacred traditions. The disputants carry on their discussion solely on the level of (international) wisdom. For that reason, the Book of Job has been compared with several extrabiblical compositions (see Appendix). This does not mean it is not Israelite. It is a book of Israelite wisdom, and it stays within the perspective of such wisdom. Its sapiential character is shown by the many explicit references to wisdom and by the abundance of wisdom themes that appear.

The most obvious and perhaps telling words concerning wisdom are in chap. 28: where is wisdom to be found (vv 12, 20)? As a class, "wise men" are addressed by Elihu in 34:2 (cf. 34:10, 34), who also admonishes Job that he will teach him "wisdom" (33:33). The traditions of the wise are invoked by Eliphaz in 15:18. Wisdom is associated with God in 9:4, 12:13, and 39:17. Job sarcastically refers to the "wisdom" of the three friends (12:2; 13:5).

More important than the explicit references are several wisdom themes that float in and out of the dialogue, and that are found also in the wisdom books:

1. A preoccupation with creation: Job 12:10–25; 36:22–37:24; chaps. 38–41.
   See Prov 8:22–31; 30:15–31; Eccl 1:4–11; Sir 42:15–43:33.

2. The importance of the name, or memory: Job 18:16–18.
   See Prov 10:7; Eccl 2:16; 6:4; 9:5; Sir 39:9–11; 41:11–13; Wis 2:4.

3. Life as onerous: Job 7:1–2; 14:1–6.
   See Eccl 2:17, 23; Sir 40:1–10.

4. The traditions of the fathers: Job 8:8–10.
   See Prov 4:1–5; 5:13; Eccl 2:13–15; 8:17; Sir 8:8–9; 39:1–2.

5. Personification of Wisdom: Job 28.
   See Prov 1, 8, 9; Sir 24; Wis 7–9.

6. The problem of retribution: see Eccl 4:1–2; 6:1–6; 8:5–15; Sir 2:1–6;
   11:4–6; 39:16–41:13.

While the Book of Job can comfortably be classified within wisdom literature, it remains wisdom of an unusual kind. Scholars often speak of a crisis of
wisdom in connection with Job and Ecclesiastes. Job is seen as an iconoclastic
attack on the traditional ideas of divine justice and retribution, which are so
firmly upheld in the Book of Proverbs. Such a reading is not mistaken, but at
the same time the problem of retribution has to be viewed in the perspective
of the entire Bible. First, the book is a broad treatment of the issue recognized already in the questions addressed by Abraham to the Lord in Gen
18:22–32, in the "confessions" of Jeremiah (e.g., Jer 12:1–5), in the Book of
Habakkuk (1:4, 13), in several psalms (37, 73), and in the Book of Jonah.
There is a tradition for such questioning at the heart of Israel's faith. Second,
the author of the book does not attempt to impose an answer. He develops
various approaches to the problem in an attempt to shed as much light as
possible on the issue of human suffering and divine justice. The book's most
positive teaching is at the same time negative: the application to Job of the
traditional theory of divine retribution is not relevant. It is even wrong, as is
made clear by the verdict of the Lord in Job's favor against the friends (42:7).
This does not mean that there is *no* truth in the traditional theory. The
author spares no effort in presenting this theory as fully as possible. The very
fact that Job is restored in the end (42:10–17), while surely not the main
point of the book, bears witness to the author's belief in the traditional
goodness and justice of the Lord. God does care for those who are faithful to
him. It is no little irony that the author destroys a simplistic understanding of
this belief by demonstrating its inapplicability to Job.

THE PROLOGUE

The prologue to the Book of Job betrays a clear structure based on several
scenes:

1:1–5, Job's sturdy piety and prosperity.
1:6–12, the interview between the Lord and the Satan in the heavenly court.
1:13–19, the disasters that wipe out Job's possessions and children.
1:20–22, Job's reaction.
2:1–6, the second interview between the Lord and the Satan in the heavenly court.
2:7–8, the affliction of Job's person.
2:9–13, Job's reaction.

The scenes have been deliberately and artfully contrived to set before the reader a picture of a living saint, one who has won divine approval for his life-style, and who holds firmly to God despite cruel afflictions. The dialogue style carries most of the action: the repetitive interviews between the Lord and the Satan; the artificial and mechanical announcements of the four disasters by Job's servants, one on the heels of the other. These disasters alternate between human (Sabaeans, Chaldeans) and natural (fire, wind) calamities.

This prologue gives rise to several questions. The first is the historicity of Job. Did he ever exist? He is mentioned in a particular context in Ezek 14. There the Lord assures the prophet that the presence of even Noah, Job, and "Daniel" in the land would not save the people from calamity. These three would save only themselves because of their virtue, but no one else (cf. Abraham's pleas in Gen 18:22ff.). It is clear that these are cited as examples of unquestionably holy men. Noah is of course familiar as the blameless man who survived the flood (saving his family). "Daniel" should probably be identified with a hero known from Ugaritic literature as a just person (see The Tale of Aqhat in *ANET*, 149–55). In such company Job must also be accounted a saint. The Noah of Gen 6–9 cannot be said to be a historical character. *Dn'l* of ancient Ugarit seems more typical than real. What about Job? He may indeed have been a historical individual whose reputation for piety was handed down for generations. But the style of the narrative in Job 1–2 is in the legendary mode and does not allow us to draw historical conclusions. The author deliberately chose the figure of a well-known holy man as the hero of his work. The artificiality of the structure and events in these chapters suggests art more than reality. Indeed the high and studied quality of the poetry throughout the speeches of the book forbids us to think they were spontaneously composed by Job (on a dung heap, according to the LXX in 2:8) and by the friends in a half-hour debate. The entire work is a sophisticated literary achievement.

This probability keeps us from historicizing the scenes in the prologue and in the actual course of the debate. Thus the meeting between the Lord and the Satan in the heavenly council is imaginative. This is not the place to discuss the development of the figure of Satan in the Bible. But the following background should be recalled. In this book Satan is one of the "sons of God," the members of the heavenly court who do the Lord's bidding and serve as his counsel (cf. Isa 6:8). Clearly he is not the "devil" of New Testament times. "Satan" designates his office, an adversary (here, of Job, and in Zech 3:1, of Joshua; cf. 1 Chr 21:1), a kind of prosecuting attorney. To fulfill this function, he "roams the whole earth" (Job 1:7), and he is in a position to know who are the saints and who are the sinners. He is unwilling to agree with the Lord's verdict about Job, but he is unable to point to a concrete sinful action. So he astutely raises the question of motivation (1:9, one of the most profound questions in the Bible, and on the lips of Satan!). Then the Lord gives approval to the testing that Satan proposes. From a perverse point of view, one might even say that Satan is concerned about God's true glory, that God not be deceived by these humans whom Satan knows so well! But perhaps we are invited to question Satan's motivations, too. Is he genuinely concerned about the divine glory, or rather is he out to score high as a prosecuting attorney? If the author does not raise these questions (explicitly, at least), it is difficult for the reader to escape them.

The scene in the heavenly court may be imaginative, but it raises a nagging question: what kind of a God is this who is willing to prove a point of honor by sorely afflicting a faithful servant? The scene presupposes an understanding of God that the modern reader may be loath to share. Ancient Israel obviously did not have such qualms. There was a dark side, or underside, to God that was simply accepted. This dark side resulted from the worldview that attributed to divine agency all that happens, evil as well as good (cf. Deut 32:39; Isa 45:7). Hence suffering remained a mystery. It could be most easily accounted for as the wages of sin, as one recognizes in the Psalms (e.g., Ps 51). But not always, and the example of the saintly Job is a case in point. How can one penetrate the mystery of divine decision, or should one say divine caprice?

The interview between the Lord and the Satan is one attempt to confront that mystery. At first sight the Lord might appear to be indifferent to the well-being of his servant. He seems to accept the Satan's wager in order to be certain of the loyalty of his subject, Job. But this may be a misreading. It fails to take into account the issue that the author wants to raise: do human beings serve God for God's sake or for their own profit (Job 1:9)? This issue has been a perennial one in theological discussion. Do I love God or myself when I love God? Is a selfless, disinterested worship of God possible?[1] The Satan brings this point to center stage when he questions the divine approbation of Job as God-fearing: Is Job pious because of the divine blessings? Does he truly fear God? Does Job act "for nought" (1:9, ḥinnām)? The phrase is deliberately taken up by the Lord in the second scene when Satan is charged with accusing Job "for nought" or in vain (2:3). The issue is not divine caprice, but human sincerity, and the author has portrayed the issue by means of the exchange between the Lord and the Satan.

Hence it is off the mark to be scandalized by the description of the Lord in Job 1–2. God seems arbitary and mysterious. Perhaps the author was not fully aware of how he had put the Lord in a "no win" situation. If God refused the Satan's challenge, would he not have seemed to be uncertain of the loyalty of his servants, and willing to be a partner to a *do ut des* arrangement whereby he "buys" obedience in return for favor? In a sense, God had to accept the challenge or else appear as one who does not (or fears to) trust the loyalty of his followers. If the Lord had not listened to the Satan, we would have been the poorer. The Satan is given leave to lay waste Job's possessions in a series of cataclysmic events that are, as it were, hurried over, till one arrives at Job's noble response: ". . . blessed be the name of the Lord" (1:21). The author is careful to note that Job remains sinless. The narrative takes over again in 2:1–3, and the Lord and the Satan go through the same question-and-answer preliminary, when the Lord taunts him about Job's holding fast to his integrity. The Satan increases the pressure, and now Job's person is the target. He is smitten with a disease whose nature is difficult to determine, except that he is driven to scraping himself with potsherds. The reaction of Job's wife has been variously interpreted.[2] She suggests to Job what the Satan had already predicted that Job would do: "bless" (i.e., curse—as in 1:11, 2:5, this is a euphemism) God. Such a reaction would have been a way out, in the sense that it would call down divine intervention to destroy Job. But Job will have none of this. He stands by the biblical view that God is the cause of all things, evil as well as good (Isa 45:6–7; Amos 3:6; Lam 3:38).[3]

Job's three friends arrive, ostensibly to give him comfort. The first sign of that is their gestures of mourning (2:12). So appalling is Job's condition that silence (for a week!) is the only suitable reaction. (Later on, 13:5, Job acidly remarks that silence is their only wisdom!)

THE DIALOGUE

The length of the dialogue between Job and the three friends would of itself suggest the importance that the author attached to it. The pattern is simple: Job alternates with each of the friends, and they have a run at each other in three cycles (3–14; 15–21; 22–27). There is a snag in chaps. 26–27, where Zophar is left without a speech. If this is not directly attributable to the author, the disappearance of Zophar's speech must have occurred very early on. The present form of the text is supported by the scroll of the Targum of Job (11QtgJob), which was discovered at Qumran only several years ago and dated to the first century C.E.[4] None of the solutions proposed by scholars for the redistribution of the lines in chaps. 25–27 are more than hypotheses.

The purpose of the dialogue is to allow the author to develop fully the best thought on the problem of the suffering of a just person. It is marked by verisimilitude, a faithfulness to reality. It must be admitted that the author has tilted the situation in favor of Job, who clearly wins the debate. The prologue in chaps. 1–2 makes this inevitable, since Job's innocence is assured by divine pronouncement. But the author intends to be fair to the traditional theology that the three friends represent. There is danger that a modern reader may find the position caricatured. This is not the intention of the author. He gives the three friends full rein in their learned discussion of the theme. They do the best they can on the principles that they accept. It is important to recall that they echo ideas that are fully in accord with other parts of the Bible (e.g., Ps 37). The author has no need to underscore how wrong they are when they rigidly interpret the tradition to infer that Job's affliction is due to his sinfulness. The temper of their words to Job increases steadily from the sympathetic opening of Eliphaz (4:1–11) to his eventual specific accusations against Job (22:1–11). The personal remarks, from both corners, enliven the debate. Job's friends accuse him of doing away with piety (15:4). He reminds them that their best wisdom would be silence (13:5) and that lying for the sake of God (13:7–9) is dangerous business.

The three friends lecture Job directly and never speak to God. Job responds to them, but significantly he turns from them often in order to address God (the Almighty, or El Shaddai). It is here that the author is once again true to life. Job oscillates between despair and ardent faith. He argues with God, and even if he cannot find God (23:8–9), he never stops yearning for a confrontation (9:32–35; 13:3, 16, 22; 16:18–22; 31:35–37). This is the stuff of spiritual conflict, the dark night of the soul, which countless people have experienced. Job's affirmation of his innocence is as inevitable as it is clear; the prologue secures that. His very integrity demands that he reject the imputation of the friends (cf. the accusations of Eliphaz in 22:6–11). Hence he has no other course but to maintain his integrity (27:6; cf. 2:3), to ask "why?" and with a certain bravado to challenge God (sarcastically in 7:12–21; somewhat lovingly in 10:1–12). He is baffled by events but he never quite gives up on God as his vindicator (or *gōʾēl*, 19:25). He is caught between two nightmares: Could the three friends possibly be right? This he clearly rejects. On the other hand, is God without care for him?

The modern reader may ask the question, which Job is more admirable? the God-fearing Job of chaps. 1–2, or the complaining Job of chaps. 3–31? Perhaps Søren Kierkegaard has given the best reply:[5]

> Job! Job! Job! Job! Didst thou indeed utter nothing but these beautiful words, "The Lord gave, the Lord hath taken away, blessed be the name of the Lord"? Didst thou say nothing more? . . . No, thou who in the ripeness of thy days wast a sword for the oppressed, a cudgel to protect the old, a staff for the decrepit, thou didst not fail

men when all was riven asunder—then thou wast a mouth for the afflicted, and a cry for the contrite, and a shriek for the anguished, and an assuagement for all who were rendered dumb by torments, a faithful witness to the distress and grief a heart can harbor, a trustworthy advocate who dared to complain "in anguish of spirit" and to contend with God. Why do people conceal this? . . . Does one perhaps not dare to complain before God? . . . Thee I have need of, a man who knows how to complain aloud, so that his complaint echoes in heaven where God confers with Satan in devising schemes against a man.

The course of the dialogue is uneven; that is, there is no logical response of one speech to another. It has often been remarked that the disputants seem to be talking past each other. Perhaps there is no other way in a discussion of such a mystery. The three are allowed to give their defense of the traditional theology, while Job is entitled to vent his feelings. The dispute is triggered by Job's powerful lament in which he curses the day of his birth and asks "why?" (chap. 3).

The response of Eliphaz, although moderate, is unmistakable: Job is clearly in the wrong. He tries to make it easy for Job to admit this: "Can mortals be righteous as against God?" (4:17). If Job would only recognize that "happy is the one whom the Lord reproves" (5:17; cf. Prov 3:11–12)! This is a test. If Job appeals to the Lord (and by implication admits to his sinfulness), the Lord will heal him. Job's "response" is taken up with describing his own agony, attacking his friends as deceitful wadis that promise water but do not deliver (6:14–30). Then he appeals to God (7:7–21), making a parody of Ps 8: what is a mere mortal, that you are so concerned with him! Bildad defends divine justice (8:3, 20) in words that are truer than he realizes: God will not reject the upright (*tām*, the word used of Job in 1:8)—indeed, that is the way the story will end! In another ironic touch, Job accuses God of afflicting him "for nought" (9:17, *ḥinnām*, the word used by the Satan and the Lord in 1:9; 2:3).[6] In chap. 10 he makes an emotional appeal to the brighter side of God, his creator (10:4–12), only to recognize that God hunts him down like a lion. Zophar in reply anticipates the tone of the Lord in chaps. 38–41: the mystery of God is higher than the heavens and deeper than Sheol—what can Job do (11:7–8)? Ironically, he wishes that God would intervene (God will!) and teach Job (11:6) the "secrets of wisdom." He can offer Job respite only if Job repents of his sinfulness. Job's answer is to single out God's power as the cause of all that happens, including his own calamity. He warns the three against their unworthy and deceitful defense of God's cause. As usual he addresses God directly, after the famous line "Slay me though he might, I will wait for him" (13:15, although the consonantal text, or *kĕtîb*, has "I have no hope"). He closes with the striking contrast between the tree (even when it is cut down, there is hope for it to grow again) and humans (once they are cut down, there is no more hope for life). In a touching outburst, he *imagines* life beyond death (14:13–22) in which God might show graciousness—only to conclude, "You destroy human hope." This description of the first cycle of speeches gives some flavor of the rather free flow of the discussion. Certain features in these and the following chapters deserve more attention. Several times the theme of a confrontation with God is discussed. According to 9:2–20, Job can see no advantage in this: one cannot win against God ("Though I am innocent, my own mouth would condemn me; though I am blameless, he would prove me perverse," 9:20). But in 13:3, 16, 22, he insists on arguing his case before God. The thought of this confrontation floats in and-out of Job's speeches. Indeed, in 16:19–21 he is able to affirm a heavenly witness who will support him. The identity of this witness is disputed; could it be God, insofar as Job opposes the bright and dark sides of God to each other? In any case, he certainly asserts in the famous text of 19:25–27 that the Lord is his vindicator (*gōʾēl;* "redeemer" is misleading in the context). However these difficult lines are to be translated, Job affirms emphatically a personal vision of God. This, and not the notion of resurrection that has traditionally been associated with this text, is the point of these lines. The declaration serves as an anticipation of the "vision" that Job will experience later (42:5). Until then, however, Job experiences the dark night of the soul (chap. 23).

If it were profitable, one could make a list of statements by Job that cancel each other out. He attacks God (7:20–21; 9:22–24; 16:7–17) and he cajoles God (10:4–12). His despair (e.g., 9:16–18; 14:18–22) is matched by his faith (13:15–16; 19:23–27). His very integrity and clear vision of himself call forth the famous series of exculpatory oaths in chap. 31. The reader knows, with all the certainty of the Lord himself in the prologue, that Job is simply stating the truth, not boasting. It has been said that ultimately Job shares in the traditional theology of the friends.[7] This is hardly fair to Job. First, this interpretation historicizes Job, as if his views were separate from the views of the author. Obviously the author is not locked into a reward system (not even by going along with the restoration of Job in chap. 42, which was part of the original Job legend). Second, for Job the issue is not prosperity versus the absence of it, but his relationship to God. This seems to be destroyed under the weight of the suffering that God has inflicted upon him. In his present condition he cannot even find God (chap. 23). He never once asks to be restored to his former greatness (which he vividly remembers, 30:1–31). At the most, Job may be at fault in saying "God must" (somehow intervene in his favor) if God is to remain credible.[8] It is always dangerous to write the script for divinity to be bound by. Like anyone else, Job is operating with a human concept of justice, which cannot be simply applied to God. In this sense, he is concerned with "the credibility of God," as von Rad put it.

But it is a mistake to define Job at any point in the book. For example, he seems to admit that he is not sinless (7:21; 10:6; 13:26), but the reader knows the divine verdict from the prologue. He even refers to his family in 19:17 in a way that is contrary to 1:13–19. Such inconsistencies are really beside the point. There is no need to make the dialogue agree with the Job legend in such details; it is more important to understand the literary character Job as a realistic figure.

We have distinguished between the author and Job himself, between the book as a whole and the role played by Job. This distinction is also applicable to chap. 28. Many scholars are of the opinion this is a later insertion in the book. Nonetheless it forms part of the total message of the book as it stands. The point of chap. 28 is simple: God alone knows where wisdom is. The position of this poem on wisdom could make it appear as a continuation of Job's words in chap. 27. But the whole tenor of the poem is tangential to the points Job is making. The mere sequence of chapters does not force one to place it in his mouth, although chaps. 26–27 are attributed to him. There is no identifying formula to specify the speaker of this sudden passage on the whereabouts of wisdom. It appears to be another view of the situation that the writer provides. The new viewpoint is that the problem is beyond the understanding of created beings, for they lack the wisdom that God alone possesses. Hence this chapter implicitly warns against even attempting to answer the problem. No answer is available. The final verse (28:28) modifies this mystery. God said to humans, "Behold, the fear of the Lord is wisdom; and avoiding evil is understanding." This conclusion lies outside the wisdom poem (vv 1–27), but it is a reasonable inference. The best one can do is "fear God," an old wisdom ideal. The verse harks back to the description of Job in 1:1 as God-fearing and avoiding evil. Chapter 28 represents still another perspective that the book brings to bear on the mystery of the suffering of its main character: humans do not have the wisdom to solve the mystery; they can only "fear" God (cf. Eccl 5:6a).

The dialogue is, in effect, over when Job makes a full-scale review of his life and assesses his present situation (chaps. 29–31). He does not even advert to the friends. Instead he describes the golden days, when the Lord's "lamp shone above my head" (29:3) and Job's "footsteps were bathed in milk" (29:6). That has all disappeared, and Job is left with the God who does not answer (30:20). Then he launches into a series of oaths, invoking upon himself divine wrath if he has contravened pious conduct (the items mentioned are counted differently by different commentators, ranging from ten to fourteen). He had already taken oaths on his right, his integrity, and his justice in 22:2–6. But in this horrendous series, Job invokes dire consequences upon himself if he has been guilty. With this goes his final challenge, "Let the Almighty answer me!" (31:35).

ELIHU

If ever the encounter with God for which Job yearned were to take place, now would be the moment. Instead, Elihu (also a non-Israelite) is introduced. After a prolix introduction (32:1–5) and bombastic preliminary remarks (32:6–22) he settles into the first of his four speeches (chaps. 32–33, 34, 35, 36–37). He is distressed at the failure of the three friends in the debate, so he directs himself primarily to Job—who never answers him. Several good reasons have induced scholars to regard these chapters as a later insertion: Elihu is never mentioned in the rest of the book; he interrupts the sequence of chaps. 31 and 38; his contribution to the theme hardly differs from that of the three friends. Even so, these chapters are present and call for some comment. First, they are meant to bolster the arguments of the friends. It has been noted that Elihu resembles a reader who has gone over the dialogue meticulously and singled out statements for further comment (e.g., 33:10–11 and 14:24b, 13:27).[9] Second, Elihu contradicts Job (33:13–14) by claiming that God *does* answer; Job's suffering is medicinal (33:19–33; 36:8–15), a point touched on briefly by Eliphaz (5:17–18). But the presupposition of both Elihu and Eliphaz is that such discipline is divinely given to turn the sinner toward God, and this is not applicable to Job. Finally, in the last speech (36:1–37:24) there is a splendid creation hymn in honor of God's greatness (36:26–37:24), which concludes with questions in the style of the Yahweh speeches in chaps. 38–41. In this respect Elihu can be said to anticipate or provide a transition to the intervention of the Lord. But his speeches are no more effective than those of the three friends.

THE LORD'S "REPLY"

One might reasonably expect the theophany in chap. 38 to settle the debate, to "answer" the question. It does contribute to a solution, but the speeches of the Lord are not what Job or the reader expect. As we have seen, this intervention is prepared for by Job's desire for a confrontation with the Lord. In 31:35 he wanted an indictment, which he confidently expected to refute. In 19:25–27 he expressed his faith in vindication that would come from his *gōʾēl*, presumably God, whom his very eyes would behold. In 13:3 Job recognized the danger in such a confrontation, but it remained a goal for him (23:3). The vaunted encounter opens with a series of questions in a divine lecture about creation. At first sight the divine reply is striking for its irrelevance. The only time the issue is joined is in 40:7–14, especially in v 8,

"Would you condemn me that you may be justified?" Here the Lord challenges Job to play king of creation (after all the changes that have been rung on the creation theme in chaps. 38–39!). The point is not pursued, but Job's impotence is underscored by the descriptions of Behemoth and Leviathan, symbols of unruly power or chaos, whom only the Lord, not Job, can dominate. The real issue of the book remains below the surface, and the reader is forced to ask what the purpose of the divine speeches is. It can be said that the speeches convey the impact of the theophany upon Job, transforming him.[10] To this end the author employed the rhetorical questions characteristic of the wisdom tradition, as an opening onto the mysteries of God and the world. There is heavy sarcasm in 38:21, "You know, for you were born then" (i.e., like Wisdom herself, before creation; cf. Prov 8:22–31; in 15:7 Eliphaz made the same point). But mostly there is pleasant irony as the Lord rolls out the questions about the works of creation. As one scholar has put it, the mood is: you know this, and you know that I know that you know.[11] There is even a playful note, which G. K. Chesterton expressed, perhaps with exaggeration: "God says, in effect, that if there is one fine thing about the world, as far as men are concerned, it is that it cannot be explained. . . . The whole is a sort of psalm or rhapsody of the sense of wonder. The maker of all things is astonished at the things He has Himself made."[12] The presupposition of the speeches is that the Lord somehow reveals self in creation, for the result of this encounter is Job's transformation. The Lord's questions add little to Job's fund of knowledge, but they do leave him changed.

There are two divine speeches and two reactions of Job. At the close of the first speech the Lord challenges him to reply (40:1–2). But Job has nothing to say. His answer is not defiant, but it is vague enough to be either humble or evasive; it is not an admission of any wrong. The reaction of Job in 42:1–6 is markedly different from the reaction to the first speech. In 42:2–4 Job acknowledges the divine purpose and also his own ignorance, with quotations from the Lord's speeches (38:2 in v 3a; 38:3b and 40:7 in v 4). Then comes his classic line: "I had heard of you by word of mouth, but now my eye has seen you" (42:5). The vision of God, pointed to so emphatically in 19:25–27 and so desperately sought for in 23:9, has now become a reality. It is enough for Job; vision has replaced hearsay. Job's experience of God in the theophany works the transformation that the lectures of the friends could not accomplish. The meaning of 42:6 is obscure. Literally, Job says, "I abhor [with no direct object; the verb could be translated also as "I dissolve"] and I repent [*nhm*] concerning dust and ashes." The entire verse is supposedly in support of his submission, but the exact meaning is not clear. It would be mistaken to see here repentance for all that he has said, or even merely for certain statements that he made. The repentance should be interpreted as a change of mind (as frequently the Lord is said to change his mind or "repent of the evil" he had planned to do: e.g., Jonah 3:9–10). Probably the *NJV*

43

captures the meaning best: "I recant and relent, being but dust and ashes."
So also the comment of M. Greenberg: "He rejects what he formerly maintained" and "is consoled for (being mere) dust and ashes."[13]

THE EPILOGUE

The epilogue in 42:7–17 returns to the style of the prologue (chaps. 1–2), and
it is not without its subtleties. If Elihu was angry with the friends (32:1–5), so
now is the Lord. The reason is that they "have not spoken rightly about me
[understanding *'ēlay* as *'ālay*], as has my servant Job" (v 7). This verdict of
approval for Job may come as a surprise after one has read Job's rebellious
speeches and the Lord's own characterization of them as "words of ignorance" (38:2). Is this simply a relative judgment, that Job is more right (closer
to the truth, as it were) than the three friends? Certainly the friends are
repudiated, but how much approval is given to Job? The question is not really
answered. The restoration of Job is part of God's mysterious freedom and
generosity, the free divine response to Job's actions and words. Now the
tables are turned: the friends are to ask Job for his prayers for them. Job
becomes the mediator in their holocaust sacrifice. The words of Eliphaz to
Job in 22:27 ("You shall pray to him and he will hear you") find an ironic
fulfillment!

The restoration of Job, who receives "twice as much as he had before"
(v 10), has sometimes been interpreted as an inconsistency in the book. Not
so; restoration is also a feature of life, which the author-editor (who has no
doctrinaire "solution") would not feel compelled to deny. Some would regard
the restoration, and the visit of Job's relatives and friends, as simply a rem-
nant from the original Job story (presumably before the debate with the three
friends was inserted). Be that hypothesis as it may, the actions of the visitors
are described in exactly the same terms as the purpose of the friends' visit in
2:11: to "console and comfort." Another ironic touch! To judge from their
"gifts," these visitors were far too practical to give lectures like those of the
three friends.

In conclusion it should be emphasized that the Book of Job is bigger than
Job himself. We need only point to the basic question raised in the prologue
(1:9; by the Satan, no less!): do humans serve God for themselves or for God?
The dialogue between Job and the friends highlights the traditional theory of
retribution, while showing how inapplicable it is to the case of Job. Chapter
28 (an independent piece?) enlightens us concerning the mystery of divine
wisdom, as if to say that there is no answer to the problem raised in the book.
Elihu attempts to salvage the traditional theory, with little success. The Lord
appears to Job and discourses like a wisdom teacher, raising all kinds of

questions about the secrets of the universe. This vision of the Lord is enough for Job to abandon himself to the Lord. The restoration of the hero shows what the Lord can do, and even does, in God's own time.

Few books in the Old Testament call for a response from the reader as urgently as the Book of Job does. It has had a long history of interpretation that also illustrates a wide range of reaction.[14] The work cannot be read without existential involvement. That is why the commentary of Gustavo Gutiérrez has been so gripping. The original Spanish title of his *On Job* is "to speak of God from the point of view of the suffering of the innocent." This title provides the particular perspective that he sees as "central to the book itself: the question of *how we are to talk about God*" especially in the context of the suffering poor of South America.[15] He has provided an enlightened and moving interpretation of Job, who has become a paradigm: "How are human beings to find a language applicable to God in the midst of innocent suffering? This question, with all its implications for our understanding of the justice and unmerited generosity of God, is the great theme of the book of Job." Even if a "Yanqui" fails to see the growth that Gutiérrez finds in the dialogue whereby Job becomes aware of his solidarity with the poor, there can be no denying the passion of the "implications" that Gutiérrez has spelled out for readers.

One of the most unexpected and successful commentators on Job has been the American poet Robert Frost, in "A Masque of Reason."[16] This short poem is practically a dialogue between Job and his wife, God, and the Satan. At the outset Job and his wife are speaking when God makes his appearance—the wife claims to know who the stranger is, because she recognizes him from Blake's pictures! When Job inquires about the heavenly bliss, the Lord begins in an apologetic vein, to the effect that it has long been on the divine mind (a thousand years) to thank Job for the way in which he helped God make the point that the old reward-punishment principle of retribution simply does not hold. There is no reasoned connection between virtue and reward, wickedness and punishment. The trial was admittedly hard for Job, who could not possibly understand what God was up to, but by now Job should know the significant role he played in showing up the folly of Deuteronomist theology (that the good are rewarded and the evil punished). Job set God free to be God by slipping him out of the bind that the three friends of Job clearly placed God in. At the end, Job's wife takes a photograph of Job, God, and Satan with her Kodak!

Has this chapter explained the message (or messages) of the Book of Job? If so, perhaps it has betrayed the work—because scholars, like David N. Freedman, ask seriously, "Is it possible to understand the Book of Job?"[17] The difficulties arise from the apparently composite character of the work (e.g., what is chap. 28 doing there, and how does it function?), but especially from the differing presuppositions that we bring to our reading. At least two of these deserve attention here: our presuppositions concerning divine justice and divine omniscience. These are *not* shared by the Old Testament author, and that is why such a puzzling book can be written. As for divine justice, it cannot be measured by any abstract code, much less by human standards. It is *sui generis* and beyond comprehension. As for divine omniscience, one can claim, as Freedman does, that it is not the correct presupposition for the Book of Job. If God had known that Job's loyalty and love were not selfish, his "wager" with the Satan would have been basically unfair (to both Job and the Satan). Something (Job's love) had to be proved or tested because by the terms of the situation it was an unknown (possibly inexistent) quality. This problem is one that exercised both Jewish and Christian theologians in the past: divine foreknowledge and human freedom. We blithely assert both of these points but cannot explain how they are to be reconciled. The Bible likewise blithely asserts both of them (not using the same terminology, of course) but does not attempt to explain them. Even more striking, in the Book of Job the issue of divine omniscience is bypassed for the sake of setting up the discussion provided by the poet. Divine omnipotence and omniscience are presuppositions of the author (and the reader?), but the tension between them remains. In a study of the "full-structure" of the work (as opposed to an interpretation guided by a piece-by-piece developmental structure), C. R. Seitz comments: "With Job, we see God testify in a whirlwind to might, power, and control over the natural realm, of which Job is a part. Yet with all this omnipotence, there is one thing the Almighty cannot do. . . . In the Prologue the reader learns something which is not revealed to Job: that God cannot coerce the love and service of mortals—or rather, precisely the best of mortals, like his servant Job. God cannot make Job serve him."[18]

Notes to "Job the Steadfast"

1. On the "degrees" of the love of God, see the classic treatise of Bernard, *De Diligendo Deo*, in *The Works of Bernard of Clairvaux* (Cistercian Fathers Series 13; Washington: Consortium Press, 1974) 91–132.

2. Her question can be construed as a taunt (note that "hold fast to integrity" in 2:9 echoes God's words in 2:3); she possibly means that Job should at least curse God before dying. Or else, Job should curse God, and the divine power would strike him dead.

3. Or is there a difference between 1:21–22 and 2:10? In his commentary on these passages in *Job* (Interpretation; Atlanta: Knox, 1985), J. G. Janzen has made a strong case for movement, for change in Job from the first to the second scene. Among other things, Janzen points to the replacing of "Lord" by "God" in a statement that is not a

profession of faith (as in 1:21), but a rhetorical question in which Job can hide under the "we." Could the text be signaling a weakening of Job's resolve? The verdict of the writer in 2:10 is expressed differently than in 1:22. Already the Talmud, followed by the great Jewish commentator Rashi, suggested that Job sinned in his heart. The way is prepared then for the outburst in chap. 3. However, the author notes for the second time that Job did nothing wrong.

4. J. van der Ploeg and A. van der Woude (eds.), *Le Targum de Job de la grotte XI de Qumran* (Leiden: Brill, 1971).

5. Cf. Søren Kierkegaard, *Repetition* (trans. W. Lowrie; Princeton: Princeton University Press, 1941) 110–11.

6. M. Greenberg astutely remarks of 9:17, "Ironically, Job has unwittingly stumbled on the true reason for his suffering." Cf. "Job," in *The Literary Guide to the Bible* (ed. Robert Alter and F. Kermode; Cambridge: Harvard, 1987) 283–304, esp. 289.

7. For example, B. Vawter, in his insightful analysis *Job & Jonah* (New York: Paulist, 1983) 62.

8. So Gerhard von Rad, *Wisdom in Israel* (Nashville: Abingdon, 1972) 219, and see p. 221 for the "credibility" of God.

9. Cf. David N. Freedman, "The Elihu Speeches in the Book of Job," *HTR* 61 (1968) 51–59.

10. Cf. R. A. F. MacKenzie, "The Purpose of the Yahweh Speeches in the Book of Job," *Bib* 40 (1959) 435–45. His analysis is articulated in his commentary on the book in the *NJBC*, 466–88, esp. 486.

11. Michael V. Fox, "Job 38 and God's Rhetoric," in *The Book of Job and Ricoeur's Hermeneutic* (Semeia 19; ed. J. D. Crossan; Missoula: Scholars Press, 1981) 53–61.

12. Quoted in Roland E. Murphy, *Psalms, Job* (Philadelphia: Fortress, 1982) 84.

13. Greenberg, "Job," 299.

14. See, for example, P. Sanders (ed.), *Twentieth Century Interpretation of the Book of Job* (Englewood Cliffs: Prentice-Hall, 1968); N. Glatzer (ed.), *The Dimensions of Job* (New York: Schocken, 1969); several essays in C. Duquoc et al. (eds.), *Job and the Silence of God* (Concilium 169; Edinburgh: Clark, 1983).

15. Gustavo Gutiérrez, *On Job* (Maryknoll: Orbis, 1987) xviii; the following quotation concerning the theme is from p. 12.

16. Cf. *The Complete Poems of Robert Frost* (New York: Henry Holt, 1949) 587–606. Artists and poets, especially, seem to have been captivated by Job. Thus, Robert Browning's Fra Lippo Lippi speaks of including Job in his painting: "And Job, I must have him there past mistake, the man of Uz (And Us without the z, Painters who need his patience)." See also the novel of G. K. Chesterton, *The Man Who Was Thursday: A Nightmare* (New York: Sheed & Ward, 1975) xix–xxvii, with the perceptive comments on the relationship to Job by Garry Wills.

17.   The title of an article by David N. Freedman, in *Bible Review* 4/2 (April 1988) 26–33, 44. Probably every reader (or at least commentator) has put that question to himself or herself. Freedman does not solve everything but leaves room for mystery and paradox (a lesson for all who study the book). He achieves a certain unity by recognizing four tests of Job: loss of material possessions and children; loss of health (physical suffering); the dialogue with friends, which ultimately turns out to be an exercise in futility; and finally the intervention of Elihu, who is, as it were, a disguise for Satan to press his case for the last time. The intervention of the Lord cannot be allowed to change the character of the test: God cannot "explain" or offer comfort to Job, but he can make a (somewhat self-serving, one may think) statement, the famous Yahweh speeches of chaps. 38–41. When Job recants (whatever is the meaning of 42:6), the Lord judges that he has passed the test and he doubles Job's former possessions (this is specified as an award for damages in cases of injustice). The final result is that Job has passed all testing, but he still has no explanation of what happened. The author seems to have created a deliberate impasse. From one point of view, the logic of the friends is correct: God is just and cannot allow unjust suffering. From another point of view (Job's), a human being can be innocent and yet suffer.

The mystery of God prevails. As Freedman puts it (p. 33), human beings "must be free of divine control and foreknowledge. Although it is highly debated in both Judaism and Christianity, the evidence of the Hebrew Bible points to a mystery at the center of the human person, a mystery that even God respects, so that the ultimate truth of human commitment can only be decided by time and testing."

See also D. N. Freedman, "The Book of Job," *The Hebrew Bible and Its Interpreters* (eds. W. H. Propp et al., Winona Lake, Ind.: Eisenbrauns, 1990) 33–51.

18.   C. R. Seitz, "Job: Full-Structure, Movement, and Interpretation," *Int* 43 (1989) 5–17, esp. 16.

CHAPTER 4

QOHELETH THE SKEPTIC?

♦

INTRODUCTION[1]

Author and Date

Ecclesiastes is the Greco-Latin form of the Hebrew Qoheleth. Both "names" have to do with a congregation (*qāhāl, ecclesia*), but the exact meaning escapes us. "Preacher" is another interpretation of the word, going back through Luther (*Prediger*) to Jerome (*concionator*). However, Qoheleth does not preach, and his book has no sermons. He is described as "David's son" (1:1; cf. 1:12), probably referring to Solomon, the accepted "author" of so many wisdom books. But this attribution has no support in the text except briefly in chap. 2, and it is negated by Qoheleth's views on royalty and on life. More concrete information is provided, probably by one of his disciples, in the epilogue (12:9–10): "Besides being wise, Qoheleth taught the people knowledge, and weighed, scrutinized and arranged many proverbs. Qoheleth sought to find pleasing sayings, and to write down true sayings with precision." It is reasonable to infer that he formed some kind of school, perhaps after the manner of Ben Sira a century later (Sir 51:23), and the present work would have been edited by his disciple or disciples. A date around 300 B.C.E. is generally suggested for the author; it would appear that his work was in circulation by 150 B.C.E., to judge from the dating of the Hebrew fragments of the book that were discovered at Qumran.[2]

If this date of 300 B.C.E. is reasonable, the question of Hellenistic influence on both Qoheleth's language and thought immediately arises. This is not a new issue, but it has been pressed vigorously in recent studies. At the present time it is safe to say that the judgment on this point is still moot (see Appendix).

The Language and Style of Qoheleth

Unlike any other biblical work of its size, the book includes an astonishing amount of repetition. Within the 2,643 words in 1:4–12:8, there are about 25 Hebrew roots (appearing as nouns, verbs, etc.) that occur at least five times, some of them thirty and fifty times—and they account for about 21 percent of the words used.[3] Among these "favorite" terms are the following: vanity, toil, work, wise, good, time, know, sun, see, fool, eat, profit, wind, death, just, wicked, portion, memory, vexation. The primary term, of course, is vanity, which occurs in various combinations thirty-eight times in the Masoretic text. The superlative expression "vanity of vanities," or complete absurdity, occurs in 1:3 and 12:8 in such a way as to suggest that it is the conclusion for the book; it obviously expresses a main theme.

The "simplicity" of this vocabulary is deceiving. The book is exceedingly difficult to translate, not because of any extensive corruption in the text, but because of our ignorance of the precise nuances of the terminology and of Qoheleth's thought. The reader can test this by comparing various translations at certain points, such as 2:8; 2:12 (sequence of thought); 3:11 (meaning of 'ōlām); 5:8; 6:8; 7:14, 18; 8:1; 10:10; 12:11—and many others could be added. The style approaches that of (later) Mishnaic Hebrew.

It is not surprising that many proverbial sayings are to be found in Qoheleth, the ḥākām. Some of these may be traditional, or even part of the repertoire to which he himself contributed. But it is frequently difficult to detect his judgment of them. Thus it is clear that the sayings in 2:13–14 proclaim the superiority of wisdom. And it is equally clear that Qoheleth rejects them in the lines that follow (2:15–16). In 4:5–6 he quotes two sayings that he considers inadequate, or perhaps he favors v 6 over v 5; it is difficult to tell. The same is true of the many sayings in chaps. 7 and 10. As a general rule one may conclude that he is usually critical of traditional wisdom, but in many cases the text has to be carefully sifted—often unsuccessfully.

Genre

Although many scholars[4] have termed the book a "royal testament," relying upon 1:1, 12 and 2:9, 12 and upon such works as the Egyptian instructions of Merikare and Amenemhet (see Appendix), this view is not adequate. The work is *sui generis* and lies somewhere between a treatise and a collection of sayings and thoughts.[5] Sayings and admonitions alternate with lengthy reflections.[6] The reflection states a thesis that Qoheleth has arrived at, and that he then develops in an unstructured way by observations, sayings, and the like.

The reflection is frequently introduced by favorite phrases, such as "I gave my heart to know" (1:13, 17; 8:16) or simply "I know" (3:12, 14). Sometimes he will relate a story to make his point (the "example story," 4:13–16; 9:13–16).

Allied to the issue of genre is the question, is this a book of philosophy or theology? In other words, should Qoheleth be regarded as a philosopher? Diethelm Michel has a helpful historical resume of modern views. Thus, E. Renan stoutly maintained that the book was clear, but theologians made it unclear. E. Podechard thought that Qoheleth's philosophical status could be justified because his viewpoint was universal (the area of wisdom), and not something specifically Israelite.[7] But it is doubtful whether the question can be answered in terms of the alleged opposition between Yahwism and wisdom (see the discussion of this in chap. 8). It is somewhat risky to use the categories of philosophy and theology because of the varying presuppositions that are implied. For example, is philosophy limited to the rational, while theology involves the revealed (faith?) or suprarational? The presuppositions determine the answer, but ultimately the characterization of philosopher or theologian tells one little about Qoheleth or his book.

However, one can pose the question of methodology. How does Qoheleth proceed in his discourse? The most recent judgments seem to be contradictory, but perhaps the difference is more verbal than real. Thus, Michael V. Fox has written that "Qohelet's epistemology is essentially (though not consistently) empirical. His procedure is to deliberately seek experience as his primary source of knowledge and to use experiential argumentation in testifying for his claims."[8] On the other hand, Diethelm Michel maintains that Qoheleth is "not an empiricist . . . but a thinker (or more exactly: an epistemological sceptic)." For both scholars, Qoheleth is a skeptic, but they arrive at this conclusion in different ways. For Fox, Qoheleth contests traditional wisdom (which Fox conceives as something static and not really experiential) by appealing to experience as a source of knowledge. For his part, Michel argues for a specific meaning to the verb rāʾâ (see). It means "to consider, to look at in a testing manner" ("betrachten, prüfend ansehen"). Qoheleth does not report an experience of "seeing" something, but is testing some statement. Thus one can distinguish between his own opinion and the view that he is criticizing. Hence one should view him not as a haphazard diarist but as a "philosopher who analyzes critically." I fail to see the difference between the Qoheleth who derives his arguments from experience to justify his views and the "philosopher" or epistemological skeptic who is consistently testing (by what he "sees") the traditional wisdom claims. It is not easy to enter into Qoheleth's world by way of "philosophy."

Structure

There has been little unanimity among scholars concerning the structure of the work.[9] There is general recognition of a prologue (1:1–11) and an epilogue (12:9–14) from another hand, but the main body has been fragmented into several sayings or unified by broad conceptual headings. To break through the arbitrary fashion in which the book has been analyzed, Addison Wright proposed a new division in the light of the principles of the "newer criticism."[10] The guide here is the text itself, not the interpretation of passages and their sequence. And the text shows some peculiar, but objective, characteristics. Thus, "vanity" and "chase after wind" are repeated several times in 1:12–6:9 and may be regarded as indicating the end of a section. The book breaks neatly into two halves of 111 verses each at 6:9. The second part also has a key phraseology: "find/not find" and "know/not know," which appear to form sections within 6:10–11:6. A final poem about youth and old age appears in 11:7–12:8. Numerological factors seem to have been at work. Thus, the numerical value of *hebel* (vanity—a key term) is 37, which is the number of times that *hbl* occurs in the book (excluding the repeated *hbl* in 9:9). The word is repeated in 1:2 three times, yielding the number 111, or the number of verses at midpoint.

The only certain addition to the book is the epilogue in 12:9–14, where an editor speaks of Qoheleth in the third person, in contrast to the first-person style throughout the work. However, many commentators have proposed the recognition of glosses and other additions to the book. These would be statements that contradict or soften the seemingly unorthodox view of life proffered by Qoheleth (e.g., contrast 8:11–12a with 8:12b–13). The tendency today, however, is to recognize such a procedure as arbitrary; the "contradiction" may well lie in the interpreter's understanding of the text, rather than with Qoheleth. Hence it seems better to take the book as all of one piece, despite the difficulties. This allows for tensions that would have existed within the author himself, and it attempts to explain the book as it stands.[11]

INTERPRETATION

History shows that the interpretation of Qoheleth's book has been very contradictory: skepticism, pessimism, Stoicism, Epicureanism, and others have all had their turn in the marketing of the work for the public. This is understandable, for the book itself provides certain starting points for these views. There are two thematic summaries. First, "vanity of vanities" and "all is vanity" (1:2; 12:8) at the beginning and end of the work (an inclusion) make a powerful characterization that suggests pessimism. Second, 12:13 is another summary, which goes in a contrary direction: "The last word . . . : Fear God and keep his commandments."[12] It matters not that this seems to be an editorial addition; it was designed to give an orientation to the work. A case has also been made for another key theme: "Enjoy life!" (e.g., 9:7ff.).[13]

The reader should be ready, therefore, for the tensions within the book, to keep them in careful balance. One must do this, moreover, without the dubious method of eliminating certain phrases or verses as being insertions of a later hand. There is another pitfall as well. Precisely because Qoheleth's viewpoints are so sharp and extreme, the modern reader may relativize them into a "biblical" homogeneity. The radical features of his thought can be tamed by the way in which the book is read in a larger context, even a biblical or ecclesial context. This is not to deny the right, or even the need, of anyone to absorb Qoheleth into a larger context. But the cutting edge of the book has to be retained.

We propose to single out various areas that can be considered as central to the author's thought, and to illustrate these with copious references to the text that the readers can verify for themselves. The themes will be intimately connected with certain key words that are repeated over and over in the book. The essential points are: vanity, joy, wisdom, fear of God, retribution, and God.

1. Vanity. Hebrew *hebel* means "vapor," "breath," hence something insubstantial and ephemeral—a vain, futile thing.[14] The repetition "vanity of vanities" is of course the normal Hebrew idiom for the superlative (as in "Song of Songs"). When Qoheleth pronounces the verdict of vanity on life, nothing is excluded. Life, in its totality, is utterly futile. This desperate judgment runs through the work, and it is not to be muted: *all* is vanity. His experiment with pleasure yields nothing (2:1–11). His toil (*ʿāmāl*) and the fruits thereof (2:18–23; 3:9; 6:7–9) give no enduring satisfaction. Riches also turn out to be a failure (5:9–16; 6:1–6). Even wisdom, which he resolutely aspired to but failed to attain (7:23–24), is not satisfying ("Why then should I be wise?" 2:15).

His verdicts are clear and forthright, but his reasons are varied and often quite circumstantial in ways that may not seem convincing to the reader. For example, he "hates" the fruits of his labor because he has to leave them to another who has not toiled for them (2:19–21, and his successor might turn out to be a fool!). There is no feeling here for family identity or the community—feeling that is so typical of traditional Israelite thought. No matter the strength of his argument, his conclusions are firm. He can always have recourse to the fact of death ("How is it that the wise man dies as well as the fool?" 2:16), which casts its shadow over all his thoughts (3:19–20; 4:3; 9:3–6, 10–12; 8:8; 11:8–12:7).

Qoheleth's judgment is also expressed in ways other than the repetition of "vanity." He questions after the "profit" (*yitrôn*) in such a way as to make it clear that there is none (1:3; cf. 2:11; 3:9; 5:15). Another ominous term is "lot" (*miqreh*, literally, "happening"), which befalls all living things (2:15; 3:19; 9:2); this is equated with death. But there is also what has been called the "falling time" when "time and a blow" ("time of calamity," 9:11) "happen" to living beings; it is the "evil time" (9:12). Elsewhere he conveys the futility of events by asserting human ignorance as fact or as a rhetorical question ("Who knows?" 3:21; 6:12).

For Qoheleth, then, the human situation is utterly bleak; it is no wonder that he can say that he "hated" life (2:17). It is possible to quarrel with his verdict and to claim that humans are not "helpless."[15] But such relativization goes beyond Qoheleth's thought, and it has to be argued from perspectives he does not envision.

2. Joy. As already indicated, a substantial number of scholars have evaluated the book in a positive way as inculcating enjoyment of life (the leitmotif, some would say); and one has even entitled Qoheleth "preacher of joy." Despite Qoheleth's emphasis on vanity, the reason is not far to seek. There are several passages in the book that can be advanced in favor of the gospel of enjoyment: 2:10; 2:24; 3:12; 3:22; 5:17–18; 8:15; 9:7–9; 11:7–10. Four of these are very similar: 3:12; 3:22; 8:15; and, with a mild emendation, 2:24. They present their conclusions as "nothing better than" (enjoyment, eating and drinking, etc.). That mode of expression is not as enthusiastic as it appears. In every case, the "nothing better" turns out to be a concession to circumstances; it is not an unqualified approval. The circumstances are that the real attainments in life are unfulfilled or unfulfilling, for whatever reason. So what to do? In that case, there is "nothing better." Qoheleth does admit that the "portion" (*ḥēleq*) of a given effort can be satisfaction or enjoyment (2:10; 3:22). What he means is that this much is *given* by God. But the tantalizing factor is that God is quite arbitrary in "giving." God gives as God pleases, and there is no consistency that Qoheleth can discover about this "giving"; it is mystery, rather than generosity. Hence there is an unmistakable quality of resignation in the "nothing better" statements. This is all that one can hope for in a very uncertain world; it is not an unqualified solution to living.

In a similar way, the other statements are weakened. In the gloomy situation of human life (5:16), Qoheleth offers (5:17) eating and drinking as man's "portion" (*ḥēleq*). Why? Because that is all humans can do, *if* they receive this "gift" (5:18) from an inscrutable divinity. In 8:15 Qoheleth recommends joy (*śimḥâ*), again as a "gift," always arbitrary, from God. In 9:7ff., he issues a positive command to enjoy life as one's "lot" (*ḥēleq*; cf. 2:10; 3:22; 5:17; 9:6, 9). But this is severely conditioned by 9:10: one is to live life to the fullest in view of the total inertia that one will eventually experience in Sheol. The same grim perspective of death haunts the enchanting recommendation to enjoy life (11:8–10): one is to remember that the days of darkness will be many (and these are vividly described in the passage on old age and death in 12:1–7). There is no denying the unquenchable thirst for life that Qoheleth himself had (9:10a; 11:7–9). But he knew only too well, and indicated explicitly, that this was severely conditioned by the fact of death, and by the inscrutable ways of the Almighty. This hardly merits for him the title of "preacher of joy."

3. Wisdom. It is a commonplace that Qoheleth goes against traditional wisdom, that with him (and the Book of Job) wisdom has entered a crisis situation.[16] The issue here is a correct evaluation of his dispute with traditional wisdom. Is it simply bankrupt, and hence to be shelved? Two things should be clear. First, Qoheleth is a ḥākām, or "wise man" (12:9), and he can be understood only in the light of this tradition with which he "quarrels."[17] Yes, he freely admits that he never attained the wisdom he sought (7:23–24), and he clearly rejects many of the claims of the sages (8:17). But the points he scores (vanity, failure of justice to be rewarded, etc.) are precisely the stuff of wisdom, the preoccupation of the sages. He reasons as a sage does, attempting to find out what is "good" for one to do (2:3; 6:10; etc.). The ever recurring question about the "profit" (1:3; 2:11, 13; 3:9; 5:8, 15; 7:12; 10:10–11) is another sign of the quest for wisdom. In his experiment with pleasure, he states twice that wisdom is the means he employed (2:3, 9). In short, his methodology is that of the Israelite sage, even if the sage has no advantage over the fool (6:8). Second, it is surely significant that he *never* considers folly a viable option. He challenges traditional wisdom and even seems to poke fun at it (1:18; 2:13–15; 9:16–17). But he never recommends folly. Indeed, folly is dangerous; just a little folly can spoil wisdom, which is extremely vulnerable (7:5–7; 9:18–10:1). He excoriates wordiness, the traditional sign of a fool (5:1–2; 10:12–15; cf. Prov 14:3; 10:19, 32; 15:17; Sir 21:16–17). Hence it is a misreading to claim that Qoheleth jettisons wisdom per se (any more than the Book of Job does). The ancients (and especially the editor of his book in 12:9–12) were not as "shocked" as modern readers are who consider Qoheleth to be in revolt against everything in the tradition. Yes, his was a deeply critical and even strident voice that did not sing in tune with the others; but the ancients made room for him among the sages.

4. Fear of God. We have already pointed out the summary in 12:13: "Fear God and keep his commandments." This frequently quoted line (regarded by F. Delitzsch as "the kernel and star of the whole book")[18] should serve as a red flag to the reader. How could Qoheleth have said this? These are not his words. They belong to the epilogist or editor of the entire book, who gave a hermeneutical direction to the book that is in line with Ben Sira's teaching on fear of God and Torah observance.[19] The nomistic understanding of fear as observance of the Torah is understandable, for the concept

itself developed various nuances within the Hebrew Bible.[20] But it is simply not appropriate for the Book of Ecclesiastes, which never mentions "commandments" (*miṣwôt*).

The phrase itself ("fear of God/Lord") is not found in the book; Qoheleth uses the verbal form, "(to) fear." The first occurence is in 3:14, where the mysterious divine activity is given a purpose: that people "may fear him." Here the verb takes on the connotation of fear before the numinous and mysterious, as the context of 3:13–22 clearly shows. On this verse W. Zimmerli astutely remarks, "Fear of God here is not travelling in paths of light which secure for those who walk therein the harvest of life's fruits and honors. Fear of God here means walking under a heaven that is mysteriously closed, walking without the assurance that lightning might not suddenly shoot out and strike you as you go—at every step relying upon the free gift of God, but with every step also summoned to suffer the riddle and oppression that God can inflict."[21]

The same connotation is present also in 5:6 in the terse command "Fear God!" This appears in a context in which Qoheleth warns against many words, rash promises, and insincerity in the worship of God. He even holds out the possibility of divine anger and ensuing destruction (5:6b). This is an instructive example of his understanding of divine wrath or judgment. He cannot rule it out, just as he cannot find it in the twists and turns of life; but it is always lurking in the background of the mysterious God whose actions cannot be programmed.

The meaning of the "God-fearer" in 7:18 is uncertain. It occurs in a context (7:15–18) that points out the uselessness of righteousness (v 15) and offers conflicting testimony about righteousness and wickedness (vv 16–17). His meaning is obscure; he seems to be pointing up once more the inadequacy of human judgment about virtue and vice. His only positive recommendation is that the one who fears God "will come forth from them all" (*RSV*) or "will win through at all events" (*NAB*). Any translation of these words remains uncertain, but the context demands a positive recommendation of the fear of God. Hence it would seem that this is the fear of the numinous, which keeps humans in check.

The only time that fear of God is used in the traditional sense is found in 8:12b, where God-fearers (hence, the just or pious) are contrasted with the wicked with respect to retribution. This surprising passage has been regarded by many scholars as a gloss, because it is a sentiment that Qoheleth totally denies elsewhere in his book. But one can allow it to remain as part of his work if one recognizes that he is repeating, even quoting, the traditional doctrine that he does not adhere to. One might paraphrase the sense thus: "There is no punishment for the sinner, although I am aware of the teaching that distinguishes between the fate of the God-fearers and that of the wicked."

5. The treatment of the just and the wicked. At several points Qoheleth laments the breakdown of the retribution that was a "given" in Israelite belief (e.g., 4:1–3; 7:15; 8:5–11). A just God prospers the good and punishes the evil; otherwise, where is the divine justice? There are many texts in Deuteronomy that enunciate this principle, and it is also the basis for the prophetic preaching against the rich who oppress the poor. In 7:15 Qoheleth registers the fact that the just perish despite their goodness and the wicked survive despite their wickedness. In 8:11 he recognizes the deleterious effect of this failure: people are emboldened to do evil because there is no penalty to be paid ("The sinner does evil a hundred times and survives," 8:12a). This lack of proper retribution he calls a vanity (8:14, *hebel*). As he says in 9:11–12, a time of calamity comes to all, because of "falling time," or the evil time that comes suddenly.

Many have argued that Qoheleth contradicts himself by proclaiming the judgment of God in 3:17 and 11:9b.[22] Hence these statements must be later "corrections" from another hand. This is not necessary. Qoheleth affirms judgment because that is part of his self-understanding as an Israelite. That God is a judge over humans is one of those undeniable factors in Israelite belief (and in belief throughout the ancient Near East, in fact). Qoheleth therefore could affirm this, but he could not draw any consolation from it; the *manner* of divine judgment is wrapped in mystery. The ways of God are simply inscrutable. It is impossible for Qoheleth to make sense out of what God is doing (3:11; 8:17; 11:5). The divine judgment is obviously not what the tradition had always accepted as "just." But Qoheleth was not one "to contend in judgment with one stronger than he" (6:10), that is, with God.

It is widely asserted that Qoheleth witnesses to the breakdown of the "act-consequence" view of retribution (discussed in chap. 8). But Qoheleth (and Job as well) is not interested in a chimera, a mechanical order that guarantees life's security. His question is with the God he knows, who has disappeared into mystery: "Who can make straight what he has made crooked?" (7:13)

6. God.[23] Who is the "God" of Qoheleth? He is never called by the sacred name, *yhwh*. The generic *ʾelōhîm* occurs forty times (twenty-six times with the definite article). This god is preeminently the creator. He has made everything "beautiful" (cf. "good" in Gen 1) or appropriate to its time (3:11), and the Masoretic text reads "creator" in 12:1. This aspect is further developed by the verbs most often used of God. He "makes" and "gives." Eleven times he is said to give (*ntn*). Among these gifts are life (mentioned parenthetically in 5:17; 8:15; 9:9), just as in 12:7 he gives the *rûaḥ* or "breath of life," which returns to him. But his gifts are often ambiguous, to say the least, such as the gift of *hāʿōlām* (3:11; a difficult term, which has been translated in various ways, e.g., duration, world, eternity) in the human heart; it keeps humans from understanding what God is up to. This is part of the

57

ʿinyan, or "troublesome task," which God has "given" to human beings to be troubled about (1:13; 3:10). More positively, he also gives wisdom and knowledge (2:26) to anyone he pleases. The joys of life, epitomized by eating and drinking, are his gift (3:13; 5:18); such things come from the "hand" of God (2:24). He also gives riches and glory to someone, only to have another take them (6:2). Hence, one never knows for certain the meaning of God's gifts. He seems to be supremely arbitrary in his generosity.

Another frequent verb is *ʿśh* (do or make). Two verses refer (with approval) to the divine action in creation: 3:11 and 7:29. Many times Qoheleth speaks of the *maʿăśeh* or "action" of God (3:11; 7:13; 8:17; 11:5) or simply of the things that are done under the sun (which are "evil," 4:3; 9:3; or "vanity," 8:14). Elsewhere in the Bible the "work(s) of God"—his creative activity (Pss 19:2; 104:24; Job 34:19) or his saving works (Pss 66:3; 111:2–7; 118:17)—are singled out for praise: But for Qoheleth the work of God is not something that stirs his admiration. It is totally unintelligible. Humans cannot know what God is doing (3:11). The work of God is something he has made crooked, and no one can straighten it out (7:13; cf. 1:15). Humans are simply unable to make sense of the action of God (8:17). Qoheleth compares the divine action to the mystery of the process of gestation, the role of the life breath in the womb of the mother (11:5).

All this constitutes a rather grim picture of the divinity. Nowhere does Qoheleth pray to this God, or even complain, as did many of the psalmists and Job. He is simply not rebellious. "God is in heaven, and you are on earth; so let your words be few" (5:1). He offers no consolation, nor does he limn the "soft" side of God that one finds in the rest of the Bible. He simply accepts God on God's terms. That is his faith. These terms are mysterious, so extreme that Qoheleth can call life's venture a vanity or absurdity (intending this as an objective fact, not as an insult). I have called this faith. It is not the faith that celebrates the saving acts of the Lord, of which we hear so much in the Bible. Hence some scholars interpret Qoheleth as honoring only an *Urhebergott* (a God of origins, or creator God), or even as rejecting the saving history of his people.[24] However, he says nothing about Israel's traditions, and it is not legitimate to extrapolate and make him say things that he has not said, or to infer that he accepted only a creator God. In view of the circumstances we learn from his writing, it is no little thing that he accepted this mysterious God, of whom he could write that divine love or hatred cannot be discerned by human beings (9:1–2). The usual signs of divine approval (prosperity or adversity) were not adequate for him.

A sympathetic interpretation of Qoheleth is in order. His is a valuable witness in the Bible to the mystery of God. He reminds us of the celebrated words of Thomas Aquinas: "When the existence of a thing has been ascertained, there remains the further question of the manner of its existence, in order that we may know its essence. Now because we cannot know what God is, but rather what He is not, we have no means for considering how God is, but rather how He is not. Therefore we must consider (1) how He is not; (2) how He is known by us; (3) how He is named."[25] Despite the general religious judgment that God is "Wholly Other," and truly mysterious, the pictures of God that human beings draw tend to be selective, optimistic, and favoring particular theological traits. Qoheleth provides a sober and necessary balance. He shows that there is more to religion than salvation. Although he failed to write of a comforting encounter with God, he did not lack reverence for the God who created a history in which his people could encounter him. There is a danger for Christians in particular to underrate this book. H. Hertzberg finished his commentary with the statement that the Book of Qoheleth is "the most staggering messianic prophecy to appear in the Old Testament." By this he meant that the "Old Testament was here on the point of running itself to death. Behind this total nothing from a human point of view, the only possible help was the 'new creature' of the New Testament."[26] This is not an adequate perspective from which to view Qoheleth. He must be taken on his own terms and not judged from a supposedly "superior" attitude. The *deus absconditus* who was real to him is sometimes hidden to those who think they know the hidden God.

This sketch of Qoheleth's thought should be weighed against the interpretations given to the book throughout its history. The history of biblical exegesis points up the presuppositions that always accompany interpretation. It also makes us aware of our own presuppositions in approaching the book.[27]

The interpretation of Ecclesiastes began with the editing of the book itself. The epilogist (whether one or many) who is responsible for 12:9–14 not only identified Qoheleth as a wise man but added a few remarks of his own.[28] In v 11 he manifests a high respect for the "sayings of the wise," which he regards as goads to thought. But v 12 has been interpreted by some as a kind of corrective: "As to more than these, my son, beware. Of the making of many books there is no end, and in much study there is weariness of the flesh." If the intention of this verse was to muffle the salvos of Qoheleth, the editor was much too indirect. Indeed, he speaks of Qoheleth in a laudatory way in vv 9–11, associating the book with the "sayings of the wise." What v 12 affirms is that the wisdom tradition, the "sayings of the wise" (to which the word "these" refers), suffices; no more wisdom books are needed after the Book of Qoheleth, which is to be included in "sayings of the wise." It is true that in vv 13–14 the book is summarized, as we have seen, in a manner that Qoheleth himself would hardly have done. In v 13, fear of God and keeping the commandments are joined together in such a way that the "judgment" of God seems to be obvious. Qoheleth would never put it that way. He does not deny that God judges (3:17; 11:9), but he denies that human beings can make sense of divine judgment or of anything that God does (3:11; 8:17; 11:5). The final verses (13–14) provide a reassuring tone to a work that may indeed have been unsettling, but that the tradition included in the canon.

In the Christian tradition, perhaps the best-known statement on Ecclesiastes is that found in the *Imitation of Christ* of Thomas à Kempis: " 'Vanity of Vanities, and all is vanity,' unless we serve God and love him with our whole heart (*Eccles* 1, 2). Oh, this is the highest and safest wisdom, that by contempt of the world we endeavor to please God."[29] This thought captures the spirit of asceticism and contempt of the world that caught on in early Christianity. Jerome set the tone for this by his commentary on Ecclesiastes, the book that he had read five years before to a certain Blesilla, "to provoke her to contempt of the world."[30] His commentary proceeded by distinguishing between the literal and the spiritual meaning. For him, as for all others before the modern period, Solomon was the author, and sometimes Solomon spoke from the point of view of another person. Such was the device that the ancients used in order to account for certain seeming contradictions in the book. This is continued in a slightly different way by modern scholars, who have recourse to later insertions! Luther, too, accepted Solomonic authorship, and the purpose of the book was "to put us at peace and to give us a quiet mind in the everyday affairs and business of this life, so that we may live contentedly in the present without care and yearning about the future."[31] He was, of course, quite opposed to the patristic and medieval "contempt of the world." Jewish tradition also accepted Solomonic authorship, and the single-minded emphasis on "profit" was understood to be the advantage of studying the word of God, which assured reward in the world to come. The words in 12:13 (fear God and keep the commandments) made a strong impression on Jewish commentators. Yet they, too, had recourse to the device of recognizing different "voices" in the book in order to explain hard sayings and apparent contradictions.[32] The history of exegesis is more than a curious collection of ancient views. It tells us of answers that disappear, but also of attempts that emerge even in modern times in our own explanations of this puzzling book.[33]

NOTES TO "QOHELETH THE SKEPTIC?"

1. The importance of these introductory issues is apparent from the volume of Diethelm Michel, who has summarized the wide range of opinions expressed in this century; cf. Diethelm Michel, *Qohelet* (EF 258; Darmstadt: Wissenschaftliche Buchgesellschaft, 1988). See his *Untersuchungen zur Eigenart des Buches Qohelet. Mit einem Anhang: Reinhard Lehmann, Bibliographie zu Qohelet* (BZAW 183; Berlin: de Gruyter, 1989) and also Michael V. Fox, *Qohelet and His Contradictions* (JSOTSup 18; Sheffield: Almond Press, 1989) 1–150.

2. Cf. J. Muilenburg, "A Qoheleth Scroll from Qumran," *BASOR* 135 (1964) 20–28.

3. O. Loretz, *Qohelet und der alte Orient* (Freiburg: Herder, 1964) 166–80 has supplied the data referred to here.

4. Notably K. Galling, "Der Prediger," in *Die fünf Megilloth* (HAT 18; 2nd ed.; Tübingen: Mohr/Siebeck, 1969) 88, and Gerhard von Rad, *Wisdom in Israel* (Nashville: Abingdon, 1972) 226.

5. As W. Zimmerli remarks, it is not a treatise with a clearly recognizable structure and a definable theme, but it is more than a loose collection of sayings. Cf. "Das Buch Kohelet—Traktat oder Sentenzensammlung?" *VT* 24 (1974) 221–30.

6. On the reflections, see Roland E. Murphy, *Wisdom Literature* (FOTL 13; Grand Rapids: Eerdmans, 1981) 127–28, with references to the studies of R. Braun and F. Ellermeier.

7. Cf. Michel, *Qohelet*, 103–7. For Michel's own views on the methodology of Qoheleth—esp. the understanding of *rā'â* (see)—see pp. 32–33 and pp. 80–81, where he lists the instances in the text where the verb means "to look at critically."

8. Cf. Michael V. Fox, "Qohelet's Epistemology," *HUCA* 58 (1987) 137–55, esp. 137, 152–54. Fox seems to have a specific definition of "empirical," for he excludes ancient Near Eastern wisdom from that sphere. He conceives of wisdom as a static body of knowledge transmitted by the sages, whose duty it was to motivate their students to accept it. In contrast to the sages' lack of argument stands the explorative character of Qoheleth's thought. It is true that by contrast Qoheleth is more exciting and provocative than the traditional sages, but they were nonetheless oriented toward experience.

9. Summaries of various proposed structures are surveyed in Addison Wright, "The Riddle of the Sphinx: The Structure of the Book of Qoheleth," *CBQ* 30 (1968) 313–34, esp. 314–17; J. L. Crenshaw, "Qoheleth in Current Research," *HAR* 7 (1983) 41–56; and esp. Michel, *Qohelet*, 9–45.

10. See Wright, "The Riddle," and also his "The Riddle of the Sphinx Revisited: Numerical Patterns in the Book of Qoheleth," *CBQ* 42 (1980) 38–51. His commentary on the book appears in the *NJBC*, 489–95.

11. To allow for such tensions, commentators have recognized "broken sentences," or "yes, but" sayings, in which a second statement modifies the previous statement; thus, 8:12b–13 represents the common wisdom, in contrast to Qoheleth's true opinion, expressed in 8:14. See Murphy, *Wisdom Literature*, 130–31.

12. Cf. Gerald T. Sheppard, *Wisdom as a Hermeneutical Construct* (BZAW 151; Berlin: de Gruyter, 1980) 125–26.

13. Cf. R. Gordis, *Koheleth—The Man and His World* (New York: Schocken, 1968) 129–31; R. Johnston, " 'Confessions of a Workaholic': A Reappraisal of Qoheleth," *CBQ* 38 (1976) 14–28; R. N. Whybray, "Qoheleth, Preacher of Joy," *JSOT* 23 (1982) 87–98.

14.   On this term see Michael V. Fox, "The Meaning of *Hebel* for Qohelet," *JBL* 105 (1986) 409–27. He argues that it does not have several different meanings in the book. It means "absurd," or "absurdity," and this is to be taken in the sense of the irrational, and not merely in the sense of the incomprehensible. But what is "reason" and the "rational" for Qoheleth? I think that the sharp distinction between absurd as irrational and absurd as incomprehensible cannot really be made (as is done on p. 413). Diethelm Michel also favors the term "absurd"; it is interesting to note that both Fox and Michel invoke the authority of *The Myth of Sisyphus* by A. Camus. For Michel, this comparison with Camus underscores the philosophical character of Qoheleth's work; cf. Michel, *Qohelet*, 86. The analysis of G. Ogden, *Qoheleth* (Sheffield: Almond Press, 1987) 22 concludes that *hebel* "conveys the notion that life is enigmatic, and mysterious; that there are many unanswered and unanswerable questions." I think this is closer to the mark, even if one disagrees with Ogden's emphasis on "Qoheleth's Call to Enjoyment" (p. 21).

15.   See B. Lang, "Ist der Mensch hilflos?" *TQ* 159 (1979) 109–24.

16.   K. Galling, *Die Krise der Aufklärung in Israel* (Mainzer Universitätsreden 19; Mainz, 1952); he is followed in this by many other scholars, such as A. Lauha and H. Gese.

17.   See Roland E. Murphy, "Qohelet's 'Quarrel' with the Fathers," in *From Faith to Faith* (Pittsburgh Theological Monograph Series 31; D. G. Miller Festschrift; ed. D. Y. Hadidian; Pittsburgh: Pickwick Press, 1979) 235–45.

18.   F. Delitzsch, *Commentary on the Song of Songs and Ecclesiastes* (Grand Rapids: Eerdmans, 1982) 438.

19.   Cf. Sheppard, *Wisdom as a Hermeneutical Construct*, 126–27.

20.   Cf. J. Becker, *Gottesfurcht im Alten Testament* (AnBib 25; Rome: Biblical Institute, 1965). For Qoheleth specifically, cf. E. Pfeiffer, "Die Gottesfurcht im Buche Kohelet," in *Gottes Wort und Gottes Land* (H. Hertzberg Festschrift; ed. H. G. Reventlow; Göttingen: Vandenhoeck & Ruprecht, 1965) 133–58.

21.   Cf. W. Zimmerli, "Das Buch des Predigers Salomo," in *Sprüche/Prediger* (ATD 16/1; Göttingen: Vandenhoeck & Ruprecht, 1962) 174.

22.   See, for example, Michel, *Qohelet*, 138, n. 14, and p. 167.

23.   The data on this topic has been assembled by H.-P. Müller, "Wie sprach Qohälät von Gott?" *VT* 128 (1968) 507–21; see also L. Gorssen, "La Cohérence de la conception de Dieu dans L'Ecclésiaste," *ETL* 46 (1970) 282–324. Further bibliography, along with discussion, is to be found in Michel, *Qohelet*, 95–103.

24.   On the *Urheberreligion*, see Müller, "Wie sprach Qohälät von Gott?" 520, and also Horst D. Preuss, *Einführung in die alttestamentliche Weisheitsliteratur* (Urban-Taschenbücher 383; Stuttgart: Kohlhammer, 1987) 174 and passim. R. B. Y. Scott implies that Qoheleth denies the salvation-history doctrine of Israel, but there is no evidence of Qoheleth's reflecting on this. Perhaps he may have regarded it as having

stopped (as many in the postexilic period might have thought): Cf. *Proverbs, Ecclesiastes* (AB 18; Garden City: Doubleday, 1965) 207.

25. *Basic Writings of Saint Thomas Aquinas* (ed. A. Pegis; New York: Random House, 1944) 25 (*S.T.*, I, 3, introduction).

26. H. Hertzberg, *Die Prediger* (KAT 17/4; Gütersloh: Gerd Mohn, 1963) 237.

27. See further Roland E. Murphy, "Qohelet Interpreted: The Bearing of the Past on the Present," *VT* 32 (1982) 331–37.

28. The epilogist is commonly considered to be distinct from Qoheleth. Fox has argued that he is the true author of the book. That is to say, Qoheleth is his *persona*, and he transmits Qoheleth's teachings in 1:3–12:7. He is the "teller of the tale," or the frame narrator of Qoheleth's tale. Cf. *Qohelet and His Contradictions*, 311–21.

29. See Thomas à Kempis, *The Following of Christ* (ed. J. van Ginneken; New York: America Press, 1937) 14.

30. Cf. *Commentarius in Ecclesiasten* (CCSL 72; Turnholt: Brepols, 1959) 249, praefatio.

31. Cf. "Notes on Ecclesiastes," in *Luther's Works* (ed. J. Pelikan; St. Louis: Concordia, 1972) XV, 7.

32. There is a lengthy exposition of Jewish interpretation in C. D. Ginsburg, *The Song of Songs and Qoheleth* (repr. New York: KTAV, 1970) 27–99.

33. An interesting example of the mixture of the ancient and the modern is Harold Fisch, "Qohelet: A Hebrew Ironist," *Poetry with a Purpose: Biblical Poetics and Interpretation* (Bloomington: Indiana University Press, 1988) 158–78. Fisch claims that the "view that would assign these closing verses of Ecclesiastes [12:9–14] to another author or editor should be resisted. This skeptical rejection of skepticism is the final twist of Qohelet's super-irony" (p. 175). Thus Qoheleth reverses the traditional wisdom saying about the fear of the Lord being the beginning of wisdom. Instead, according to 13:13 he tells us that to fear God and keep his commandments is "the end of the matter," or "the whole of man." As Fisch remarks, Qoheleth's "final statement seems to say that the *end point* of ḥokmâ is the fear of God!" (p. 175). This approach fits a current hermeneutical tendency to interpret a book holistically (as a whole, including *all* the parts), and not merely genetically (i.e., from the point of view of how the book was put together in various periods of time).

CHAPTER 5

Ben Sira—Wisdom's
Traditionalist

♦

INTRODUCTION

Author and Date

In what appears to be a colophon to the book, the author has given us his name: Yeshua (Greek form "Jesus") ben (son of) Eleazar ben Sira (50:27). This is a departure from the style of Old Testament writings, which are usually unsigned. The author has transmitted the name of his father and then his grandfather, but he is commonly referred to as either Ben Sira or Sirach (the Greek form of Sira).

There is universal agreement that Ben Sira was actively engaged in his teaching and writing in the first part of the second century B.C.E. Indeed, the first quarter of the century is more accurate, because the book does not reflect the problems that arose in Palestine with the advent of Antiochus IV Epiphanes to power in 175, and the ensuing Maccabean revolt triggered by the desecration of the Temple in 167. Hence the year 180 is generally assigned as the date of the work. This inference is strengthened by the prologue to the Greek translation written by Sirach's grandson. This grandson mentions his arrival in Egypt in 132 B.C.E., the thirty-eighth year of the reign of King Euergetes (Ptolemy VII), when his activity as a translator could have begun (perhaps in Alexandria). This provides a suitable time period between his grandfather and himself. Another sign is the praise of Simon the high priest in 50:1–24; he is to be identified with Simeon II, who was high priest from 219 to 196. Sirach describes his Temple ministry, as it were, from the point of view of an eyewitness, although 50:1 implies that Simon has (just) died. It is generally presumed that the work was composed in Jerusalem.

The Man

Whatever we know about Ben Sira is derived from the prologue that his grandson prefixed to the book when he translated it, and from the book itself. There are three significant passages (24:30–33; 33:16–18; 50:27–29) that reveal Sirach's self-understanding. In 24:30–33 he develops the metaphor of water and applies it to himself. Wisdom, or Torah, is comparable to the great rivers of antiquity (24:23–25), and he is a rivulet that channels the water into the garden he has planted. He registers a naive astonishment: "This rivulet of mine became a river, and my river became a sea" (v 29). Indeed, his teaching will shine like the dawn, illuminating far-off places. More than that, he calls it "prophecy," which is destined for future generations (vv 30–31). This gives an idea of the importance he attached to his work. He wrote not for himself but for those who seek wisdom (33:18). At the same time he is somewhat self-effacing; he is surprised at what has happened. We learn in 33:16–18 that this is due to the Lord's blessing. He modestly compares himself to one who gleans after the vintage that was prepared in Israel's traditions. Then in the final colophon, where he identifies himself by name, he speaks of the teaching that he has poured forth. "Happy the one who meditates on these things," for if he acts on them, he can cope with anything (50:27–29). Hence Sirach can invite the "untutored to take up their dwelling in my house of instruction" (51:23). He may be speaking in literal terms of a school building (although we know nothing of the circumstances) or merely referring to his teaching. Teacher that he is, he asks for an earnest desire for wisdom on the part of his students, and he promises them (without cost!) the riches for which he himself labored.

The aforementioned passages from Sirach are fairly straightforward and revealing. It is also possible to infer more from the description of the sage in 39:1–11. In a sense this is an ideal self-description, for it is clearly the goal that Sirach set for himself. In context he reviews various professions in relation to that of the scribe (sōpēr; 38:24–39:11). Some have compared this passage with the Egyptian Satire on Trades (*ANET*, 432–34), but this is misleading. Sirach's perception of other callings is far from ridicule; he is remarkably enlightened, and even enthusiastic. His description is vivid, almost as if he had worked on a farm, or cut seals, or labored in a smithy, or toiled at a pottery kiln. He ends up praising the noble work of various artisans: "Without them no city could be lived in" (38:32). At the same time, he ranks higher the vocation of the sage, who devotes himself "to the study of the Law of the Most High," and Sirach describes him in 39:1–11. This person is concerned with the Torah, wisdom, and the prophecies (a threefold division of the Hebrew Bible—as in the prologue to the Greek translation, but now in a different order). The wise man's concern with parables, proverbs, and the like is not surprising (39:3), but in 39:4 Sirach notes the sage's travels and appearance before rulers (did he himself travel?). It is noteworthy that prayer is underlined. The wise man prays to be purified, and only then does the Lord bestow his gift of understanding and wisdom (39:5–6). Sirach becomes very effusive in describing the fame that the wise man achieves (39:9–11). Even if this is an idealized portrait, not a biographical note, it fills out the author's vision of himself, the goal to which he aspired.

His grandson, in the important prologue to his Greek translation, tells us more about the temper of the man, and his observations are borne out by the character of the book. He notes that his grandfather had devoted himself to an intense study of the Hebrew Bible and, out of a desire to help others, had written the present work. The prologue speaks not of "the Hebrew Bible" but of a threefold division: "Law, the Prophets and the later authors." Already a threefold division that came to be termed "Law, Prophets and Writings" (TNK)[1] was recognized in the translator's time (after 132). The grandson notes that Ben Sira was thoroughly familiar with these works. His judgment is quite correct. The work is filled with allusions and deliberate repetitions of phrases from earlier books of the Bible. Modern scholarship has called this *style anthologique,* or "anthological composition." The writer knows the Bible so well that he expresses his thoughts in the phraseology of previous biblical books; his work becomes, as it were, a mosaic of biblical terms and images. This style of writing has been verified in many other compositions of this era, such as the Wisdom of Solomon (written in Greek, and using the earlier Greek translation, or Septuagint, as its source) and the *Hodayot* psalms from Qumran.

The Book: Title and Text

The original title, if any, has not been transmitted in Hebrew, but the Greek tradition calls it The Wisdom of Jesus, Son of Sira. Another commonly used title, Ecclesiasticus, derives from many Latin Vulgate manuscripts, although most Latin manuscripts are in harmony with the Greek: The Book of Jesus, Son of Sirach. The term Ecclesiasticus refers to the book (*liber ecclesiasticus,* "church book"). Nothing is known about the origin of this title, which dates back to the time of St. Cyprian (d. 258 C.E.), but it has been surmised that the title is due to the extensive use of the book as a *vade mecum* for Christians, or perhaps as a claim for its canonicity. In any case, the book was not received as canonical in the Jewish tradition (followed by Protestants), although it is quoted in the Talmud and other Jewish writings, sometimes even with the formula "it is written," the usual sign of a canonical work. It is part of the canonical Old Testament for Catholics and most Orthodox groups.

The text of Sirach has a unique history, chiefly because of the practical disappearance of the original Hebrew text from the Western world for about fifteen centuries (from Jerome to about 1900).[2] Although the Hebrew was known in the Jewish tradition, it was not conspicuous. In the Christian tradition it was known from the Greek and Latin translations, from daughter versions (e.g., Coptic) of these sources, and from the Syriac version. Then came the discovery, in 1896 by Solomon Schechter, of medieval Hebrew manuscripts of Sirach that had been fortuitously preserved in an old Jewish *genizah* (a storeroom for used liturgical and biblical Hebrew manuscripts) in Cairo.

By 1900 fragments from four different Cairo manuscripts (A, B, C, D) were published. Later, in 1931, a fifth manuscript (E) was brought to light. By 1960 more portions from manuscripts B and C were made available by J. Schirmann. The Dead Sea Scroll discoveries turned up small fragments of Sir 6:20–31 in cave 2 at Qumran, and also Sir 51:13–20, 30 in the Psalms Scroll from cave 11. Then the excavation of the Masada fortress (1964) led to the discovery and publication of Sir 39:27–44:71.[3] This manuscript was written about a hundred years after the book was composed. At the present time we possess a little over two thirds of Sirach in the original language.

But do these copies represent the original, or are they Hebrew translations of, say, a Greek text that had been the primary text in the Western world? Minute and exacting scholarly analysis quickly established that these were copies of an original Hebrew. Paradoxically, the establishment of the text of Sirach became ever more complicated. In both the Hebrew and Greek traditions two basic forms of the text, one short and one long, came to be recognized. It is not to be thought that the recensions in the Hebrew manuscripts discovered since 1896 are impeccable. Most of these are of medieval provenance and give evidence of some contamination. In fact the Cairo manuscripts betray a short and a long (expansion) form of the Hebrew text. This conclusion is not surprising in view of the evidence provided by the ancient versions. There are also short and long forms in the Greek tradition: short in the famous uncials, such as Codex Alexandrinus and Vaticanus, and long in Codex 248 and in ancient translations from the Greek such as the Old Latin, which Jerome took over into the Vulgate with practically no change.

The phenomenon of short and long forms of a biblical book is not unusual, as can be seen from the differences between the Hebrew and Greek texts of Jeremiah and of Job. Many of the expansions in Sirach are typical of the fate of any book that is handed down over the years, such as marginal glosses that creep into the text. But the expanded (long) form of Sirach provides considerable interest in that it supplies an eschatology that goes beyond the views of the author. This eschatology is attested in the Greek and Old Latin traditions that imply a judgment after death, with suffering for evildoers and joyous eternal life for the righteous. Similar ideas are found in the ancient Syriac version, which stresses union with the angels in the next life. Whether or not Ben Sira held such views will be discussed later.

From this discussion of the forms of the text emerges an interesting theological issue: must one choose between the texts, and if so, which is the "canonical" text? C. Kearns proclaims the long form as the canonical text, and he has recourse to the Council of Trent, which considered canonical those books "in their integrity with all their parts" that were found in the Catholic tradition represented by the Vulgate Bible.[4] The issue here is not new. Many Catholic authors have sided with Augustine in claiming that the Septuagint form of the Bible is inspired (i.e., the translation itself) because this form was the one used by the early Church.[5] Normally, one would assume that a translation is, objectively speaking, "inspired" only to the extent it agrees with the original autograph. But the claim here would include the expansions that are not due to the hand of Ben Sira.

However, the proper issue is not text, but book.[6] No council or theological opinion has determined the canonical character of later additions to a text. It cannot be said that Trent intended to settle the problems of textual criticism (of which the council fathers had little understanding). But they did want to ensure that such passages as the deuterocanonical parts of Esther and Daniel be considered part of the Bible because the centuries-old Vulgate contained them. They were of course ignorant of the Hebrew text of Sirach and the corresponding textual problems. Hence one may conclude that only the identity of a biblical book (Genesis, for example) is determined as canonical. Issues of textual criticism have to be distinguished from canonicity and left open to whatever evidence textual critics can muster. Additions by later hands to an original autograph testify to the later history of the book, how the book was interpreted by later readers, but not to the original text and meaning of the book.

This summary of the history of the text of Sirach has an important practical bearing. It alerts the reader to the problem of the translation of the work. In modern times various kinds of English and other modern-language translations have been made. Some settle for a translation from a Greek text, with occasional footnotes about Hebrew readings (e.g., *RSV, NJB, NEB*). Others (*NAB*, AB) rightly attempt to establish a critical text of Sirach on the basis of the Hebrew, Greek, and other ancient versions, and translate this critical text into the vernacular. The results are twofold: there are significant differences among the English versions, and also the chapter and verse references will often differ, sometimes by one or several verses. The plea has been made that all should follow the numbering of a critically established Greek text, and that practice is followed in this book.[7]

Structure

Efforts to detect a structure in the book have not been successful. Every proposal suffers from subjective factors, and none have rallied any consensus. It is generally agreed that chap. 51 is an addition or appendix to the work (like the acrostic poem that ends Prov 31, an acrostic is found in Sir 51:13–30). In the rest, the reader is confronted with a collection of minitreatises on various topics: wisdom, friendship, poverty and riches, and the like. The ancients seem to have recognized the absence of any structure. In both the Hebrew and Greek manuscript traditions, subtitles were added at various places, and this practice is followed by some modern translations (NAB, NJB).

A comparison with the Book of Proverbs is helpful. Sirach's various compositions resemble the wisdom poems in Prov 1–9. The most obvious example is chap. 24 on the personification of Wisdom, which is modeled on Prov 8. The point is that Sirach has organized his discourses in a relatively logical and consecutive fashion. It is still more instructive to compare the similarities and differences between Prov 10ff. and Sirach. At first sight, the discrete sayings in these chapters of Proverbs stand out in contrast to the smooth discourses in Sirach. But careful examination illustrates the art of Ben Sira. The collection of sayings in Prov 10ff. is relatively haphazard in the sense that each verse stands on its own. In Sirach, however, there is a sense of unity and development of thought to a topic, even though many of his verses could be excerpted and seen clearly to be proverbial sayings in their own right. Thus, Sir 13:1–14:2 deals with attitudes toward the rich and the poor, and it reads quite smoothly—so smoothly that one may overlook the fact that there are several (independent) sayings that have been worked into the flow of thought (e.g., 13:18, 21, 23). What the Book of Proverbs has separated in Prov 10:15; 18:23; 19:4, 6 (on riches and poverty) is found together in Sirach: Sir 13:21–23 consists of separate sayings about the treatment of the rich and poor (the differences that wealth creates), but they are so strung together that a unity is created. A different kind of example is the way in which Sirach will expand on a given saying. Thus Prov 21:3 (cf. Prov 15:8) on justice and sacrifice is reflected in a kind of homily in Sir 31:1–11. An outstanding example is the multiple development of the traditional wisdom theme, fear of the Lord (Sir 1:11–30; 10:19–23; etc.), a theme that can be compared to the motto in Prov 1:7 (9:10). Sirach develops this theme in a creative way (1:11–30 contains twenty-two lines, the number of letters in the Hebrew alphabet), mixing in sayings (vv 11–14) with commands (vv 28–30).[8] It has been pointed out that Ben Sira has a tendency to round off a discourse with a proverb, or rather an admonition (cf. 7:36; 28:6–7; 35:12–13).[9] But overall, one has the impression of reading a unit, not merely a collection of sayings. He succeeds in mixing imperative commands, "better" sayings, and quotations, as in 29:21–28, which manifests a sense of continuity despite the wide range of literary forms.

This prompts the question of Ben Sira's originality. It lies more in his presentation than in the content, and perhaps this is to be expected in a sage who conserves and hands on the tradition. However, when one considers the wide range of his topics, and the fruitful development of his themes, one recognizes the magnificent control that he had of wisdom lore. While one may not always be able to single out individual verses as the original creation of Sirach, there can be no doubt about his deft orchestration and expansion of traditional ideas. Among the excellent examples of his ability should be mentioned the treatment of the fear of the Lord (1:11–30); the association of creation with divine goodness (16:24–18:24); the miseries of life (40:1–10); the hymn to God's works (42:15–43:33). Finally his "praise of famous men" in chaps. 44–49 is a tour de force that builds on Old Testament sources. For a judgment on Ben Sira's attitude toward Hellenism, see the discussion in the Appendix.

Literary Forms

Sirach mastered a wide range of forms, and this has contributed to the liveliness and variety of his message. We have seen his adroitness in combining the proverbial sayings with relatively lengthy poems. Among the long poems, these hymns are conspicuous: 16:24–18:14; 39:12–35; 42:15–43:33. The first one illustrates the thin line that exists between wisdom reflection and praise. It begins with a didactic opening ("my son") and then proceeds to a description of the manner in which God has ordered creation. The creation of humankind is the main emphasis as Sirach lingers over the data of Gen 2:7 and 3:19. The detail of creation is touching: tongues, eyes, and ears (17:6), and also an "understanding heart" (Solomon's request in 1 Kgs 3:9). The destiny of humankind is to praise God. This has been made possible for Israel through the covenant and Torah. The Lord is aware of human sinfulness, which will be requited, but Sirach praises the divine mercy toward those who will convert. The final verses (18:1–14) are a lively contrast between the ephemerality of human existence and the Lord's patience and shepherding qualities.

The second hymn announces a definite theme: the works of God are all of them good (39:16, with inclusion in 39:33). This theme is illustrated by the right *kairos*, or "time": "In its own time every need is supplied" (vv 17b, 33b). Unlike Qoheleth, he never seems to advert to the fact that God's *kairos* is out of kilter with human ideas of time (cf. Eccl 3:11). This hymn is even

71

challenging: who can say, "What is the purpose of this?" Qoheleth would have supplied him with unexpected answers. Sirach reaffirms the traditional view of retribution (39:24, 27) as if the Books of Job and Qoheleth had never been written. But he stubbornly sticks to his point (39:32–35).

The third hymn (42:15–43:33) is marked by a sequence of natural phenomena, reminiscent of Job 38–41. It is a creation hymn in praise of the master, omniscient and omnipotent, whom all the works of creation obey, especially the hail, lightning, rain, and the like (cf. Pss 147–48). In an outburst of admiration he concludes in 43:27, "He is [the] all" (hû' hakkōl). This seems to mean that God is the source and sustenance of all that exists.

Two prayers of petition occur: 22:17–23:6 and 36:1–22. The first is a personal request of Sirach for control of his tongue and his sexual appetite. Interestingly, the prayer ends in an instruction on these topics (the tongue, 23:7–15; passion and adultery, 23:16–27). The second prayer clearly has a political bent: a request that the Lord raise his hand against the goyim, or "gentiles"—that is, the Seleucid rulers who have begun to dominate Palestine (after 198 B.C.E.). Just as God manifested his holiness by punishing his people, so now he is to show his glory by granting them victory over their oppressors (cf. Ezek 28:22–25). The "signs and wonders" of the Exodus are to be repeated, and the Jews of the Diaspora are to be brought home to Palestine—to Zion and the Temple, where the divine glory will be manifested. In 50:25–26 Sirach expresses his loathing for the Edomites, Philistines, and Samaritans, but his prayer in chap. 36 is clearly directed against the Seleucid yoke. It is the only "eschatological" passage in his book. He wants to see the people united, and his vehemence is a harbinger of the aggressive spirit that was shortly to be manifested during the Maccabean revolution.

Naturally, Sirach exploits all the usual wisdom forms, such as sayings, numerical proverbs (e.g., 25:7–10, ten beatitudes [emended text]; 26:5–6, and admonitions. A particular form of the admonition is the "say not" prohibition. This recommends against a saying that is quoted and usually gives a reason for the command. The form occurs also in Eccl 7:10 and in Egyptian wisdom (Amenemope 18, 21, ANET, 423–24). A series of these occur in Sir 5:1–6 (cf. also 15:11–12; 16:17–18). In the context of Sirach's treatment of human freedom, 15:11 is typical: "Say not, 'It was God's doing that I fell away'; for what he hates he does not do."

CONTENTS

It is impossible to summarize the contents or message of this book. Two ways of reading Sirach can be suggested. One can begin with chap. 1 and be agreeably surprised in meeting the variety of topics that are treated, and even repeated. It is also possible to put together an index of the various topics that occur, in order to gain a more synthetic view of this thought. The following informal table of contents may be helpful.[10]

Almsgiving and lending: 29:1–20.
Autobiographical references: 24:28–32; 33:16–18; 34:9–13; 50:27–29; 51:13–30; see also the evaluation of professions in 38:24–39:11.
Counsel: 37:7–15.
Creation: 16:24–18:14; 39:12–35; 42:15–43:33.
Death: 14:11–19; 38:16–23; 41:1–4.
Discretion and moderation: 11:7–28.
Fear of the Lord (see "Wisdom"): very frequent, perhaps over sixty times, and especially prominent in 1:9–2:18.
Forgiveness: 28:1–7.
Friendship: 6:5–17; 9:10–16; 11:29–12:18 (friends and enemies: 22:19–26; 27:16–21; 37:1–15).
Humility: 3:17–24; 7:16–17; 10:28.
Hymns:
(a) creation: 16:24–18:14; 42:15–43:33.
(b) providence: 32:14–33:18; 39:12–35.
Joy: 14:11–19; 30:21–25.
Law: 9:15; 11:1; 17:11; 19:20; 24:23; 32:14–33:3; 35:1; 39:1.
Miscellanea: 4:1–6:4 (commands and prohibitions; cf. also 7:1–8:19).
Paradoxes: 20:9–31.
Parents and children: 3:1–16; 7:23–25; 16:1–4; 30:1–13; 41:5–10.
Physicians: 38:1–15.
Praise of the ancestors: 44:1–49:16 (50:24).
Prayers: 22:27–23:6; 36:1–17; 50:22–24; 51:1–12.
Riches: 11:10–21; 14:11–19; 31:1–11; cf. 13:1–14:10 (rich and poor).
Sacrifice: 34:21–35:13.
Self-control: 18:30–19:3; 37:27–31.
Shame: 41:17–42:8.
Sheol: 14:16–17; 17:27–28.
Simon, high priest: 50:1–24.
Sin and folly: 16:5–23; 19:18–20:32; 21:1–22:2.
Social justice: 4:1–10; 34:21–27; 35:14–26.
Table etiquette: 31:12–32:13.
Tongue: 5:9–15; 23:7–15; 28:8–26; cf. 20:1–8 (silence).
Wisdom: 1:1–10; 4:11–19; 6:18–37; 14:20–15:10; 24 (see chap. 9); 51:13–30; cf. also 19:20–20:31; 21:11–26; 32:14–33:6; 37:16–26; 38:24–39:11.
Women (wives, daughters): 9:1–9; 23:22–26; 25:13–26:18; 36:26–31; 42:9–14.

At least three topics in Sirach deserve more detailed consideration: retribution, the union between wisdom and Israel's election/covenant traditions, and fear of the Lord.

1. Retribution. It will strike the reader immediately that Ben Sira, for all his acquaintance with the previous books of the Bible, does not seem to have been affected by the Books of Job and Qoheleth. His work resembles Proverbs not only in style but in teaching as well. Along with the sages of old, Ben Sira presented wise conduct as the means to prosperity and the good life in the here and now. The only immortality is that of name or memory, and one's descendants (30:4–5; 37:26; 41:12–13). There is evidence of the typical Israelite resignation to the finality of death:

> Give, take, and treat yourself well,
>   for in Sheol [Hades] there are no joys to seek. (14:16)

His advice to the mourner is practical: one can weep and pay the tribute of sorrow, but not to excess. There is no hope of return, and one must face the future resolutely (38:16–23). In a brilliant passage (41:1–4) he describes various reactions to death, how bitter it is to the one who is well off, but how welcome to others:

> Whether one has lived ten years, a hundred, or a thousand,
>   in Sheol [Hades] there is no claim on life. (41:4)

Hence the reader should not be deceived by certain passages that seem at first sight to give an indication of some kind of judgment at death. For example, 7:36 reads:

> In whatever you do, remember the end,
>   and you will never sin. (cf. also 28:6)

The "end" does not connote judgment or a transition to a better life. It is merely a sober reminder of human mortality. One should live righteously, or one's "end" will be somehow marked by grief, a premature death, a parting from the things one has prized more than wisdom. The Lord can repay on the day of death; hence by how one ends, one is known (11:26–28). In the Greek tradition of this book,[11] a personal eschatology was read into such passages by the translator. However, this view is foreign to Sirach, who consistently affirms that Sheol/Death is the ultimate end of human beings (e.g., 14:16–19; 41:4).

The tradition confronted Sirach with a real problem in the matter of divine retribution: how does God differentiate between the faithful and the sinner in the order of providence? Scholars have used the term "theodicy" in describing his understanding of the working out of divine justice.[12] This is too ambitious a word to characterize his thought, but perhaps one can state the principles that govern his optimistic point of view. First of all, he begins with the accepted biblical principle of determinism. All that happens is the Lord's doing:

> Like clay in the hands of a potter,
>> to be molded according to his pleasure,
> So are humans in the hands of their Maker,
>> to be assigned by him their function. (33:13)

This does not deny human responsibility. In fact, Sirach says that God has made human beings free to choose (15:14–17), and in that context he admonishes those who would try to blame God for their failings ("Say not: 'It was God's doing that I fell away.' . . . 'It was he who led me astray,'" 15:11–12). No, before us are life and death, and we receive what we choose (15:17). Like the rest of the biblical writers, Sirach makes no effort to reconcile these two factors—determinism and free choice.

Second, he proclaims the principle that all the works of God are good. Such is the refrain that opens and closes his hymn in 39:12–35 (cf. vv 16, 23). Indeed, he rejects the right to say that one thing is not as good as another (39:34). He points to the basic gifts of God, such as water and fire, milk and honey (39:26). These are good for the godly, but they turn out evil for sinners (here the typical law of retribution is at work). In addition, Sirach is operating with a second premise: the right time. He continually affirms the *kairos*, or timeliness of events (39:16, 33, 34). There is even a proper time for "fire and hail, famine and disease" (39:29). These are mere servants of God, which have their tasks to perform.

A third principle is also at work—the doctrine of opposites (33:7–15):[13]

> Good is the opposite of evil,
>> and life the opposite of death;
>> so the sinner is the opposite of the godly.
> Look at all the works of the Most High;
>> they are in pairs, the one the opposite of the other.
>> (33:14–15)

The same idea is expressed in his enthusiastic hymn in 42:15–43:33.

> All things are in twos, one the opposite of the other,
>> And none of them has he made in vain. (42:24)

It is clear from these affirmations of Sirach that he had no answer to the problems that modern (and ancient) theodicy puts before us. The astonishing fact is that the only mention of Job is the casual reference in the shadow of Ezekiel in 49:8–9 (cf. Ezek 14:14, 20). Sirach was not unaware of hardships and difficult problems. In a moving passage he exclaims:

> Mock not the worn cloak
>   and jibe at no one's bitter day;
> For strange are the works of the Lord,
>   hidden from men his deeds. (11:4)

This verse shows that Sirach, like Qoheleth (Eccl 3:11; 8:17; 11:5), appreciated the mystery of the "work of God," but he resolutely refused to question God in the manner of Qoheleth. The hard question of (unjust) suffering is to be regarded as "trials" and testing (2:1–5). The one who trusts in God will eventually win out. Yet the works of God are mysterious, hidden (11:4), despite the rhapsody of his praise in 42:15–43:33.

This optimism is difficult to explain. It is aimed at the consolation and strengthening of the faithful, but it obviously does not confront the hard questions. Perhaps this is due to Sirach's understanding of humility (cf. Ps 131):

> The greater you are, humble yourself the more,
>   and you will find favor with God. . . .
> What is too sublime for you, seek not,
>   into things beyond your strength, search not. . . .
> What is committed to you, attend to;
>   for what is hidden is not your concern.
> With what is beyond your tasks, meddle not;
>   for things beyond human understanding are shown you. (3:18–23)

One can detect here a caution against overextending oneself; one is to perform the job at hand. But what did Sirach conceive as being "sublime" and "hidden"? It has been suggested by some that he is warning against the "new wave" that Hellenism was bringing about in Palestine.[14] But could it not be equally well directed against prying into the mystery of God, which was prominently discussed in his own wisdom tradition?

2. Wisdom and Israel's sacred traditions. Ben Sira is the first to have created a bond between wisdom and the typical traditions of Israel. This is manifest particularly in the identification of Wisdom with Torah (chap. 24, which is treated in detail in chap. 9), and in the list of Israel's heroes (chaps. 44–50). Perhaps the most important move is the identification of Wisdom and Torah. This is not a casual connection, as the several references to Law

in the table of contents earlier in this chapter demonstrate. Wisdom has become for Ben Sira a new expression of Israel's self-understanding. She hears the astonishing command from the Most High—"In Jacob make your dwelling, in Israel your inheritance" (Sir 24:8)—and so she does (24:10–12), and Ben Sira identifies her with the "Law which Moses commanded us" (24:23).

Chapters 44–49 (with an appendix in 50:1–24 about Simon) are commonly known as "the praise of the fathers" after the title that appears in many Greek and Latin manuscripts. Like chap. 24, this section stands out in contrast to the rest of the book. Also, it is something new in the Bible that men are praised, and not God. Where the Old Testament recalls its past heroes—such as Moses or Joshua or David—it is not to sing their praises; the emphasis is rather on what the Lord did through his servants, as the hymns of the Psalter clearly illustrate. Sirach's creation is a compact sequence of historical figures that occurs nowhere else in the Bible. The immediately preceding hymn (42:15–43:33) praises the works of God in creation; it ends with the line that God has given wisdom to his *ḥăsîdîm* ("loyal," "faithful" ones). This serves to unite it to 44:1, in which it is the praises of *'anšê ḥesed* (men of loyalty) that are sung. The opening lines are very general: wisdom, prophecy, governors, and the like. No names are given, but the heroes will be specified. Their name and memory will be perpetuated (44:1, with an inclusion in v 14).

Burton Mack[15] has described the literary structure of the individual items: (1) designation of office (prophet, etc.); (2) mention of divine choice ("found," "formed"); (3) a reference to covenant (except for prophets); (4) virtues (according to their offices); (5) historical setting (especially the background of threat against the people); (6) rewards (namely, the honor or praise that the heroes receive from the people). Looked at from the point of view of office, the list can be broken down into the fathers (Noah, Abraham, Isaac, and Jacob); priests (Aaron, Phineas); judges (Joshua and Caleb receive explicit mention); prophets (Moses, Samuel, Elijah, and Elisha, plus the twelve, and the three major prophets); kings (only the good kings are explicitly named—David, Hezekiah, and Josiah; Solomon is criticized). Several figures have more than one office (e.g., Moses, who is teacher, prophet, and ruler). To this roster of heroes is added an emphatic and lengthy description of Simeon II, high priest, but also a ruler who protected his people (50:2–4). Sirach follows a chronological sequence, but he omits freely. It is striking that he mentions Zerubbabel, Jeshua, and Nehemiah from the restoration period, but omits Ezra.

For many, these chapters have evoked the memory of the Roman genre *de viris illustribus,* or the Hellenistic genre of encomium (praise), or even an epic poem.[16] Whatever Sirach's debt to contemporaneous forms, a larger and even more difficult question remains: what precise significance did he attach to this list of heroes? This is obviously more than a catalogue, and it is placed in a prominent position at the end of his book. Perhaps we must be satisfied with his words in 44:7–9, contrasting these heroes with others whose names have been forgotten. At least the achievements of these "godly people" will live on, thanks to his efforts.

3. Fear of the Lord. For Sirach, wisdom and fear of the Lord are practically one, in line with the slogan found in Prov 1:7; 9:10; Job 28:28; and Ps 111:10, and repeated in Sir 1:14, "The beginning of wisdom is the fear of the Lord."[17] An impressive introduction is given to the book by the initial discourse on Wisdom (1:1–10), which will find echoes in chap. 24. The mood is that of Job 28, but Sirach moves beyond it. Yes, Wisdom is with God, beyond human reach. However, the Lord who created and *saw* Wisdom (cf. Job 28:27; Sir 1:9) has communicated this Wisdom, lavishing her upon creation, upon all that lives, and especially upon those who love him (Sir 1:10). Wisdom has now become accessible, despite her locus with God. Job 28:28 had the added note that wisdom is the fear of the Lord. This concept now is developed by Sirach (1:11–30) in a series of strong metaphors: fear of the Lord is the beginning (1:14), fullness (1:16), crown (1:18), and root (1:20) of wisdom. Attitudes characteristic of the wise person are mentioned: self-control, correct speech, sincerity, humility. A new and significant addition is made: keeping of the commandments (1:26). Fear of the Lord constitutes a two-way street with wisdom; it leads to wisdom, but wisdom in turn feeds the God-fearer with choice foods and long life (1:16–20; cf. 24:19–21).

Sirach uses the language of love to describe the relationship between the faithful and Wisdom (4:11–19; 6:18–31; 14:20–27; 51:13–30). The youth is to search out and seek her, and "when you take hold of her, never let her go" (6:27; cf. Cant 3:4). He is to pursue her, peeping through her windows, listening at her doors (14:23; cf. Cant 2:9). The youth's devotion will be matched by Wisdom's response (4:11–19). "Like a young bride" she will embrace him (15:2; cf. Cant 2:6; 4:9–12) and will give him food and drink (15:3; cf. Cant 8:2). The teasing and testing (Cant 5:3) that go along with lovemaking are also characteristic of Wisdom's approach, for she will test her lover (Sir 4:17). Sirach even speaks of Wisdom's "yoke," which the lover assumes (6:25; 51:26), but her cords are a sign of majesty: he will wear her as a robe of glory (6:31), for "whoever loves her loves life" (4:12; cf. Prov 8:35), and Wisdom will "reveal to him my secrets" (4:18).

Therefore it is not surprising when Sirach equates fear of the Lord with love and hope:

Those who fear the Lord do not disobey his words;
    those who love him keep his ways. (2:15)
Whoever fears the Lord is never alarmed;
    never afraid, for the Lord is his hope. (34:16)

This interiorization of fear of the Lord, the intense commitment that it signifies, gives an insight into Sirach's emphasis on the Law. Throughout his work he keeps coming back to the relationship of wisdom, fear of the Lord, and the Law:

> All wisdom is fear of the Lord,
>   and in all wisdom is the fulfillment of the Law.
>   (19:20; cf. 15:1)

Lady Wisdom is communicated by God, who sends her to Israel to take up residence in the Temple, and Sirach explicitly identifies her with "the Law which Moses commanded us" (24:23). This is best described as "Torah piety," the joyful and enthusiastic pursuit of God's will, which permeates Pss 1, 19, and 119. It is not legalism; it is the manifestation of the divine will, "a lamp to my feet and a light to my path" (Ps 119:105).

It is appropriate to conclude with a reference to the acrostic poem on Wisdom with which the book ends, since it forms an inclusion with 1:11–30.[18] It describes the intensity of Sirach's pursuit of Lady Wisdom, and it ends on the paradoxical note of human industry and divine beneficence, which Sirach understood so well:

> Work at your tasks in due season,
>   and in his own time God will give you your reward. (51:30)

NOTES TO "BEN SIRA—WISDOM'S TRADITIONALIST"

1. TNK is the acronym, spelled out often as Tenach or Tanakh, for the threefold division of the Hebrew Bible into *Tôrāh* (Law), *Nĕbî'îm* (Prophets, both former and latter), and *Kĕtûbîm* (Writings).

2. For the history of the text and versions, see C. Kearns, "Ecclesiasticus," in *A New Catholic Commentary on Sacred Scripture* (ed. B. Orchard et al., London: Nelson, 1969) 546–51, and esp. P. Skehan and A. Di Lella, *The Wisdom of Ben Sira* (AB 39; Garden City: Doubleday, 1987) 51–82.

3. Cf. Y. Yadin, *The Ben Sira Scroll from Masada* (Jerusalem: Israel Exploration Society, 1965) and the review by Skehan in P. Skehan, *Studies in Israelite Wisdom and Poetry* (CBQMS 1; Washington: Catholic Biblical Association, 1971) 245–46.

4. See Kearns, "Ecclesiasticus," 551. M. Gilbert has argued that both text types, the short and the long, are canonical and inspired; cf. "L'Ecclésiastique: Quel texte? Quelle autorité?" *RB* 94 (1987) 233–50.

5. Notably D. Barthélemy, "La Place de la Septante dans l'Eglise," in *Etudes d'histoire du texte de l'Ancien Testament* (OBO 21; Fribourg: Editions Universitaires, 1978) 111–26.

6. Rightly argued by L. Hartman, "Sirach in Hebrew and in Greek," *CBQ* 23 (1961) 443–51.

7. So Skehan and Di Lella, *The Wisdom of Ben Sira*, x; Di Lella reasonably proposes that all should adopt the numbering of the critically established Greek text (by J. Ziegler) in order to introduce some uniformity in references to Sirach. The NRSV also follows suit.

8. On the several poems in Sirach of twenty-two and twenty-three lines, see Skehan and Di Lella, *The Wisdom of Ben Sira*, 74.

9. See J. T. Sanders, *Ben Sira and Demotic Wisdom* (SBLMS 28; Chico: Scholars Press, 1983) 15, who makes further comparisons of Sirach with Proverbs; see also H. Duesberg and I. Fransen, *Ecclesiastico* (LSB; Rome: Marietti, 1966) 64–71.

10. Other lists can be consulted: W. Oesterley, *An Introduction to the Books of the Apocrypha* (London: SPCK, 1935) 229–32; Di Lella, *The Wisdom of Ben Sira*, 4–6. For a detailed summary, see R. Pfeiffer, *History of New Testament Times* (New York: Harper, 1949) 352–408.

11. For the details, see Kearns, "Ecclesiasticus," 549–51.

12. See J. L. Crenshaw, "The Problem of Theodicy in Sirach: On Human Bondage," *JBL* 94 (1975) 47–64; G. L. Prato, *Il problema della teodicea in Ben Sira* (AnBib 65; Rome: Biblical Institute, 1975).

13. The doctrine of opposites is akin to the two levels of meaning (*Doppeldeutigkeit*) that J. Marböck points out in Sirach's writings: true and false shame (4:20–26; 41:14–42:8); true and false honor (10:30–11:6); the relativity of prosperity and adversity (11:25); the mixture of good and evil in a human being (10:8; 37:17–18); speech and silence (20:5–7); loans and alms (29:1–20); true and false sacrifice (34:21–35:5); true and false counselors and friends (37:1–6, 7–18). It is not for nothing that Marböck concludes his list with 37:28: "Not every food is good for everyone, nor do all dishes appeal to every taste." Ben Sira was well trained in the discernment that the sages practiced. Cf. J. Marböck, *Weisheit im Wandel* (BBB 37; Bonn: Hanstein, 1971) 153.

14. Cf. Martin Hengel, *Judaism and Hellenism* (Philadelphia: Fortress, 1974) I, 139–40, following R. Smend; J. L. Crenshaw, *Old Testament Wisdom* (Atlanta: Knox, 1981) 35. Fuller information about the relationship between Ben Sira and Hellenism can be found in the Appendix.

15. Burton Mack, *Wisdom and the Hebrew Epic* (Chicago: University of Chicago Press, 1985) 11–36.

16. See the study of the encomium in T. R. Lee, *Studies in the Form of Sirach 44–50* (SBLDS 75; Atlanta: Scholars Press, 1986) 81ff. Burton Mack, in *Wisdom and the Hebrew Epic*, considers the poem as more than an encomium—he considers it as an

epic (p. 136). Read in the light of Sir 24, it leads from the order of covenants down to the climax, the glorification of Simon in chap. 50. Thus, "the hymn may have functioned as a mythic charter for Second Temple Judaism" (p. 56).

17. The basic study of this topic in Sirach is J. Haspecker, *Gottesfurcht bei Jesus Sirach* (AnBib 30; Rome: Biblical Institute, 1967); see also Skehan and Di Lella, *The Wisdom of Ben Sira*, 75, for the quotation from R. Smend: "Subjectively, wisdom is fear of God; objectively, it is the law book of Moses (chap. 24)."

18. For a careful translation based on the Hebrew text from cave 11 at Qumran, see Skehan and Di Lella, *The Wisdom of Ben Sira*, and P. Skehan, "The Acrostic Poem in Sirach 51:13–30," *HTR* 64 (1971) 387–400.

CHAPTER 6

THE WISDOM OF SOLOMON— A VIEW FROM THE DIASPORA

◆

INTRODUCTION

Title

The title according to the Greek tradition is The Wisdom of Solomon, but the Latin tradition calls it simply The Book of Wisdom. The latter is more adequate in terms of the content of the work, which never mentions Solomon by name, but only an "I." This "I" is not called "son of David, king in Jerusalem," as Qoheleth is (Eccl 1:1), but it is clear that the author assumes the mantle of Solomon and speaks in his name (e.g., 9:7–8, 12). Thus the work fits into the wisdom tradition that is dominated by the figure of Solomon (Proverbs, Ecclesiastes, Song of Songs).

Date

The identity of the author cannot be ascertained, despite the many guesses (e.g., Philo). His date is a matter of inference. The work shows a dependence upon the Septuagint, the Greek translation of the Hebrew Bible, which would make 200 B.C.E. the *terminus a quo*. On the other hand, it was written before Romans and Ephesians, which seem to utilize it (Rom 1:18- 22; Eph 6:11–17). Hence a first century B.C.E. date is generally agreed upon, perhaps in the last half of the century. It is reasonable to suppose that the work originated in Alexandria, a large Jewish center of the Diaspora, which was also an intellectual pivot of the ancient world. This is in harmony with the author's knowledge of Greek ideas, and also the attention given to Egypt in chaps. 11–19.

Language

Although it was once argued that the first part of the work (chaps. 1–5, or even 1:1–11:1) was a translation from a Hebrew original, it is now generally agreed that the work is an original Greek composition. It retains the parallelism of Hebrew poetry, but it abounds in such literary devices as paronomasia and alliteration, which are less likely to occur in a translation. Not only is the original language Greek, but there is one author throughout, despite the obvious differences between chaps. 11–19 and the first half of the book. The unity has been demonstrated by the forty-five "flashbacks" that J. Reese has recognized in the work; these are short repetitions "of a significant word or group of words or distinctive idea in two different parts of Wisdom."[1] Reese points to the association between 6:12 and 13:5–6. In both of these passages contemplation (*theōreō*, used in the sense of mental vision) is the beginning and the means for one to "seek" and "find" Wisdom and God (for the Greeks also wanted to find God).

Audience

Surprisingly, the book is addressed to those "who judge the earth" (1:1), to "kings" (6:1), as if the unnamed Solomon were addressing his colleagues. The reason for such address is not clear. Wisdom is of course associated with kingship, but the author is not really interested in instructing monarchs. He has his own Jewish sisters and brothers in mind, and he wants to strengthen them in their traditions. Although the author never claims the name of Solomon, he is clearly writing in the name of that personality (cf. chaps. 8–9). This king fiction adds a certain weight to his words and perhaps disguises the identity of his real audience. Solomon was the classic wise person in Israel's tradition, and wisdom was seen as a royal prerogative.

Character

This work stands out as intensely Jewish and, at the same time, thoroughly stamped by Greek culture. It could have been written only in the Hellenistic period, and the preoccupation with the Exodus suggests its relevance for the large Jewish population in Alexandria. The author knew the Hebrew text of the Bible, but most of the time he reflected the Septuagint (LXX) Greek in the style that has been called anthological composition—the use of words and phrases from the Bible in the presentation of one's thought (as Ben Sira did with the Hebrew Bible). This is not so much a question of quotations, even implicit, as it is a studied use of biblical data (e.g., chap. 10). He shows a

84

marked preference for Genesis, Isa 40–66, Proverbs, and Psalms.[2] Certain portions of the Bible are the subject of elaborate developments, such as 1 Kgs 3:5–15 and Proverbs in chaps. 7–9, Genesis in chap. 10, and Exodus in chaps. 11–19.

The influence of Hellenism is striking. It has been calculated that the book contains a vocabulary of 1,734 different words, of which 1,303 appear only once, and 335 (about 20 percent) are not found in any other canonical book of the Old Testament.[3] More significant than this is the influence of contemporary Hellenistic (rather than classical Greek) thought. Obvious examples are the four cardinal virtues in 8:7 or the philosophical treatment of the knowledge of God in 13:1–9. It is difficult to trace the dependence of the author upon given books or writers. The judgment of C. Larcher and J. Reese suggests that the author was eclectic in his use of contemporary popular Greek philosophy.[4] In any case, we have an interesting example of a biblical writer who took seriously the culture of his day, while elaborating his own vision of faith.

Considerable discussion has focused on the precise genre that is represented by the Book of Wisdom. D. Winston and J. Reese agree in calling it a protreptic, a form of didactic exhortation.[5] This form goes back as far as Aristotle, but it developed more in the Hellenistic period. M. Gilbert thinks that the genre is epideictic, that is, an encomium or praise, as this was practiced in Greek and Latin rhetoric.[6] All would agree that within this genre individual literary forms are used, such as the diatribe found in chaps. 1–6. Diatribe is characterized by such features as the address to kings, the argument for moral integrity, and the use of imaginary opponents. Chaps. 11–19 are marked by the Greek figure *synkrisis*, or "comparison." But the entire work is unusual in that it breaks new ground. It is addressed to kings (1:1; 6:1), but from 10:20 to 19:9 the addressee is God, who is at the center of the author's concern.

Outline

The outline proposed by Addison Wright, implemented in the *NAB* translation and in his *NJBC* commentary, commends itself.[7] Better than others, he has pointed out the many instances of literary *inclusio* (a word or phrase used at the beginning of a section and repeated at the end, e.g., "justice" in 1:1, 15). These are not obvious in an English translation, but the original Greek text makes them clear, and they serve to mark off units within the whole. In addition, Wright has shown that there was a careful symmetry intended by the author: the book can be divided into two parts of 251 poetic verses. The break is after 11:1 (which others are inclined to see as the title of the second half).[8] Within the two parts are further refinements in structure—such as concentric and linear arrangement, and proportionality—which need not detain us here. The analysis follows a threefold division.

CONTENTS

1:1–6:21, The Reward of Wisdom: Immortality

The message of the first six chapters deals with justice/wisdom and immortality. Wisdom is the way to God for human beings who are designated as body/soul (1:4), a Greek combination that differs from the traditional Hebrew life breath, or spirit, and material dust (cf. Eccl 12:7). A warning is in order: through the all-pervading spirit of wisdom (1:6–7) God is aware of wrongdoing and will punish with death. This is really contrary to the divine plan, since life and not death is the divine purpose, because "justice [*dikaiosynē*] is undying [*athanatos*]." The statement is electric. It is one of the few in the Old Testament that refer to immortality (cf. Dan 12:1–3), and it does so in a unique way. One might have expected that the writer would have utilized the Greek notion of the natural immortality of the spiritual soul. No doubt he was aware of Greek conceptions of the soul (*psychē*, cf. 9:15), but he adopts a typically biblical approach. Immortality is not rooted in the human makeup, but in one's relationship to God. Justice or righteousness is a relationship, not a human achievement: "Abraham put his faith in the Lord, who credited it to him as an act of righteousness" (Gen 15:6). The same idea is reflected in Ps 73:23–24: "With you I shall ever be; you have hold of my right hand. With your counsel you guide me, and in the end you receive me in glory." Admittedly, this relationship could be broken by human choice. But on the part of God, it was a situation that would be honored beyond death for those who remained faithful. The long, dark night of Sheol, which cast its shadows across the pages of the Bible, was ended, for the just. What about the wicked? The book does not tell us much about their fate. Dire things are said about them in 4:19, and their judgment is recorded in 5:1ff. But there is no breath of immortality here. It appears as if immortality is so positive a concept (life with God before and beyond death) that the wicked are considered not to live on in any real sense. The author is not greatly interested in their fate, since they have simply failed. They have made a "covenant" with Death (1:16; obviously death is more than physical demise here), which they experience because they belong to the devil's "lot" (*meris*, 2:24). In a sense, death is denied for the just. They seem to have died in the eyes of the wicked, "but they are in peace" (3:2–3), for "their hope is full of immortality" (3:4). In contrast to the wicked, whose "lot" (*meris*) is with the devil, the "portion" (*klēros*) of the just is with the holy ones, the "sons of

God" (5:5), who constitute the divine family. No reference is made to the resurrection of the body. The author was interested not in the mode but in the meaning of immortality—to be with God permanently.

This manner of thought is also consonant with the sages' accent on life. According to Proverbs, life is the goal of the wisdom enterprise (Prov 8:35). Wisdom is a "tree of life" (3:18), not merely in the sense of "length of days" (although the sages' teaching provided this also—cf. Prov 3:2), but qualitatively, the *kind* of life that came to the wise person: "favor and good esteem" (3:4), "honor" (3:35). This was, however, limited by the reality of Sheol, the inevitability of death; in the Book of Wisdom now the grip of death is broken by a deeper vision of the life that wisdom brings.

The description of the wicked in chap. 2 of the book (and their remorse in 5:1–13) serve as a foil for the doctrine of immortality. These are the people who have no future, whose memory will perish (Wis 4:19). It is difficult to identify the particular Greek philosophies that lie behind their materialism and hedonism in 2:1–9 (but the author probably does not have Qoheleth in mind, as some have asserted).[9] The views of the wicked come to focus upon the ideal just person (Wis 2:10–20), who is a "censure" to them. These verses seem to be a model followed by the passion narratives of the Gospels.[10] The malice of the wicked is more clear than their identity (hostile Hellenists? renegade Jews?). But they provide the author with the contrast to the just, which he develops in 3:1–12. The just are with God. Yes, they were tried, but they showed they were worthy of God. The explanation of the trials of the just leads into the problem of childlessness, which would normally be considered a tragedy, even a punishment, in the ancient world ("Better is childlessness with virtue," 4:1). Similarly, the premature death of the just is a mystery that the wicked cannot understand (4:17). But in fact, honorable age does not mean mere passing of time or years. The sage explains that premature death is due to God's love (4:10–14).

Chapter 5 is the counterpoint to chap. 2. In chap. 2 the wicked had given full vent to their own philosophy and hatred of the just person. Now in chap. 5 they are filled with remorse and overcome by their folly; in a striking judgment scene they exclaim about the just person, "This is he whom once we held as a laughingstock. . . . fools that we were! . . . See how he is accounted among the sons of God. . . . What did our pride avail us?" (5:3–8). Blessed immortality had been described in 3:9 in terms of the abstract words "love," "grace," and "mercy." Now it is presented concretely: one is a member of the divine family; one's lot is "with the holy ones" (5:5). One can recognize a concentric circle in chaps. 1–6: an address to rulers about wisdom (chaps. 1, 6); the speech of the wicked (chaps. 2, 5); and the fate of the just and wicked relative to suffering, childlessness, and an early death (chaps. 3–4).

While wisdom is merely mentioned in 1:4–7, it becomes the principal concern of chap. 6. Pseudo-Solomon begins with an exhortation to this audience ("kings," 6:1) to "learn wisdom" (6:9). According to 1:4 she could not dwell with a sinner, but because she is a spirit ("the spirit of the Lord," 1:7), she knows all that goes on, and punishment ensues for the sinner. This cosmic quality of Wisdom will appear also in 7:27–8:1. The king fiction of 1:1 appears in the exhortation to kings in chap. 6. This exhortation is remarkable for its description of Wisdom's initiative and the use of the Greek style of sorites. Although one should seek out Wisdom (a theme already present in Prov 9:4–6 and Sir 6:23–31), she anticipates the desire for her and seeks out those who are worthy of her (6:12–16). The chain of reasoning in the Greek sorites (6:17–21) is that the predicate of one statement becomes the subject of the next (A = B; B = C, etc., then Z = A). The style is elastic in that there is not an exact repetition of words (e.g., "desire" becomes "care" for discipline in v 17). The conclusion goes back to desire (v 17) as leading to incorruptibility and a kingdom (synonymous with being close to God). The emphasis on kingdom is of course in harmony with this address to "kings."

6:22–11:1, Solomon and Wisdom

Solomon describes a personal experience of Wisdom with a low-key approach about his own sincerity and honesty; note the parallelism of sage and king in the introduction (6:22–25), and his humanity (no divine origin for him! 7:1–6). He attained Wisdom because he prayed (an allusion to 1 Kgs 3:5–9; cf. 2 Chr 1:9–10), and she came to him as the spirit she is (7:7; cf. vv 22–24). He continues in a very intimate vein about his love of her and the joy he experienced in the incomparable gifts that she bestowed upon him. He again refers to the need of prayer because God is the "guide of Wisdom" and "we and our words are in his hand" (7:15–16).

Solomon claims (7:17–21) to have received an encyclopedic knowledge that would make any Greek envious (contrast the modest description in 1 Kgs 5:9–14 [4:29–34]): cosmology, time, astronomy, zoology, demonology ("powers of the winds"), psychology, botany, and pharmacy—knowledge taught him by Wisdom, the "artificer of all" (perhaps he understood Wisdom in Prov 8:30 as artisan; cf. Wis 13:1). This very Hellenistic passage is followed by another (7:22–23), enumerating twenty-one attributes of Wisdom as spirit which explain how she can teach all these things. As spirit, Wisdom is of utter purity, acting on all other spirits and penetrating all things (v 24). At the same time, this immanence is balanced by transcendence: holy, unique, all-powerful, all-seeing. Scholars have pointed out the influence of the Stoic pneuma and the Platonic world soul in the terminology and ideas of 7:22–24.[11] The purity (vv 23 and esp. 24) of Wisdom's spirit leads into the images of vv 25–26, which describe the relation of Wisdom to

God. She is an expression of the divine power, glory, light, and goodness. The author returns in vv 27–30 to Wisdom's activity, especially among her followers, those who "cohabit" (v 28) with her and are therefore beloved of God. She is a "super-sun" whose light conquers even the darkness of evil. The effusive description of Wisdom closes with the affirmation of her universal providence.

Solomon proceeds to relate his love affair with Wisdom in language that is reminiscent of the Song of Songs (e.g., Cant 1:15; 4:9–10). The theme of marital love is clearly emphasized in 8:2, 9, 16, 19. In 8:2 he falls in love with her "beauty" (a Greek touch; cf. 6:12; 7:10), but he quickly describes the other qualities of this ideal spouse, such as nobility and "living with" (*symbiō-sis*) God (8:3). She has taught him the four cardinal virtues (temperance, justice, prudence, and fortitude) that were a staple of Greek moral teaching; it is the only time they are enumerated in the Bible (8:7). These remarkable qualities stir Solomon in his desire to have her as spouse, for he will become a glorious king whose memory (that is the sense of "immortality" in 8:13) will perdure. The essential means to gain her is by prayer (oddly enough, there is no prayer for Wisdom in Proverbs, Job, or Ecclesiastes). In a somewhat parenthetical aside (8:19–21), he mentions that he possesses a noble nature, but prayer will be necessary in order to gain Wisdom. Verses 19–20 have been interpreted to indicate a belief in the Platonic preexistence of the soul: having a good soul, Solomon came to an unsullied body. This idea seems remote from the text. Pseudo-Solomon nowhere else gives any evidence of such a belief, and here he is explaining his noble nature by emphasizing the soul—as it were, the "ego"—which is united to the body. The point is that his noble nature does not suffice for him to be wise; for the gift of Wisdom he must pray to the Lord.

Solomon's prayer is neatly structured in three strophes: 9:1–6, 7–12, 13–18.[12] The keynote is the request for Wisdom in vv 4 and 10 and presumed in v 17. The motive in the first strophe is that Solomon is human and imperfect, and thus unable to govern God's people (cf. 1 Kgs 3) unless he has the divine Wisdom that was already manifested in creation. In the second strophe, Solomon claims a need for the Wisdom that was present when the world was made if he is to build a Temple. The final strophe moves off from Solomon's immediate concern to contemplate the human condition. Our thoughts are simply remote from the divine plans, and we are worn down by our own physical weakness (v 15, a reminiscence of the Platonic notion of soul and body—in the sense of physical weakness, not the impurity, of the body). Without the gift of Wisdom we cannot know what God is about, namely in the history of those who were saved by Wisdom (v 18, which is then articulated in the stories of chap. 10).

Chapter 10 presents a new development: Wisdom is now credited with salvation.[13] The verbs "deliver" (*ryomai*) and "preserve" (*phylassō*) are repeated in a series of examples in the lives of "the just"—a code name, as it were, for specific characters: Adam, Noah, Abraham, Lot, Jacob, and Joseph. Most surprisingly, the key event of the Exodus deliverance is attributed to Wisdom: "She brought them across the Red Sea" (v 18). The "Lord's servant" is Moses, also identified as prophet in 11:1; this latter verse serves as a transition to the second part of the book, which deals with the plagues. The chapter stands in contrast to Sir 44–50. There also, Wisdom and history came together. But here theology of history is presented from the viewpoint of saving Wisdom. It has the same bold sweep as the Old Testament itself, from Adam to the Exodus from Egypt (Genesis and Exodus).

11:2–19:22, God's Providence During the Exodus

The second half of the book is a kind of meditation or homily on the plagues. It is unusual in that it is addressed to God (11:4, 7, 8, 10, etc.). In all, seven plagues are treated, and quite freely, since the author means to draw lessons from them. The theme running through the presentation is a simple one: by the things through which the Egyptians were punished, the Israelites were benefited (11:5). Another principle is introduced in 11:16: the Egyptians are to recognize that they are punished by the very things through which they sin. To this end five tableaux or contrasts (*synkrisis*) are set up, comparing the experiences of the Israelites with those of the Egyptians.[14] In a sense this is another discussion of the fate of the just and the wicked, which was treated in chaps. 1–5. Now the Israelites are the just in contrast to the wicked Egyptians. The Lord's fidelity to his people during the Exodus is the same as to individual just ones (chaps. 1–5). The Exodus has become, as it were, a type or model of the way God acts to save the just. There are even specific allusions to the earlier chapters, such as the "testing" (11:9–10 and 3:5–6), the "doom" of the wicked (13:10 and 3:11), and the like.

An outline of the structure (adapted from Addison Wright in the *NJBC*) is in order if the reader wishes to follow the development of thought:

I. God's fidelity to his people in the Exodus (11:2–19:22)
    A. Introduction (11:2–4)
    B. Theme: Israel benefits from the very things that punish Egypt (11:5)
    C. Theme illustrated by five contrasts:
        1. Water from rock instead of Nile plague (11:6–14)
        2. Quail instead of plague of little animals (11:15–16:15)
            (a) 11:15–16 with digression on God's power and mercy (11:17–12:22)
            (b) 12:23–27 with digression on false worship (13:1–15:17)
            (c) 15:18–16:4 with digression on serpents in desert (16:5–15)

3. Manna from heaven instead of rain, hail, and fire (16:16-29)
4. The pillar of fire instead of the plague of darkness (17:1-18:4)
5. The tenth plague instead of the Exodus, by which God punished the Egyptians and glorified Israel (18:5-19:22)

The theme (11:5) is immediately exemplified in the first contrast (11:6-14). In the first plague, the punishment of the Egyptians (Nile water turned into blood and ensuing thirst) corresponds to the benefit of the Israelites (water from rock, to quench their thirst). The example is quite dense, since the author elaborates upon it as a testing and discipline (vv 9-10; cf. the testing of the just person in 3:5-6).

The second contrast (11:15-16:15) is between the plague of little animals (locusts, flies, etc.) and the quail that provided food for the Israelites. The unwary reader should note that this contrast is prolonged through five chapters, from 11:15 to 16:4 (11:15-16; 12:23-27; 15:18-16:4), with digressions corresponding to each mention of the contrast: God's power and mercy (11:17-12:22); false worship (13:1-15:17); and the serpents in the desert (16:5-15). The punishment of the Egyptians is appropriate in the author's view: in suffering from the animals, the Egyptians are being punished by the very things through which they sin (a principle enunciated in 11:16 and 12:27; cf. Ps 7:15-16).

The digressions are more interesting than the contrast itself. In the first digression, God is said to be merciful because he loves (11:17-12:8). He could have destroyed the enemy by terrible means, but instead he gave them warnings as he did to the Canaanites, to whom he gave a chance to repent, for he loves his creatures (11:23-12:8). After all, his spirit is in all things (12:1; cf. 1:7). God's lenient treatment of the Canaanites derives from his very power, "the source of justice" (12:16). This justice of God is not lost on his own people—they too are to be kind to others (12:19, *philanthropos*, "loving humankind"), and they are to expect God's merciful justice for their own wrongdoing.

Pseudo-Solomon returns to the animals-quail contrast in 12:23-27 and enunciates the familiar principle that the Egyptians were punished by the very things through which they sinned (vv 23-27; cf. 11:16). Indeed, their real sin was that after recognizing the true God (cf. Exod 10:16), they continued in their wrongdoing and received the "final condemnation." The example of the Egyptians provides the opportunity for a second digression, dealing with false worship—of nature and of idols (13:1-15:17).

The passage on nature worship in 13:1-9 (cf. Acts 17:27-31; Rom 1:19-25) is unlike anything else in the Bible and is clearly influenced by Greek philosophical thought (cf. "analogy" in v 5).[15] The author is not out to prove the existence of God; the existence of God or gods was simply a given in the ancient world. Rather, the claim is that those (especially the Greeks, incidentally) who identified nature and divinity were mistaken. If they had applied their own principle of analogy, that principle would have recognized the true creator God. There is a certain excuse in that the very beauty of the world seduced them, but then they are still to be faulted because they did not find the Lord of the world. The beauty and power of created things should have led pagans away from nature worship to the one who was "their original author." This passage breathes the monotheism of the Hebrew and the aesthetics of the Greek. It looks out upon the mutual reaction of humans and nature. What do the marvels of creation say to us? The question was already suggested in the personification of Wisdom and her role in creation (Prov 8). Pseudo-Solomon understands creation as the revelation of "him who is" (13:1; cf. Exod 3:14 in the LXX). While he underscores the fact that humans may err in hearing this message, the approach "through" the greatness and beauty of created things (13:5) is clearly affirmed as a path to God (see chap. 8).

The condemnation of idolatry· (13:10–15:17) draws on several biblical books that contain polemic against idols (Isaiah, Deuteronomy, Hosea, and Psalms). First the carpenter is singled out for his role. With biting irony the author describes how the idol is made out of refuse wood, fastened to a wall so that it will not fall, and then, utterly lifeless, it becomes the object of worship and prayers for life and prosperity. Sarcastic jibes are continually made throughout these chapters, but one must remember that this is polemic, a polemic all the more bitter in the light of Israel's own failures in the past. For an empathetic understanding of the "graven image," one has to recall that the ancient image had a symbolic aspect, and "image worship" is by no means as crass as the biblical writers made it out to be. In the words of Thorkild Jacobsen, "the god—or rather the specific form of him that was represented in this particular image—was born in heaven, not on earth. In the birth the craftsmen-gods that form an embryo in the womb gave it form. When born in heaven it consented to descend and to 'participate' (in L. Lévy-Bruhl's sense) in the image, thus transubstantiating it. The image as such remains a promise, a potential, and an incentive to a theophany, to a divine presence, no more."[16]

Carpentry leads into shipbuilding: can one pray to a wood that is more unsound than the boat itself (14:1)? It is the providence of the Father that guarantees the welfare of the seafarer, as in the case of Noah. Idolatry itself is described as originating in worship of those who have died, and in the construction of an image of an absent ruler. All kinds of moral evils are attributed to this abomination, for which there will surely be retribution. In a beautiful aside (15:1–3), the writer claims Israel's privileged relationship to the living God, to know whom brings justice and immortality (in contrast to lifeless idols). He returns to his topic in another sarcastic description of the clay images that the potter creates. The acme of folly is exemplified by one who creates a god out of the very clay from which he was made—all for the sake of profit. Thus a lifeless thing is made, and the worshiper is better off than his god, for he at least lives (15:17).

After this long digression on idolatry, pseudo-Solomon returns in 15:18 to the second contrast (cf. 11:15ff.), the plague of little animals that afflicted the Egyptians in contrast to the quail that benefited the Israelites. The topic triggers a development on the serpents that afflicted Israel in the desert (Num 21:6–9). Whereas the Egyptians were slain by the animals (16:9), the Israelites were merely given a warning and ultimately saved from the serpents, not by what they saw (the bronze serpent), but "by you, the savior of all" (v 7), "your all-healing word" (v 12).

The third contrast is between the rain, hail, and fire (thunderbolts and lightning) that devastated the Egyptians and the manna that God rained down upon the Israelites (16:16–29). The author plays on the fact that fire destroyed the food of the Egyptians, while Israel was nourished by the "bread from heaven" (vv 19–20). The underlying principle is that creation fights for Israel, fulfilling the divine purpose (vv 17, 24). Many embellishments are given to the Exodus story, such as the taste of the manna (v 20; cf. Num 11:6; 21:5), the admonition to thank God before sunrise (v 28), and the lesson that is conveyed by the food (God's words give life, v 26; cf. Deut 8:3–4).

The fourth contrast is between the plague of darkness and the pillar of fire (17:1–18:4). The effects of the darkness upon the Egyptians are presented in vv 3–19 with vividness and imagination. And certain bold psychological conclusions are drawn: cowardly wickedness testifies to its own condemnation and is driven by conscience (*syneidēsis*, the first mention of conscience in the Bible) to magnify its misfortunes; fear is the surrender of the aid that comes from reason (vv 11–12). It is fear that begets the paralysis described by the vivid reactions (vv 18–19) to even the most ordinary sounds. On the other hand, the pillar of fire provided great light and guidance for God's people, "through whom the imperishable light of the Law was to be given to the world" (18:4).

The fifth and final contrast is between the tenth plague (death of the firstborn) and the Exodus experience (18:5–19:22). Several minor contrasts accompany this description, such as the punishment of the death of the firstborn for the Egyptians, who had decreed death for Israelite males (Exod 1:16, 22) and who were oppressing God's firstborn, Israel (Exod 4:22–23). The Passover prayers of Israelites are matched by the wailing of the Egyptians, as the all-powerful Word leapt from the heavenly throne on a mission of death (18:8–19). A parenthesis (18:20–25) describes the plague suffered by Israel because of the revolt of Korah, Dathan, and Abiram (Num 16–17). It is the intercession of Aaron, the "blameless man," that stops the plague. The

Exodus experience is the counterpart to the tenth plague, and it is described in rather fanciful terms (19:8–9). The whole event is portrayed as a renewal of creation (v 7, and note the harmonious melody of the elements in vv 18–21, a Greek touch). The punishment of the Egyptians is for their inhospitality, worse than that of the Sodomites (19:13–17). The abrupt conclusion in v 22 is a doxology on the Lord's faithful providence, and it seems to have a bearing on the people for whom the book is written.

CONCLUSION

The wisdom movement within Israel is not without surprises. The security preached by Proverbs is jarred by the experience of Job and buffeted by the hard-nosed insistence upon vanity by Qoheleth. Unruffled, Sirach seems to put it all together again with his emphasis on traditional wisdom and Law. Perhaps the most surprising twist is the appearance in the Diaspora of the Wisdom of Solomon. Here Greek language and culture make a significant entree into the Bible, but under the aegis of Solomon, no less. Wisdom and salvation history come together; both are recognized as integral to the experience of the people. Yet it is remarkable that this book is relatively silent about the Torah, despite the identification of Wisdom and Torah in Sir 24:23. Now Wisdom is identified with spirit (recall the twenty-one qualities of 7:22–23), "pervades all things" (7:24), and is ever more closely identified with God (7:25–26). Such characteristics are in sharp contrast to the modest references to the "imperishable light of the Law" (18:4; cf. 16:6).

Whereas a blessed immortality after death was not within the purview of older wisdom, it is now proclaimed with vigor, and in a vein explored but never exploited by traditional wisdom. The sages had always taught that wisdom secured life, and now this is pressed to the full—to life that is undying, incorruptible, eternal (Wis 1:15; 2:23; 5:15). The "heavenly court" that played a large role in Hebrew thought (Ps 29; Job 1:7; etc.) now is seen as a goal, a group to whose ranks one might aspire (Wis 5:5).

Personified Wisdom (see chap. 9) is now light (Wis 7:10, 25–26, 29) and spirit (Wis 1:6; 7:22; 9:17). She had been traditionally associated with creation (Prov 8:22ff.), and she even roamed the created world (Sir 24:5). Now she penetrates all things (Wis 1:7; 7:24; 8:1). While the Jews of the Diaspora doubtless recognized that she dwelt in the Temple in Jerusalem (Sir 24:8–12), they recognized her in their Greek world as well (Wis 7:16–28). Hence "Solomon" could address (the kings of) the world and speak of his coming into Wisdom (Wis 6:22ff.), and even of taking her as his bride (8:2). The vision of this unknown author was a powerful one.

NOTES TO "THE WISDOM OF SOLOMON— A VIEW FROM THE DIASPORA"

1. J. Reese, *Hellenistic Influence on the Book of Wisdom and Its Consequences* (AnBib 41; Rome: Biblical Institute, 1970) 124; see also 130.

2. Cf. C. Larcher, *Etudes sur le livre de la Sagesse* (EBib; Paris: Gabalda, 1969) 102–3. Larcher also has many helpful pages on the relationship of the book to Enoch, Qumran literature, and Philo (pp. 103–78). For another summary of the ideas shared by Philo and the Book of Wisdom, see D. Winston, *The Wisdom of Solomon* (AB 43; Garden City: Doubleday, 1979) 59–69, who thinks the book was likely to have been composed ca. 37–41 C.E. and hence was dependent upon Philo.

3. Cf. Reese, *Hellenistic Influence*, 3; he provides many examples of Hellenistic religious and philosophical vocabulary, pp. 6–25.

4. Larcher, *Etudes*, 232–36; the conclusions in Reese, *Hellenistic Influence*, 88–89, are only slightly different. For a comparison of the Book of Wisdom and the oeuvre of Philo, see also Burton Mack, *Logos und Sophia* (SUNT 10; Göttingen: Vandenhoeck & Ruprecht, 1973) 63–184.

5. Winston, *Wisdom*, 18–20; Reese, *Hellenistic Influence*, 117–21.

6. M. Gilbert, "Sagesse de Salomon," *DBSup* XI, 58–119, esp. 83ff.

7. For details, see the basic studies of Addison Wright: "The Structure of the Book of Wisdom," *Bib* 48 (1967) 165–84; "The Structure of Wisdom 11–19," *CBQ* 27 (1965) 28–34.

8. So Gilbert, "Sagesse de Salomon," 73, 89, and in contrast see the commentary of Wright in the *NJBC*, 512–13.

9. See the careful discussion of Wis 2:1–11 in P. Skehan, *Studies in Israelite Poetry and Wisdom* (CBQMS 1; Washington: Catholic Biblical Association, 1971) 213–36.

10. For the history of the exegesis of this passage, see C. Larcher, *Le Livre de la Sagesse ou La Sagesse de Salomon* (EBib; Paris: Gabalda, 1983–85) I, 258–63.

11. See the discussion in Larcher, *Etudes*, 367–402, and also T. Finan, "Hellenistic Humanism in the Book of Wisdom," *ITQ* 27 (1960) 30–48.

12. Cf. M. Gilbert, "La Structure de la prière de Salomon (Sg 9)," *Bib* 51 (1970) 301–31.

13. Roland E. Murphy, "Wisdom and Salvation," in *Sin, Salvation, and the Spirit* (ed. D. Durken; Collegeville, Minn.: Liturgical Press, 1979) 177–83.

14. Other scholars recognize seven contrasts or diptychs; see Gilbert, "Sagesse de Salomon," cols. 72–77.

15. Cf. the commentary on 13:1–9 in Larcher, *Le Livre de la Sagesse*, III, 748–73.

16. Cf. Thorkild Jacobsen, "The Graven Image," in *Ancient Israelite Religion: Essays in Honor of Frank Moore Cross* (ed. P. Miller et al.; Philadelphia: Fortress, 1987) 15–32; the quotation is from p. 29.

CHAPTER 7

WISDOM'S ECHOES

♦

Much has been written on the presence of wisdom throughout the Old Testament, and even some radical conclusions have been drawn.[1] Wisdom has been found from the *Tôrāh* to the *Kĕtûbîm*, from beginning to end of the Hebrew Bible. The previous chapters have dealt only with literature that is acknowledged by all as wisdom. Now we take up other parts of the Bible where the "influence of" or "borrowings from" wisdom have been alleged. It will soon become apparent that the problem is the establishment of adequate criteria for such judgments.

THE CLAIMS

We may begin with one admittedly extreme statement: "Evidently I have identified the wise men of Israel with the historians, and thus effectively designated the historical books as wisdom literature."[2] J. L. McKenzie had no criteria for this, but only broad presuppositions, such as the conviction of the sages about the validity of collective as well as individual experience, and their role as scribes who collected the memories of the people. L. Alonso Schökel detected specific wisdom ingredients in Gen 2–3: the sapiential motif of "knowledge of good and evil"; the "shrewdness" of the serpent; Adam as sage; the discussion of the four rivers. The sage attempted to answer the origin of sin by the Genesis story, with sapiential and mythical motifs.[3]

One of the first efforts (1953) to find wisdom in the Old Testament was Gerhard von Rad's analysis of the Joseph story.[4] In Gen 37–50, Joseph is smarter than the Egyptian sages (Gen 41:8), he gives solid advice, and he is finally called by the Pharaoh a "man intelligent and wise" (41:33, 39) In von Rad's view, the story of Joseph illustrates the rise of a wise courtier, and in fact it is designed as "a didactic wisdom-story" influenced by the Egyptian educational ideal. A similar method was adopted by R. N. Whybray in his study of the Succession Narrative (2 Sam 9–20; 1 Kgs 1–2). Whybray argued that the author "has consciously created his characters and situations as

concrete examples, in narrative form, of the teaching we find in Proverbs."[5]
A massive study of Deuteronomy has pointed to the "wisdom substrata" in
this work and in the Deuteronomist history (Joshua to 2 Kings), and also to
the sapiential humanism and retribution that is to be found there.[6] Individual prophets have been studied for evidences of wisdom—for example,
Amos[7] and Isaiah.[8] Repeatedly the Psalms have been analyzed for wisdom
content, although there is no list of "wisdom psalms" on which everyone
agrees. Finally, the Book of Esther has been considered as presenting a "gen-
eralizing wisdom-tale and traditional wisdom-motifs in a specific historical
setting."[9] More could be added to this list of claims, but it suffices for our
purpose.

METHODOLOGICAL CONSIDERATIONS

One can detect a certain ambiguity in what is written about the appearance
of "wisdom" in historical or prophetic books. (1) Does it mean that the piece
in question was written by a sage, just as Job or Qoheleth are clearly the
productions of a professional wise man? Such a contention cannot be proved,
and indeed the anonymity of authorship for many biblical works suggests that
it is futile to deal in such hypotheses. Hence the claim of J. Fichtner[10] that
Isaiah was a professional sage before he became a prophet does not have
sufficient foundation. (2) One might mean that a passage contains elements
that one expects to find in admitted wisdom books, and hence one can speak
of "wisdom influence." This is the type of argument presented, for example,
by H. W. Wolff for the prophet Amos. Presumably this kind of claim must
be shown by vocabulary, by literary forms, or by content. One can perhaps
mount a cumulative argument by drawing on all these factors.

    1. Vocabulary. There is a limited range of terminology that is character-
istic of wisdom. Admittedly the whole spectrum of Hebrew vocabulary remained open to any Israelite writer. But when certain wisdom terms appear
in rather concentrated fashion, this may be a sign of wisdom influence. R. N.
Whybray[11] has submitted a list of nine words that are "apparently" exclusive
to the wisdom tradition. In a narrower investigation, A. Hurwitz[12] singled
out terminology that is indicative of "wisdom psalms" (Pss 30 and 37). For
example, he shows that the word *hôn* (riches) is a typical term: eighteen of
twenty-six occurrences are in Proverbs. Moreover, comparable texts in the
Torah and Psalms use a synonym (*kesep*), not *hôn*. In addition to the repeated occurrences in Proverbs, *hôn* appears in Pss 112 and 119, which have
been associated with wisdom for other reasons. The advantage of this kind of
argument is that it is relatively independent and autonomous. It does not
have the weakness of hypothetical arguments derived from an alleged wisdom

setting or worldview. At the same time, it is to be admitted that our knowledge of Hebrew vocabulary and its distribution is relatively meager; the argument needs support from other sources.

2. Literary forms. The forms characteristic of Old Testament wisdom have been discussed in chap. 1. The sayings (and their various kinds) and admonitions appear in the books commonly recognized as "wisdom" (Proverbs, etc.), and there is no dispute about such a characterization. Even the Wisdom of Solomon, which is short on typical forms, is long on the emphasis on wisdom (chaps. 6–10) and fits into the category of wisdom literature.

The issue becomes somewhat cloudy when an accepted sapiential form is used in books that are clearly of another genre. Is the presence of a saying, an admonition, a parable or comparison, to be taken as a sure sign of wisdom influence? The Book of Isaiah begins with an indictment of disobedient people and immediately uses a comparison that some would claim is a wisdom parable:

> The ox knows its owner,
>> and the ass its master's crib;
> but Israel does not know,
>> my people does not understand. (Isa 1:3; cf. Jer 8:7)

Or one can point to the so-called parable of the farmer (Isa 28:23–29):

> Give ear and hear my voice;
>> Give heed and hear what I say:
> Is the plowman forever plowing,
>> Loosening and harrowing his land for sowing?
> When he has leveled its surface,
>> does he not scatter dill and sow cumin,
>> put wheat in a row, barley in place
>> and spelt as a border?
> He has learned the right way,
>> his God teaches him. . . .
> This, too, comes from the Lord of Hosts,
>> wonderful in counsel,
>> great in wisdom.

(Verses 27–28 contain further description of the farmer's methodology in working the ground.)

This passage is couched in typical wisdom language (listen, learn, teach, counsel, wisdom [tušiyyâ]). The observation is based on the farmer's experience, and it claims that his agricultural skills come from God. It makes no difference how this parable of the farmer is used by Isaiah (probably an *a fortiori* argument in defense of the Lord's wise action in history); the prophet is pointing up a lesson from nature.

What conclusions are to be drawn from examples such as these? As regards Isa 1:3, it is simply not meaningful to speak of wisdom influence. One does not have to be a sage or be directly indebted to the wisdom tradition before one can use a simple comparison, such as that of the people and dumb animals. On the other hand, the extended parable of the farmer (Isa 28:23–29) can probably be claimed as an example of wisdom. The prophet analyzes the way farmers operate and establishes an analogy between that and the Lord's activity in history. This is not a casual comparison, but an elaborate literary analogy: "Isaiah, arguing like a wise man, saw a fundamental affinity between agricultural activities and historical events: both bore the stamp of Yahweh's wisdom and counsel."[13]

At the same time, it should be remarked that the sages had no monopoly on specific literary forms. They favor short sayings and admonitions, but comparisons, parables, stories, and the like belong to the common cultural inheritance, and hence they can hardly be singled out as proofs of wisdom influence. Otherwise, the language of the sages would have been a jargon, relatively unintelligible to their audience. There was a broad range of intelligence and education that was common to prophet and people. To demand wisdom influence for every admonition would be a stultifying division of literary analysis and an unreal compartmentalization of human beings. Instead of characterizing certain passages as examples of wisdom influence, almost as if they were deviant from the broad interests of priest or prophet, we should recognize them as part of the mainstream of Israelite thought. These literary forms reflect simple reality, not the views of a particular school or group, and hence can be used universally.

There is often a kind of circular reasoning involved in the arguments that are advanced to show "wisdom influence." The wisdom writings make statements about the way things are. If a historical narrative also reflects reality, it can conclude to the same points as the wisdom writing, without any "influence." Why should the Joseph story be characterized as a wisdom tale? Yes, it concerns the rise of a courtier (Joseph) in Pharaoh's court; it underlines Joseph's cleverness, his self-control, his love of peace, and these are all desirable virtues that can be documented in the Book of Proverbs. But why were they singled out for attention by the sages? Because they are real factors that reflect the way things are (people are clever; they are virtuous; they receive blessings). Hence one is justified in concluding that the story itself separately —on its own, as it were—reflects the reality that the wisdom sayings in Proverbs are also dealing with, and that it is not a "wisdom tale."

Wisdom insights result from observation and experience, and hence they reflect real life—the same is true of stories. One might, however, claim that certain examples of elevated speech and diction, of powerful stories, bespeak a refined cultural level of both writers and readers. One thinks of the literary quality of Nathan's parable to David (2 Sam 12:1–7) or of Isaiah's parable of the vineyard (Isa 5:1–7). This kind of literature presupposes a high cultural level that made such achievements possible. It is not meaningful to speak of "wisdom influence" in such instances. Rather, the literature of Israel, priestly, prophetic, and sapiential, arose from a cultural matrix that was broadly gauged.

3. Content. This is a rather slippery criterion. The sages were concerned in a broad way with (right) living, but they were not ethicists or framers of the law. Because human conduct is the common denominator between wisdom and law, it is sometimes difficult to separate the two and to determine the direction of influence (compare Prov 22:28 on the "ancient landmark" with Deut 19:14). These difficulties also occur with respect to the social concerns of the prophets: It is commonly accepted that these spring from the law codes and also from cultic demands (Pss 15, 24) rather than from wisdom preoccupations. But the sages were also sensitive to the plight of the poor and the oppressed (e.g., Prov 14:31; Job 24:4–12; 29:12–17). Here again is a thin line of separation.

One of the most frequent topics in wisdom literature is the problem of retribution: the prosperity of the good, and the fate (punishment) of the evil. One need merely recall the sayings about the righteous/wise and wicked/foolish in Proverbs, the central problem of Job's suffering, the denial of retribution by Qoheleth (8:14; 9:1–2; etc.). One is tempted to think that the issue was exclusive to the sages. But of course it was not, as the "confessions" of Jeremiah ("Why does the way of the godless prosper?" 12:1) demonstrate. The problem of divine justice is widespread, and it appears in such disparate writings as Habakkuk (1–2), Lamentations (chap. 3), and Ps 89. Hence the motif of retribution must be used carefully in determining a wisdom writing, as with Ps 73. Retribution is not sufficient of itself to constitute a definitive criterion. Other characteristics have to be advanced in addition to the alleged "retribution." Even the presence of a poem on the personification of Wisdom, surely a criterion of "content," does not necessarily affect the rest of the composition, as the presence of the poem in Bar 3:9–4:4 demonstrates. The issue of "wisdom influence" is more subtle than that.

The presentation of these considerations on vocabulary, form, and content shows that the determination of "wisdom influence" has to be based on cumulative arguments, none of which alone suffices. The danger of circular reasoning has been pointed out. Instead of considering "wisdom influence" as an outside factor impinging on priest or prophet, one should perhaps regard it as reflecting the outlook of any human being who tries to draw a lesson from human experience. From this point of view, the "influence" comes not from without but from within: from the reflections of individuals on their experience. In a narrow sense, then, one might speak of wisdom only where there is a didactic purpose, where teaching is going on. Such is clearly the case in the five books that all recognize as wisdom. A didactic purpose is not explicit in other parts of the Old Testament. Even where it is explicit, as in the final verse of the Book of Hosea (14:10), it does not change the nature of the book. It is merely an additional remark that calls the reader to a more attentive reading and broader appropriation. A wisdom thrust is also apparent when recourse is made to tradition: this is what one has always said or done. The argument from tradition is used in an effort to persuade someone to accept a given point. We are in the realm of motivation, as when Bildad tries to convince Job by pointing out the harmony of his doctrine with that of the "fathers," or past generations (8:8).

Does the presence of alleged wisdom influence in various portions of the Old Testament suggest that there was no class of sages as a distinct professional group, but rather merely "men of superior intelligence," "an educated class, albeit a small one, of well-to-do citizens who were accustomed to read for edification and for pleasure, and that among them there arose from time to time men of literary ability and occasionally of genius who provided the literature which satisfied their demand"?[14] R. N. Whybray has indeed argued that there was no class of sages in Israel to whom the traditional wisdom literature is to be attributed. The prickly question of the existence of schools in Israel (and thus, who were the teachers?) aside, the issue here is the existence of a professional class of *ḥăkāmîm*. One can hardly controvert the evidence of the usage of the *ḥākām*, or "sage," in Jer 8:8, 9:22 [23], and 18:18. However undefined their tasks are, the "wise" are designated as beyond the ordinary, and they are contrasted with other professionals (priests, prophets). Similarly, the titles ("words of the wise") in the Book of Proverbs at 22:17 (emended text) and 24:23 (cf. 1:6; 30:1; and 31:1) are indicative of a class. Probably the activity of the *yôʿēṣ* or "counselor" should be considered here as substantially the same as the *ḥākām*, but channeled in a more restricted style in court life.[15] All things considered, it seems impossible to eliminate the sages (certainly not Qoheleth or Sirach!) as a class among the literati who pursued their own purposes: writing, teaching, and these within the specific field of human experience as opposed to meditating upon the sacred traditions of Israel. This is not a hard-and-fast line; there could have been crossovers of both persons and influence. Thus, one can point to Deut 32 as a hymn that betrays wisdom concerns; similarly Ps 78, which draws lessons from Israel's early existence.

These methodological considerations remain somewhat abstract without concrete examples. Three quite different books can be proposed for analysis: Psalms, Deuteronomy, and the Song of Songs.

PSALMS

The great advances made by the studies of H. Gunkel and S. Mowinckel established two firm conclusions for biblical scholarship: an approach to the Psalms by way of the particular literary forms (characteristic vocabulary, life setting, motifs) and the liturgical background into which they fit. These criteria seemed to leave little room for such a category as wisdom psalms. Nonetheless, there was a sufficient number of psalms that fell between the cracks. Are they wisdom psalms, and what are the criteria to be used to establish the existence of such a genre? Both Gunkel and Mowinckel spoke of such a category. Gunkel[16] entitled his treatment "wisdom poetry in the Psalms" but was not explicit about the number of psalms he would so classify: perhaps 49, 1, 9, 112, 128, 37, and 73. Mowinckel[17] spoke of "learned psalmography" and listed the following as "non-cultic poems": 1, 19b, 34, 37, 49, 78, 105, 106, 111, 112, 127. Since then many other studies have appeared, and there is no unanimous decision as to the identity of the wisdom psalms. A recent study by J. Luyten[18] has concluded that "a genre 'wisdom psalm' as such cannot be reconstructed." But the author goes on to draw up a pragmatic description of the dimension of wisdom in the Psalms: "the entirety of characteristics: stylistic, thematic and functional through which a psalm demonstrates a special relationship with wisdom literature." Such a cumulative argument best supports the designation of a psalm as in some sense a wisdom psalm. It is somewhat drastic to claim that there is no genre of wisdom psalm, but in any case, Luyten's description of the wisdom dimension is a welcome one to characterize certain psalms.

Following the standards of Gunkel, one can look for the signs of wisdom diction: *'ašrê* formulas ("blessed be"), numerical sayings, "better" sayings, the address of a teacher to a "son," alphabetic structure, admonitions, and comparisons. Obviously the presence of a few of these characteristics (and perhaps even of all) cannot be considered conclusive. One should look also for wisdom themes, such as the contrast between the two ways and also the two types (just and wicked), practical advice, preoccupation with the problem of retribution, mention of fear of the Lord. On such bases I urged many years ago[19] that the following psalms could be considered "authentic wisdom psalms": 1, 32, 34, 37, 49, 112, 128. This list is minimal; for example, why should 119 be excluded when 1 is included, or 111 excluded when 112 is included? The judgment remains tenuous. J. K. Kuntz[20] expanded the methodology, added Ps 127 and 133, and classified wisdom subtypes. Others[21] have argued that further psalms be included, such as Ps 73 and 119. The reader is invited to form his or her own criteria for wisdom, and challenge the number of psalms that have been classified as "wisdom."

DEUTERONOMY

Obviously, Deuteronomy is not a book of wisdom. It presents itself in its final form as a series of discourses, a valedictory oration, given by Moses shortly before his death: 1:1–4:40; 4:44–11:32; 12:1–26:19 (containing the Deuteronomic code, or book of the law). The final section (chaps. 27–34) contains various elements, including another speech of Moses, chaps. 28–30. The entire book is characterized by a unity of diction and purpose. It is clearly a theological interpretation of history and law, composed with an intensity and fervor that make it stand out within the Pentateuch. It is not a work of one or a few years. It was composed over a period of at least two centuries, with a high point coming during the reign of Josiah in 621, when "the book of the law" (some form of Deut 12ff.) was found in the Temple (1 Kgs 22–23).

Deuteronomy seems at first sight not to be a prime choice to illustrate wisdom influence. The Israeli scholar Moshe Weinfeld,[22] however, has argued that "it is more plausible to assume that the book of Deuteronomy was influenced by the ancient sapiential ideology that found expression in the book of Proverbs and the wisdom literature of the ancient Near East." As in every instance where "wisdom influence" is at issue, his argument is a cumulative one, and some arguments are stronger than others. Not all of Weinfeld's arguments can be treated here, but a selection will give the reader a sense of the way in which scholarship has proceeded in discovering the influence of wisdom literature.

A theme common to wisdom and Deuteronomy is life. This is almost too frequent to document: Life is the kerygma of the Book of Proverbs, as we have seen, and it is the great promise of wisdom: the good life, longevity, a large family, prestige, joy, and (inheriting the) land.[23] The same vision permeates Deuteronomy, and perhaps the most vivid presentation is the choice laid out in Deut 30:15–19: "Here then I have put before you today life and prosperity, death and doom. If you obey . . . loving God . . . you will live and be numerous, and the Lord your God will bless you in the land you are entering to occupy. But if you turn away your hearts . . . you will certainly perish. . . . I have set before you life and death, the blessing and the curse. Choose life, then, that you and your descendants may live." In Deuteronomy this emphasis arises out of the covenant that is at the heart of Deuteronomic preaching, not from the wisdom perspective. But the fact remains that the goal of wisdom and the promise of Deuteronomy are basically the same. It should be remembered that this perspective is not absent from the promises of the prophets (e.g., Amos 5:6, 14), or from the ideals of the ancient Near Eastern cultures.

Fear of the Lord/God is another ideal that is common to wisdom and Deuteronomy. One need merely consult a concordance to verify the many times the phrase appears in both areas. Again, there are different nuances, but covenant devotion is the point of sentences like Deut 10:12: "Now, Israel, what does the Lord your God ask of you but to fear the Lord your God and to walk in his ways and to love him and to serve the Lord your God with your whole heart and soul . . . ?" Covenantal love and fear are joined together. This precise nuance does not appear in wisdom until Ben Sira (e.g., Sir 2:15–17; cf. Eccl 12:13). Likewise the collective nuance is missing from the individualistic emphasis of the wisdom teacher. But one should not draw a hard-and-fast line in terminology that develops through a book and a culture. Thus Weinfeld comments, "Fearing God 'all the days' means constant awareness of God. No wonder, then, that the author of Deuteronomy exhorts the Israelites not to forget the Lord (6:12; 8:11, 14, 19). The causes of such forgetfulness are the pride and arrogance which come with material wealth and satiety (6:10–11; 8:12–13; 17:16–20; cf. 31:20; 32:13–15). The notion that affluence and satiety bring one to deny and forget God also belongs to wisdom ideology."[24] The mixture of covenantal and wisdom fear is thus illustrated.

A third example can be drawn from legal stipulations. Perhaps the most outstanding is the prohibition to remove the neighbor's landmark set up by past generations (Deut 19:14; cf. 27:17; Prov 22:28; 23:10; and Amenemope 6 [ANET, 422]). Similarly there is an emphasis on honest weights (Deut 25:16; Prov 11:1; 20:10, 23; and Amenemope 16 [ANET, 423]). Other items deal with vows (Deut 23:22–24; Eccl 5:1–5; Prov 20:25; Sir 18:22–23); with impartiality in judgment (Deut 1:17; 16:19; Prov 24:23; 28:21); with the pursuit of justice (Deut 16:20; Prov 21:21).

Finally, the didactic mood of Deuteronomy is matched in many places by the intensity of speech in Proverbs, as a comparison of Deut 6:7–9; 11:18–20 with Prov 6:20–22; 7:3; 8:34; and other verses readily demonstrates. Words like listen, heart, teach, and discipline are frequent in both Deuteronomy and the wisdom literature.

What is to be concluded from all this? Weinfeld is convinced that there are "wisdom substrata in Deuteronomy and Deuteronomic literature."[25] It is difficult to determine the direction of influence. Perhaps the view of J.-P. Audet is more objective and realistic. He pushed the question back beyond the monarchy and the class of sages. He advanced the hypothesis that the wisdom tradition is rooted in pre-school and pre-city civilization, in the family (as later examples of Tobit 4:1–19 and Ahiqar [see Appendix] would illustrate).[26] One must postulate family training or *paideia* as the basis for people to live together. Out of these insights grew a certain family ethos that sustained the social fabric.[27] This undifferentiated mode of living gradually separated into what we call wisdom instruction and also what came to be called law. But for all their differentiation, they had a common root. Primitive structures of society slowly became more sophisticated in teaching and in law.

THE SONG OF SONGS

Needless to say, the Canticle is not a wisdom book; it is a collection of love poems. However, it is worth discussing in more detail since it illustrates an interesting hermeneutical issue, the levels of meaning within the Old Testament. On one level, these are love songs. However, *as edited*, do these poems have a sapiential character on another level of understanding? E. Würthwein thinks that the Song derived from wisdom circles, and B. Childs argues that "the Song is to be understood as wisdom literature."[28]

First, there is the fact that ancient Jewish tradition, followed also by the Christians, attributed the work to Solomon (Cant 1:1). This suggests a sapiential interpretation of the work, and the impression is confirmed by the ancient canonical lists that rank the Canticle among the (wisdom) books of Solomon along with Proverbs and Ecclesiastes.[29] All this does not constitute proof of the book's wisdom character. But it does indicate that the Canticle was read as a work in the Solomonic (wisdom) tradition.

Second, it is eminently reasonable to look upon the sages as the ones responsible for the preservation and handing down of these songs. The Canticle upholds the values of fidelity and mutuality in love between the sexes, which are a concern in the training of youth (see Prov 1–9; esp. 5:15–20). Thus the sages would have interpreted the Song in the literal historical sense as love poetry that promoted the same ideals they nourished. Perhaps the mention of marriage (Solomon's) in Cant 3:11 was a factor in such thinking.

Third, there is an affinity between wisdom and eros in the wisdom literature: the quest for wisdom is a quest for the beloved.[30] The essential point is this: the language and imagery used to describe the pursuit of Lady Wisdom (see chap. 9) are drawn from the experience of love. Although the Canticle speaks of love between man and woman in the literal historical sense, it is by that very fact open to a wisdom interpretation. Wisdom is to be "found" (Prov 3:13; 8:17, 35), just as one "finds" a good wife (Prov 18:22; 31:10). In verses that are remarkably parallel, Wisdom and wife are termed "favor from the Lord" (Prov 8:35; 18:22). The sage advises the youth to "get Wisdom," to love and embrace her (Prov 4:6–8). The youth is to say, "Wisdom, you are my sister" (Prov 7:4), just as the beloved in the Song of Songs is called "sister" (Cant 4:9–5:1).

The association of wisdom and eros is not peculiar to the Book of Proverbs. As we have seen, Sirach tells his students to take hold of Wisdom and not to "let her go" (Sir 6:27), just as the woman in the Song found her lover and would not let him go (Cant 3:4). The one who pursues Wisdom is one who "peeps through her windows" (Sir 14:23), much in the style of the lover in Cant 2:9. Wisdom is compared to a young bride who will nourish the youth with her food (Sir 15:2–3; cf. Prov 9:5) just as the woman in Cant 7:14–8:2 offers food to her lover. In 51:13ff., Sirach speaks with passion of his pursuit of beloved Wisdom, just as "Solomon" describes his love affair with Wisdom in Wis 8:2, "I sought to take her for my bride." "Solomon" loved Wisdom beyond all else (Wis 7:10), and he discovered that she responded in like manner; one would find her "sitting by his gate" (Wis 6:14).

Within the Canticle itself is a passage that is didactic—different in style from the warm exchange of sentiments between a man and a woman. It is reflective in nature, making a statement about human love:

> Strong as Death is love,
>   hard as Sheol is ardor,
> Its darts, fiery darts,
>   a flame of Yah. (Cant 8:6)

Love is directly described here, and in terms of the great force that the ancient Israelite experienced as unconquerable: the dynamic power of Death and Sheol, which seek out their human victims without fail. Even during life, Death and Sheol pursue every human being. To the extent that the Israelite experienced nonlife, he or she was in the grip of Sheol (cf. Pss 30:4; 49:16; 89:49). Moreover, love is declared to be a "flame of Yah." This can be understood, as many translations render it, as a superlative, "a most vehement flame." However, Yah (the short form of the sacred name, *yhwh* (can refer to the Lord, as in the *NJB*, "a flame of Yahweh himself." This is the supreme compliment to the power of (human) love—it has some mysterious relationship to the Lord. The relationship is not spelled out further, but enough has been said!

It is precisely the link between eros and wisdom that opens the Song of Songs to another level of understanding. While it is not wisdom literature, its echoes reach beyond human sexual love to remind one of the love of Lady Wisdom—a "flame of Yah."

CONCLUSION

It is not surprising that the broad area embraced by wisdom should inevitably be reflected in the various literary genres of the Bible (exhortation, lament, story, etc.). Wisdom developed its own peculiar genres (saying, parable, etc.), and these serve as typical signs. The problem is the middle ground, where sapiential stylistic features (and ideas as well) are mixed with other parts of the Bible. The mixture itself is not surprising. Reciprocal influence is at work among all the Old Testament traditions. No one lived sealed off from other writers and traditions. From this point of view the influence of one area upon another can be seen as something perfectly natural. But the claims call for analysis and some kind of clear evidence. The survey of the issues in this chapter is an illustration of the living mix of literary activity reflected in the Bible.

NOTES TO "WISDOM'S ECHOES"

1. See the treatment, with copious bibliography, in D. F. Morgan, *Wisdom in the Old Testament Traditions* (Atlanta: Knox, 1981) 167–73.

2. J. L. McKenzie, "Reflections on Wisdom," *JBL* 86 (1967) 1–9.

3. L. Alonso Schökel, "Sapiential and Covenant Themes in Genesis 2–3," in *SAIW*, 468–80.

4. Gerhard von Rad, "The Joseph Narrative and Ancient Wisdom," in *SAIW*, 439–47; see p. 447.

5. R. N. Whybray, *The Succession Narrative* (SBT 9; Napierville: Allenson, 1968); quotation is from p. 72.

6. Cf. Moshe Weinfeld, *Deuteronomy and the Deuteronomic School* (Oxford: Clarendon, 1972).

7. Cf. H. W. Wolff, *Amos the Prophet* (Philadelphia: Fortress, 1973).

8. J. W. Whedbee, *Isaiah and Wisdom* (Nashville: Abingdon, 1971); R. N. Whybray, "Prophecy and Wisdom," in *Israel's Prophetic Tradition* (P. Ackroyd Festschrift; ed. R. Coggins et al.; Cambridge: Cambridge University Press, 1982) 181–99.

9. Cf. S. Talmon, "Wisdom in the Book of Esther," *VT* 13 (1963) 419–55. "Thus both the Joseph-story and the Esther-narrative represent the type of the 'historicized wisdom-tale' " (p. 453).

10. So J. Fichtner, "Isaiah Among the Wise," in *SAIW*, 429–38. There is more substance in Whedbee, *Isaiah and Wisdom*, and also in J. Jensen, *The Use of tôrâ by Isaiah: His Debate with the Wisdom Tradition* (CBQMS 3; Washington: Catholic University of America, 1973) esp. 122, 135.

11. R. N. Whybray, *The Intellectual Tradition in the Old Testament* (BZAW 135; Berlin: de Gruyter, 1974) 142–49.

12. A. Hurwitz, "Wisdom Vocabulary in the Hebrew Psalter: A Contribution to the Study of 'Wisdom Psalms,' " *VT* 38 (1988) 41–51.

13. So Whedbee, *Isaiah and Wisdom*, 63.

14. Cf. Whybray, *The Intellectual Tradition*. The quotations are from pp. 54 and 69.

15. Cf. P. de Boer, "The Counsellor," in *Wisdom in Israel and in the Ancient Near East* (VTSup 3; H. H. Rowley Festschrift; ed. M. Noth and D. Thomas; Leiden: Brill, 1955) 42–71.

16. H. Gunkel, *Einleitung in die Psalmen* (GHAT; Göttingen: Vandenhoeck & Ruprecht, 1933) 381–97.

17. S. Mowinckel, *The Psalms in Israel's Worship* (Nashville: Abingdon, 1967) II, 104–25; see p. 111.

18. Cf. J. Luyten, "Psalm 73 and Wisdom," in *La Sagesse de l'Ancien Testament* (BETL 51; ed. M. Gilbert; Leuven: Leuven University Press, 1979) 59–81; see pp. 63 and 64.

19. See Roland E. Murphy, "A Consideration of the Classification 'Wisdom Psalms,' " in *SAIW*, 456–67.

20. J. K. Kuntz, "The Canonical Wisdom Psalms of Ancient Israel," in *Rhetorical Criticism* (J. Muilenburg Festschrift; ed. J. J. Jackson and M. Kessler; Pittsburgh: Pickwick Press, 1974) 186–222.

21. See Luyten, "Psalm 73 and Wisdom," and also the study of J. J. van der Ploeg, "Le Psaume 119 et la sagesse," in *La Sagesse de l'Ancien Testament*, 82–87.

22. Weinfeld, *Deuteronomy*, 297; see also pp. 244–319.

23. Roland E. Murphy, "The Kerygma of the Book of Proverbs," *Int* 20 (1966) 3–14.

24. Weinfeld, *Deuteronomy*, 280.

25. Weinfeld, *Deuteronomy*, 244; so runs the title of the section.

26. J.-P. Audet, "Origines comparées de la double tradition de la loi et de la sagesse dans la proche-orient ancien," *Acts of the International Orientalists' Congress* (Moscow, 1960) I, 352–57; see also Guy Couturier, "La vie familiale comme source de la sagesse et de la loi," *Science et Esprit* 32 (1980) 177–92.

27. E. Gerstenberger, *Wesen und Herkunft des "apodiktischen Rechts"* (WMANT 20; Neukirchen-Vluyn: Neukirchener, 1965). See also W. Richter, *Recht und Ethos* (SANT 15; Munich: Kösel, 1966).

28. E. Würthwein, "Das Hohelied," in *Die fünf Megilloth* (HAT 18; Tübingen: Mohr/Siebeck, 1969) 31; B. Childs, *Introduction to the Old Testament as Scripture* (Philadelphia: Fortress, 1979) 571–79; the quotation is from p. 574.

29. Cf. J.-P. Audet, "Le Sens du Cantique des Cantiques," *RB* 62 (1955) 197–221, esp. 202.

30. Cf., e.g., Gerhard von Rad, *Wisdom in Israel* (Nashville: Abingdon, 1972) 166–69. M. Pope has pointed out, "In the late sixteenth century a new idea was proposed by the celebrated Don Isaac Abravanel who saw the protagonists of the Song of Songs as Solomon and Wisdom rather than God and Israel. . . . This line of interpretation . . . was adopted and adapted in the present century by Gottfried Kuhn (1926), who identified the Bride with Wisdom, but saw the Bridegroom as a type of the seeker after wisdom rather than as the historical Solomon"; cf. *Song of Songs* (AB 7C; Garden City: Doubleday, 1977) 110. See also Roland E. Murphy, "Wisdom and Eros in Proverbs 1–9," *CBQ* 50 (1988) 600–3.

CHAPTER 8

WISDOM LITERATURE AND THEOLOGY

♦

At first sight "theology" seems not to be in character with the experiential thrust of biblical wisdom. This is also suggested by the typical study of Old Testament theology, which is centered on promise, covenant, the prophetic literature, and other areas that are deemed more crucial. Such theology seems creedal, even academic, compared to a treatment of modest proverbs and unassuming admonitions. The most nakedly theological feature of the sapiential books is the personification of Lady Wisdom, which merits separate treatment (chap. 9).

It will be helpful at the outset if the concept of theology can be discussed more fully, if not clarified. "Biblical theology" is the broadest term for the area that concerns us. It is determined by the Bible one recognizes. The Christian accepts both Testaments; the Jew recognizes only the Tanakh. Further divisions are possible: New Testament theology,[1] Old Testament theology,[2] and Tanakh theology.[3] We can perhaps offer a working definition that can be accepted by all: a theology of the Bible (however the canon or extent of that Bible be defined) is an organized presentation of the biblical data concerning God, humans, and the world, according to biblical categories. Organization implies some systematization in the explication of the data; biblical categories are important because the basic material is the Bible itself. This is an attempt to capture biblical thought at its purest and also with the inconsistencies and changes it may have acquired throughout the history of the composition of the biblical literature. The method is the widely used and sometimes much maligned "historical methodology" or "historical criticism," which strives to interpret the Bible as objectively as possible.[4] This goal is difficult to attain because every interpreter is influenced by his or her presuppositions, no matter how "objective" one attempts to be. One simply has to allow for a certain margin of error. Another important factor is the recognition of biblical categories and the historical conditioning of biblical thought as it comes to expression through the centuries of its formation. This is not to fall into the error of sacralizing "biblical" thought as though its linguistic and cultural vehicle were unique.[5] But one has to begin with the biblical data and work within its context.

Can all the biblical data that is retrieved by assiduous application of the historical methodology to the text be systematized and organized? The many biblical theologies (of either Testament or both) that exist are all systematizations of one kind or another. The decisive question is, how successful have they been? Two facts tell against a *systematized* biblical theology: (1) None of the many attempts at systematizing the biblical data have succeeded in commanding a consensus. They have been helpful; they deserve the attention of every student and much can be learned from them. (2) Despite many recent attempts, there is no center or *Mitte* of either Testament that can adequately express its theology (either *in nuce* or in expanded form.)[6]

When one goes beyond biblical theology and incorporates it into the ongoing tradition and teaching of a community of faith, systematic (also called dogmatic) theology is the result. That is not our concern here, because it is a synthesis based *upon* the Bible, and it is not directly the meaning that the Bible acquired in its origin. Despite protests to the contrary, one may claim that everyone operates on this basis; there is no *pure* biblicist, even if some might think they are such. There is hardly any need to draw attention to the outstanding achievements of such systematicians as Karl Barth or Karl Rahner.

How does biblical wisdom fit into all this?[7] The usual approach in Old Testament theology is by way of the biblical record of God's revelation to the people by prophets and deeds—the rigid axis of history—which leaves little room for wisdom literature.[8] We shall discuss later the limitations of this approach and the impasse it has created for biblical theologians. We propose to treat wisdom and theology from points of view that will enable us to escape this impasse. The following remarks treat of four perspectives that are essential to a theology of biblical wisdom: the understanding of reality, the search for order, creation theology, and Yahwism and wisdom (the wisdom experience).

THE UNDERSTANDING OF REALITY

It seems at first too large a question to ask, even perhaps having little relevance to theology: How did the sages view reality? What was their *Weltanschauung?* But the answer to this question profoundly affects the way one can construe a theology of wisdom. Gerhard von Rad was the first to properly focus the issue, and he came back to it time after time in his ingenious *Wisdom in Israel.* Already in his brief foreword he invited his readers to contemplation—almost as if he felt this was the necessary step to the *Wirklichkeitsverständnis*, or "understanding of reality," that was exposed in this literature. He never made a list of items—perhaps that was part of his challenge to contemplation—and there is no intention of doing that here.[9] At the same time, his insights are important and should not be lost sight of. Here we shall examine a few, both to agree and to disagree. One must be careful not to treat the sapiential understanding of reality as something foreign to the rest of Israel and merely the private property of the sages. If the sages did not share an understanding with their audience, they would never have been understood. Hence we are dealing with an aspect of the Israelite worldview, as this was manifested in a particular portion of the literature.

1. Wisdom does not view reality in an unhistorical manner.[10] It is important to state this explicitly.[11] We have seen that the sages do not investigate the saving events in Israel's tradition as part of their repertoire (Sirach and Wisdom of Solomon are notable exceptions, and at the end of the wisdom development). They draw upon daily experience as this was framed in the traditions handed down in the family and by teachers. But their lessons are not timeless or unhistorical. They deal with the concrete, how and when and why certain actions are to be performed and certain insights to be appropriated (cf. Prov 15:23; 25:11; Sir 4:23). The effective literary presentation of these views in pithy sayings tends to set them apart, without a concrete context to explicate them. But their original context was in history, and their further application is in the historical order. History is not merely the recollection of times past, but also the analysis of daily experience in which the variable and the incalculable often appear.

2. Wisdom recognizes a dynamic relationship between humans and their environment. Gerhard von Rad has written that "the most characteristic feature of her [Israel's] understanding of reality lay, in the first instance, in the fact that she believed man to stand in a quite specific, highly dynamic, existential relationship with his environment."[12] The sages analyzed the environment—the created world and its inhabitants—for signs and for conclusions (Prov 17:1; 25:13). They drew analogies and made comparisons between things, living and nonliving (Prov 25:14; 26:2). In the animal world there were the very small that were, at the same time, very wise: ants, locusts, and lizards (Prov 30:24–28). Job could taunt the three friends to ask the beasts and birds of the air to teach them (Job 12:7). It has been well said that when the Lord "replies" to Job he lets nature do the talking (Job 38–41).

In a sense, this is a "worldly" understanding, an appreciation of the autonomy, the independence, of created things. It is not the same as "secularism." The autonomy of creation is recognized for what it can teach humans about themselves, about God's creation, and even about God's own self. The recognition of such autonomy is on the level of immediate sense perception. There were certain lessons to be drawn from what one saw, but there were mysteries as well: "Which is the way to the dwelling place of light, and where is the abode of darkness that you may take them to their boundaries and set them on their homeward paths?" (Job 38:19–20). Obviously there was only a rudimentary knowledge of what we could call natural sciences. Nevertheless, they developed a practical wisdom, a creation theology, from their accumulated experience: nature and its mysteries were observed and weighed, even if by the most elementary of methods (cf. Prov 30:18–19). More significantly, there was no separation of the world from the creator. The cosmos was not a machine that was wound up at creation and then let go. The Lord was active at all levels, both good and evil. This basic fact of Israelite belief stands in a certain tension with what we have called autonomy. Both the autonomous actions of creatures and the all-pervasive causality of God are affirmed. Humans bear responsibility for their actions; we might say they have "free will." On the other hand, the Lord is the cause of everything, both good and evil. Israel never tried to correlate human freedom and divine activity, as later Christian theology attempted to do. Sirach is aware that one might try to blame personal wrongdoing on the Lord, but he does not deny the divine causality (Sir 15:11–20); if one chooses, one can keep the commandments. Job knows who is to blame for his sufferings and for evil in the world: "If it isn't he [the Lord], then who is it?" (9:22–24).

The "environment" of which we have been speaking is not simply creation, but God as well. As Gerhard von Rad put it, "The experiences of the world were for her [Israel] always divine experiences as well, and the experiences of God were for her experiences of the world."[13] The theological implication is that the world is never experienced as purely secular, as apart from the Lord who controls it and who is revealed in it (see what is said about the personification of Wisdom in chap. 9). The Christian distinction between faith and reason is not applicable to Israel. She did not "believe" in the Lord who spoke through the prophets in contrast to "knowing" him through his creation and the experience of it.

Undergirding this dialogue is the virtue of trust.[14] In order to deal with experience the sage had to trust in the relative stability of human relationships, and in the integrity and meaningfulness of daily events. If the complexities of human activity did not somehow lend themselves to human insight, sheer chaos would be the result. The resulting harmony was understood within the perspective of the all-pervasive divine presence. Ultimately, trust in the patterns of human experience was trust in God, who was responsible for the reality that confronted the sages.

Trust in the Lord did not eliminate a lively respect for the mystery of divine activity. The teachings of the sages were open to experience and verification—up to a certain point. Beyond that lay the mystery of God's free activity (Prov 20:24; 21:30; Job 11:7–8; Isa 40:13–14, 28). The basic paradox of wisdom appears: on the one hand, wisdom is something acquired by discipline and docility, but on the other hand, it is a gift of God. Sayings about the Lord appear cheek by jowl with sayings about human experience. Ultimately wisdom is never secular, nor does it rest on presuppositions alien to faith in the Lord. Although von Rad claimed that Qoheleth had lost the trust that characterized traditional wisdom, one may wonder if he ultimately had a deeper faith than those who "trusted." He rejected the easy acceptance of the tradition, questioning it severely, but ultimately he accepted God on God's terms.[15]

WISDOM AS A SEARCH FOR ORDER

It is practically a commonplace in wisdom research to maintain that the sages were bent on discovering order, or orders, in the realm of experience and nature.[16] This means that the sages recognized a certain autonomy (granted that nothing could escape the divine sovereignty) in the actions and experiences of the world. Once the order of such events could be discovered, wisdom could be achieved, lessons made apparent, and laws for conduct established.[17] This is not an irreligious view, nor even totally pragmatic or eudaemonistic, as if one should follow rules solely for the success that they bring. Behind the order stands the divinity, the creator, who has set up his world according to certain laws. Creatures are to abide by the divine set of orders.

This point of view has been reinforced by the role of *ma'at* in the Egyptian wisdom literature (see Appendix). *Ma'at* is virtually untranslatable, but it can be rendered as "justice" or "truth" or "order." Siegfried Morenz describes the concept thus:

> What is ma'at? This is like asking Pilate's question—for ma'at does indeed mean "truth" among other things—and it cannot be answered by a simple translation of the Egyptian term. At least four sentences must be added by way of explanation. Ma'at is right order in nature and society, as established by the act of creation, and hence means, according to the context, what is right, what is correct, law, order, justice, and truth. This state of righteousness needs to be preserved or established, in great matters as in small. Ma'at is therefore not only right order but also the object of human activity. Ma'at is both the task which man sets himself and also, as righteousness, the promise and reward which await him on fulfilling it.[18]

This Egyptian mentality is accepted by many biblical scholars as part of the ancient worldview and is transposed, as it were, to the thinking of the Israelite sages in particular.[19] Their sayings and admonitions are aimed at ferreting out and establishing the order that governs the world.

Is the reconstruction of this "order" mentality truly helpful in understanding the teachings of wisdom? A straightforward reading of the literature hardly suggests that the sages were in quest of an order "out there," the knowledge of which would make the task of living easier and more profitable. They deduced from observation or experience that certain actions lead to good or bad results: what are the effects of a soothing word, of self-control, honesty, humility, and so on? Experience teaches certain lessons: laziness usually leads to poverty and diligence to prosperity. But did such generalizations assume the status of an innate, static, order of things? The ambiguities that the sages noted, and their awareness of their limitations, suggest that they did not operate with this concept.[20] The scholarly postulate of "order" is a reconstruction of Israel's mentality. It raises a question never asked by Israel: on what is your wisdom insight based? *Our* answer to this (for silent Israel) might possibly be, on the order in and of creation. It may be a logical and correct answer, but Israel never raised the question nor consciously assumed the answer we give to it. The orderly Greek *kosmos* (for which there is, in Hebrew, no exact verbal equivalent) was not the world in which Israel lived.

There is no intent here to deny that Israel was sensitive to certain regularities in the world (such as the cycle of seasons), or even to a customary way of doing things (as the "impossible questions" demonstrate; cf. the emended text of Amos 6:12, "Can one plow the sea with oxen?"). But such accepted regularities are not the same as an "order" that is envisioned as operative in the reality of everyday experience and as the goal of the wisdom enterprise. Analogies are not the same as order. One can point to many comparisons: pleasing words can be compared to a honeycomb (Prov 16:24), the lazy sleeper to a door turning on its hinges (Prov 26:14), and so on. But where is the evidence of an all-embracing order that regulates human conduct? The wisdom sentences are largely concerned with human activity; they supply data about reality to human beings, inculcating ideals of action. To this end comparisons and analogies with the world of nature are used, correlations between actions and results are made.

The preoccupation of wisdom research with order comes to full expression with K. Koch's theory about deed and consequence.[21] Order is applied to the area of retribution, or reward/punishment. Koch gave this the name of "fate-producing context," that is, the view that deed and consequence are aspects of one reality. There is an intrinsic connection between the good act and the good result, between the bad act and the bad result. God does not "intervene"; he has set up reality that way, and he acts as a "mid-wife"

(Koch's term) watching over the operation of this law. Thus a mechanical correspondence is perceived to operate in the fortunes of the wise and foolish. One can point to many sayings in Proverbs (and elsewhere, as Ps 7:15–18) that reflect such correspondence. Prov 26:27 (cf. Ps 7:16; Eccl 10:8; Sir 27:26) is typical:

He who digs a pit falls into it;
    and a stone comes back upon him who rolls it.

The diligent person becomes prosperous (Prov 10:4). The foolish/wicked will not prevail (Prov 10:30; 11:21; 13:25), while the wise/virtuous will inevitably succeed (10:2, 30; 13:25). The correspondence between deed and consequence can even be compared to the laws of nature, such as the rain brought by the north wind (Prov 25:23).

It is certainly true that the *verbal expression* of many sayings allows one to infer a correspondence, even a mechanical correspondence, between a good/bad action and its good/bad result. But along with such statements is the view that directly connects good and bad results with the Lord who rewards and punishes. This is found not only in the wisdom literature but throughout the Bible. God is directly involved in the weal or woe that humans experience. The prophets recognized this in the arena of history (cf. Isa 45:7; 43:13; 1 Sam 2:6), and no less did the sages in the reality of daily experience (Prov 16:4; 20:22; 22:12).

Is it necessary to choose between these two points of view of retribution, or could both of them have been operative in Israel's experience? Probably the latter. There is something profound in the thought that evil somehow corrupts and that the good will not be without its effect. Moderns might call this "poetic justice." But one cannot exclude the basic biblical understanding of the all-pervasive causality of God in human affairs. Koch's interpretation is in harmony with many biblical statements about retribution. But one must also recognize the biblical emphasis upon the *reaction* of God to human conduct (e.g., Abraham's questioning of God in Gen 18:16–33; Deut 4:3–4; 5:9–11; etc.). In most cases the biblical text does not leave room for a hypothetical reconstruction of a mechanical law of retribution. There is no zone of "order" that separated the Israelite from the Lord.

The concept of order has been pushed as far as it can conceivably go (and, I think, over the edge of plausibility) by Hans H. Schmid. Order, which is expressed almost equally by Egyptian *ma'at* and Hebrew *ṣĕdāqâ*, was initially seen as the basic goal of international wisdom. Then wisdom theology came to be understood as creation theology. The next move was to postulate creation as the unifying theme of order—cosmic, political, social—in the ancient world. Thus, the biblical prophets were merely trying to restore this order (on the basis of the deed-consequence syndrome proposed by K. Koch) when they condemned Israel. The salvation preached by *both* Testaments is alleged to be inherent in the structure of the universal world order, and thus a total salvation. Creation theology has become the horizon (*Gesamthorizont*) in which Jewish and Christian faiths are to be interpreted. As Schmid puts it, "The doctrine of creation, namely, the belief that God has created and is sustaining the order of the world in all its complexities, is not a peripheral theme of biblical theology but is plainly the fundamental theme. What Israel experienced in her history and what the early Christian community experienced in relation to Jesus is understood and interpreted in terms of this one basic theme."[22]

WISDOM AND CREATION

"Wisdom theology is creation theology." This is practically an axiom in biblical studies, and it is the insight of W. Zimmerli.[23] His concern was not creation but wisdom: how is wisdom to be fitted into biblical theology, since it is so atypical? He interpreted the wisdom phenomenon as an outgrowth of Gen 1:28, in which God addresses the man and the woman: "Be fertile and multiply; fill the earth and subdue it. Have dominion over the fish of the sea. . . ." Wisdom represents the human effort to fulfill the divine command to master the world. Thus wisdom became "respectable," because it was overtly connected with the divine word. For the moment we can bypass Zimmerli's concern about the theological locus of wisdom, and dwell on his true insight that wisdom has to do with a theology of creation. Here creation can be viewed as "origins" or "beginnings," and also as the world that humans learn from and react to, "the surface of his earth" (Prov 8:31) on which Lady Wisdom plays.

    1.   Origins. The opening pages of Genesis usually dominate any discussion in the Old Testament about creation. The liturgical majesty of "creating" in six days, with a rest on the sabbath, is presented in Gen 1:1–2:3. The Lord God is the divine potter shown at work in Gen 2:4–7. There is just a hint of a chaos motif in the mention of the waters, darkness, and the abyss (Gen 1:2). This motif of the battle of divinity with chaos became a celebrated feature in many psalms (74:12–17; 104:6–9, 24–26) and in passages of the prophets (Isa 51:9–11). It has been argued that the chaos motif has to be taken more literally, in the sense that chaos is never totally eliminated. In other words, creation for Israel was not intrinsically irreversible.[24] It is important for wisdom theology to take cognizance of this view, since "evil" and divine retribution figure so largely in the wisdom books. This interpretation does not allow for the fact that the chaos motifs in the Old Testament had long since been demythologized. In fact, this imagery was used at the plea-

sure of the writer. Thus the waters of chaos are used to extol the Lord's supremacy in Ps 29, or even as a divine weapon (Exod 15; Judg 5:20–21; 2 Sam 22:10–16).[25] One cannot really explain the persistence of evil in the world as the upper hand that chaos has over the Lord. While the Israelites argue with God to conquer chaos, the underlying presupposition is precisely that the Lord is truly omnipotent; the present distress is puzzling and oppressive because it is not intelligible in the light of the Lord's omnipotence. Chaos serves to underscore the problem, but it is not part of the problem.

Within the wisdom literature itself there is not much interest in origins per se. The famous passages that clearly bear on this subject are Prov 8:22–31 and Job 38–41. But the creative activity of God is not the direct object of the poetry. In Prov 8:22ff. Wisdom is describing her status with God as having been present with him before creation as an 'mwn. As indicated in chap. 9, the meaning of this word is uncertain, either "crafts [wo]man" or "nursling." Hence we cannot be sure what role, if any, she may have played in creation (although in Wis 7:22 and 8:6, she is understood as a "crafts [wo]man," *technitis*). In Job the speeches of Yahweh take up creation, but not in order to inform Job about the beginnings. Rather, it is the Lord's turn to score points against Job, pitting the divine creative activity against Job's ignorance and limitations. Israel lived easily with the Lord and creator of all, as the frequent use of creation in the psalms of praise (e.g., Pss 95–98) demonstrates.

2. Wisdom and the world. This was the prime concern of the Israelite sages and their writings. The world is constituted first of human beings, the most mysterious creatures of all ("Sometimes a way seems right to a person, but the end of it leads to death," Prov 14:12 = 16:25). But Sirach hints at the puzzling generosity of God: "With wisdom and knowledge he fills them; good and evil he shows them" (Sir 17:7). The human condition is only part of the sages' perspectives. The world of nature, animate and inanimate, came within their purview (see the discussion of Prov 30:18 in chap. 2).

Israel's perception of the world in which one lived is to be found throughout the Old Testament, and there are various emphases according to various interests—the emphasis of the Yahwist, for example, differs from that of the priestly tradition in Gen 1–11. But there is a primary characteristic that is important for theology: the world is the showcase for divine activity. It is not contemplated in and for itself, but in relation to the creator and to living things that occupy it. It is not a cosmos that works mechanically, but a happening that occurs over and over for all its inhabitants (Ps 104). Hence the human *experience* of the world is so important. As Odil Hannes Steck describes it, Israel deduces from its encounter with the world "the fact of being endowed with length of life, space for living, the means for food to sustain life, and the power of multiplying life. All these are things that actually precede human activity and are not at man's disposal either. . . . In this elemental experience of the nondisposable gift of life and its equally nondisposable withdrawal, the individual in Israel actively experienced Yahweh the creator as acting in the event of his life."[26] In support of this statement, Steck refers to such texts as Ps 22:10 (dependent upon God from birth) and Job 10:8ff. (God's loving care in the creative act). This deep sense of not disposing of one's own existence begets an attitude toward creator and creature that parallels Israel's understanding of herself as called into being as the people of God. This kind of experience is exposure not only to the world but to the Lord: "To be exposed to Yahweh in absolutely everything, to encounter him, to find meaningful existence solely in orientation toward him, in what he gives and what he takes away, in his reliably revealed activity and in the activity that is mysteriously unexplorable—this was the determining background against which Israel perceived the natural world and environment, perceived it in experience, knowledge, and formative activity."[27] It was through the experience of the world, of creation so perceived, that the Old Testament sages were stimulated (in contradistinction to stimulation from the events of sacred history).

Is this perception of the world, as presented in Israel's wisdom literature, really theological? Yes, because it is inseparable from the experience of God. The union of the two has been expressed in the theology of Karl Rahner, and has been described thus:

> The God experienced in this "mysticism of everyday things" is not the distilled essence of things, not the highest abstraction from the world, but the experience of God's life at the very heart of the world, in flesh, in time and in history. Perhaps the greatest dualism that Karl Rahner overcame is that between God and the world. For him they are never identical, but neither are they ever separate, so that God and the world are experienced and known together. Presence to self, presence to world and presence to God are all aspects of one and the same experience, the experience of God's real presence in the world which he created to be his real symbol.[28]

There is some connection between wisdom and the praise of God for his created world. Gerhard von Rad pointed out "a very close connection between the hymns and wisdom."[29] The world is not dumb; it proclaims a message for all to hear (Pss 19:2; 145; 148). The attitude of the wise man was perhaps more of wonder than of praise, although this is a very thin line, as Ps 104 indicates. This psalm rehearses several examples of God's providential care of the world: water, grass and vegetation, home even for inconsequential animals like rock badgers, and the like. Then the psalmist exclaims:

> How manifold are your works, O Lord!
> in wisdom you have wrought them all! (Ps 104:24ab)

It is this reverential attitude that is important. The creation doctrine of wisdom does not speak directly to the ecological concerns that have agitated recent discussions. But it does contribute to forming a basic human attitude that can have an ecological "fallout," so to speak.[30]

YAHWISM AND WISDOM
(THE WISDOM EXPERIENCE)

The issue here is whether the wisdom literature deserves to be considered a valid expression of Israel's faith. The assertion that it is invalid might seem to be an oddity, but it is unfortunately not a rare item. Perhaps the most vigorous exponent of the theological illegitimacy of Old Testament wisdom is Horst D. Preuss, who has also written extensively and well about the sapiential books.[31] In his view, early wisdom (as reflected in Prov 10ff.) is essentially a foreign body within the Old Testament. It is allied to international wisdom and has as its object the ensuring of a successful human life. Success is achieved by ascertaining the order of things over which the divinity (who is in this view an *Urhebergott*, a God of origins and sustainment) presides— especially the order of retribution (see the discussion of deed and consequence earlier). Preuss considers the religion in Prov 10ff. a form of "Poly-yahwism,"[32] a contaminated faith in a God who is quite different from the Lord that is revealed in the rest of the Old Testament (history, prophets, cult). This religion met its crisis with the Books of Job and Qoheleth, but it was eventually preserved in the Old Testament by various factors (identification of wisdom and Torah in Sirach, etc.). It is well-nigh impossible to unite such wisdom with the New Testament; at the most it is an indirect witness to Christ (in the style of Bultmann's understanding of the Old Testament) insofar as it is bankrupt and thus calls for another (read: Christian) understanding of God.

This position is a logical development of earlier views about Old Testament theology that could find no room for wisdom. G. E. Wright wrote that wisdom "does not fit into the type of faith exhibited in the historical and prophetic literatures."[33] W. Eichrodt asserted that there is a "strongly secular flavour" about wisdom, and it "is only loosely connected with religious faith."[34] Many more examples of such benign neglect, if not indifference, to Old Testament wisdom could be given.[35] The astonishing thing is the revival of interest that has occurred, even if the results have not been altogether satisfactory. The first sign of the revival was an attempt to find a locus within

Old Testament theology for this refractory literature. Right there an important methodological move appeared: the assumption that wisdom is to be justified by its relationship to a Yahwism that is defined by a narrow historical axis.[36] W. Zimmerli presented in 1964 a carefully thought-out case for wisdom as creation doctrine, specifically derived from Gen 1:28.[37] Wisdom is the theological development of the divine blessing bestowed upon humans: they are to fill the earth and master it. Thus wisdom could be safely located within the cocoon of salvation history. However, Zimmerli returned to the issue of the integration of wisdom into Old Testament theology in 1973, and raised two interesting questions: "Must one always have an historical explanation, explicitly referred to and fully formed, as the center [of theology]?" And also: "Did not Israel know the "I am who I am," whom she recognized only from the historical experience that explained the name of Yahweh, also as the One who is attached to his creation without being a captive of it?"[38] In other words, both creation and Sinai are vehicles of revelation for God's people.

Already a second methodological problem was on the horizon. One may justify wisdom from the creation theology of Gen 1, but is creation really part of Israelite belief? Not for C. Westermann. He located creation under the category of blessing—the blessing issued by the Lord in Genesis. Creation is not a *credendum*, or "item of belief": "The Old Testament never speaks about faith in the creator; or faith in being created" (because "belief" for Westermann has to allow of an alternative, a possibility of not believing). It is similar with wisdom: "The significance of wisdom as an integral part of the Bible resides above all in the fact that it makes it clear that the creator gave man the capacity of becoming properly oriented in his world, of understanding himself in his world, and of mastering the daily tasks given him. This requires neither revelation nor theological reflection. Wisdom is secular or profane."[39] One can hardly imagine greater embarrassments than those that wisdom has bequeathed to these biblical theologians.

Gerhard von Rad came up with a clear answer. He stubbornly maintained that wisdom was a form, if an unusual one, of Yahwism. In his *Old Testament Theology* he included wisdom literature and especially the Psalter as "Israel's answer" to the saving acts of God, but he came to see that this was unsatisfactory. In *Wisdom in Israel*, he defined his view more precisely: "The wisdom practiced in Israel was a response made by a Yahwism confronted with specific experiences of the world. In her wisdom Israel created an intellectual sphere in which it was possible to discuss both the multiplicity of trivial, daily occurrences as well as basic theological principles. This wisdom is, therefore, at all events to be regarded as a form of Yahwism, although—as a result of the unusual nature of the tasks involved—an unusual form and, in the theological structure of its statements, very different from the other ways in which Yahwism reveals itself."[40]

At an early point in his thinking, von Rad was inclined to tie in creation with salvation history. Thus, he viewed the positioning of Gen 1–11 as an introduction to the history of election and promise that was to be unfolded.[41] He tied creation into Yahwistic faith by means of the prohibition of images contained in the Decalogue (Exod 20:4).[42] Israel was aware of the various creation stories current in the ancient Near East (Enuma Elish and Atrahasis could be mentioned). She expressed her own faith in the Lord as creator and sustainer (Gen 1–2; Ps 104; Isa 40ff.). An analysis of the Israelite view of creation shows its distinctiveness: the effortlessness of the Lord's word; supreme dominion; the goodness of creation. For von Rad, Israel's unique view came from the recognition that the Lord was totally transcendent, completely other from the world—the Lord could *not* be imaged. "The prohibition surely enshrines a decisive and fundamental recognition of the fact that God is theologically transcendent relative to the world, so that the creation narrative must be understood in a certain sense as the immensely diversified exposition of a theological datum which was already embedded in the most ancient form of Yahwism." This is an important consideration, but the emphasis on transcendence fails to allow for the immanence and intimacy implied in the personification of Lady Wisdom (Prov 8:22–31; Job 28; Sir 24).

Thus far we have been discussing the problem (or embarrassment) that wisdom has given to various academic theologians. Even in the case of von Rad, there is the presupposition that one begins with historical Yahwism and is then under the obligation to justify the existence of wisdom literature as a legitimate expression of Israel's faith. The basic assumption is that Israel's understanding of the Lord as working in the historical communal order is somehow more orthodox, more Yahwistic as it were, than her understanding of the Lord through nature or by human experience. But it is a mistake for logical or theological clarity to be granted the right to determine the quality of faith in God. One must look at the reality of life in Israel.

Two considerations deserve discussion here: first, the centrality of the Sinai revelation and the ensuing acts of the Lord in Israel's history, and second, the relationship of wisdom to so-called "natural theology." The touchstone for biblical revelation and theology has long been the acts of God in Israel's history. This was severely shaken when B. Albrektson pointed out that divine action in human history was not a view unique to Israel, but could be found elsewhere.[43] Revelation by divine acts in history might possibly be neither unique nor all-sufficient. However, Israel's concept of itself and its history with God still remains unique, in my view, despite the parallels offered by Albrektson. Nowhere else is there to be found such a consistent, even rigorous, historical sequence of a nation's understanding of its God and itself. The relationship between the one Lord and Israel is ongoing and open, fraught with historical vicissitudes but never dying. The total Israelite view is not found elsewhere in the ancient Near East. However, even if it is fundamental to Israel, it does not exhaust the relationship between God and people.

Second, there is the resemblance of wisdom literature to "natural theology," which has been much shunned during this century, thanks to Karl Barth. It would be a mistake to characterize the wisdom experience as a species of "natural theology" within the Bible.[44] True, it deals with creation and with day-to-day living, but this is in a concrete supernatural situation to which God has called his children; God is available to them through this experience. The Israelite sages were Yahwists. What they learned about the Lord from creation and experience was necessarily associated with what they learned from their historical traditions. The manner and style may have differed, but it was the one Lord who was communicated. Here I am relying upon the theological views of Karl Rahner. In his terms, biblical wisdom is a thematic expression of God's revelation as mediated through creation. Humans live in a de facto supernatural order. Whatever knowledge (not even necessarily "conceptual" or thematic) they have of God is the lifeline to the free and faithful submission that they can make to him.[45]

It would probably be fair to say that the traditional theological approach to Yahwism/wisdom has developed along prejudicial lines. That method consisted in a logical academic procedure: wisdom is to be judged from the vantage point of God's revelation in history. This view is biased. Rather, one should look directly at the wisdom experience (which is also historical!) that the worshiper of the Lord actually had. What is the religious dimension of this wisdom experience?[46] It is an appropriation of the lessons that one can draw from day-to-day living, from the realm of personal intercourse and the surprises of creation. The dialogue between the Israelite and the environment was also a dialogue with the God who was worshiped in Israel as creator and redeemer. The covenant relationship to the Lord does not figure directly in the wisdom experience; it is bracketed, but not erased. The world of the sage was hedged about, but not directed, by the sacred traditions rehearsed in the cult (the liturgical experience). It was from the experience of the world, the give-and-take between human beings and their environment, that the sages derived their lessons.

It is true, the Decalogue proposed certain ultimate ideals: commands concerning reverence for parents, prohibitions against murder, adultery, and other crimes. But there were other areas of human life, no less important, that were left untouched. In the smaller concrete details of life one found innumerable situations that called for attitudes, actions, and decisions that ultimately had a profound effect on the individual. This sphere was not felt to be withdrawn from the Lord and his activity; God was as much at work here as in the heady experiences of Israel's history and liturgical worship. The Lord's dominion over the created world is at the core of wisdom's effort to help one to live in the world. As von Rad puts it, "We hold fast to the fact that in the case of the wise men's search for knowledge, when they expressed their results in a completely secular form, there was never any question of what we would call absolute knowledge functioning independently of their faith in Yahweh. This is inconceivable for the very reason that the teachers were completely unaware of any reality not controlled by Yahweh."[47]

The sages did not analyze nature in the subject-object manner that is ours. Ps 104 and the sayings in Prov 30 show this. All things, especially all living things, were appreciated for simply existing, for being alive. The happiness of being alive runs as a current through Israel's attitude toward the world (Ps 104). The creator was not experienced by way of a cosmological argument that concluded to transcendent being ("natural theology"). He was a "given," along with being the redeemer ($g\bar{o}\bar{}el;$ cf. Exod 15:13) of the Exodus. Israel encountered this creator in her experience of daily events. If one met the incalculable, this was an encounter with the Lord, mysterious and free. The world and the experience of it were intrinsic to this encounter.

J. Marböck has expressed this unity of the everyday and theology very well. He has noted in Sirach the mixture of theological and religious interpretation of Wisdom with "profane" notices (e.g., Sir 4:23–24, following on 4:11–19: the right word at the right time, following upon Wisdom's speech to those who love her). This kind of juxtaposition seems to suggest a double message: "Wisdom in the theological sense of God's presence, of an intimacy and community with God, is not separate from the world, but is in the midst of everyday life with its customary, even petty events. At the same time this world, which is accepted with its own cleverness and wisdom, receives a midpoint, a secret center: the Wisdom of Israel's religion."[48] He distinguishes between a wisdom "from above" (e.g., Sir 24) and one "from below" (e.g., a whole list of "profane" recommendations, such as table manners in 31:12–32:13). Modern presuppositions of the "spiritual" should not prevent one from recognizing that Ben Sira deepens rather than dispenses with the wisdom "from below."[49] Marböck rightly differs with Martin Hengel, who judged that Ben Sira excluded any wisdom that is not identified with pious observances. (Sirach is very much concerned with everyday actions or *Alltagsweisheit.*)

In short, the wisdom experience is to be described as a faith experience. The shaping of Israel's views of the world, and of the activity of God behind and in it, was done in an ambience of faith, and was characterized by trust and reliance upon God. Moreover, the sages penetrated into the divine mystery in a manner that even the prophets never equaled. God drew the people, through their daily experience of themselves and creation, into the mystery of God's dealings with each individual human being. Yahwistic belief has doubtless colored and affected Israelite doctrine on wisdom. After all, the sages believed in Yahweh and what he had done for Israel. But it would be impossible (perhaps illegitimate?) to separate out within the wisdom books what is due specifically to Yahwistic belief. The epigrammatic association of wisdom and fear of the Lord (Prov 1:7) is an example of this profound and inextricable unity, because "fear of the Lord" would have certain nuances from Israelite history (Gen 28:17; Exod 3:6; 20:18 [LXX]) and worship. The fact that Yahweh sayings occur (Prov 16:1ff.) says nothing about the wisdom operation itself. The mere use of the divine name has no intrinsic importance, as if it made the secular into something religious and Yahwistic. "Lord" (*yhwh*) is Israel's God, the one who is encountered in the wisdom experience, whether or not the "official" name is used.

Wisdom literature provides a biblical model for understanding divine revelation apart from the historical mode (salvation history) in which it is usually cast. We have portrayed the dialogue with divinity that takes place essentially via human experience and creation. It is also clear that the issues of life and salvation emerge in this dialogue, and especially in the invitation of personified Wisdom (Prov 8:35). On this level the Israelite encountered the Lord in a vital faith relationship that is as valid as the liturgical experience in the Temple, or the Exodus event itself.

What does this model suggest for nonbiblical religions and their clients who have never heard of *yhwh* or Christ? It points to a faith response that is not explicitly related to a particular historical revelation of God. Israel learned of her Lord also through experience and through creation. This is saving faith, even if it is not centered on the promises or the Exodus. Moreover, the openness of Israelite wisdom to the wisdom of Israel's neighbors— the clearly international character of the wisdom movement, the actual borrowings from Egyptian wisdom, the controlling references to creatures and creation—provides a biblical basis for the possibility that the non-Israelite can also respond in saving faith to the creator, who is the God revealed in Israelite and Christian experience.

This theological position does not take a particular stand on truth or falsehood, or on the superiority or inferiority of any belief. It is not the theoretical expression of belief that is at the heart of the matter; rather, it is the dialogical relationship with God in which a faith response occurs, through God's free and gracious communication. Neither does this view derogate from the centrality of Jesus Christ in the Christian understanding of the redemptive plan of God. One can still theologically affirm universal redemption through Christ. It is his redemptive, sacrificial life that makes possible and fruitful the faith engendered in the wisdom encounter. The understanding of biblical faith as reflected in the wisdom literature is a profitable insight into a relatively new (or newly appreciated) situation in a non-Christian world where God's relationship to millions of his children is at issue.

NOTES TO "WISDOM LITERATURE AND THEOLOGY"

1. For a summary review of New Testament theology, see Gerhard Hasel, *New Testament Theology: Basic Issues in the Current Debate* (Grand Rapids: Eerdmans, 1978); G. Strecker (ed.), *Das Problem der Theologie des Neuen Testaments* (WF 367; Darmstadt: Wissenschaftliche Buchgesellschaft, 1975); C. K. Barrett, "What Is New Testament Theology?" *HBT* 3 (1981) 1–22.

2. Cf. the summaries of H. G. Reventlow, *Problems of Old Testament Theology in the Twentieth Century* (Philadelphia: Fortress, 1985) and, esp. for the relationship between the two Testaments, his *Problems of Biblical Theology in the Twentieth Century* (Philadelphia: Fortress, 1986). Cf. also Gerhard Hasel, *Old Testament Theology: Basic Issues in the Current Debate* (3rd ed.; Grand Rapids: Eerdmans, 1989).

3. It may be said that this is in its infancy, in view of the plea (as well as the program) of M. Goshen-Gottstein. Cf. his "Tanakh Theology," in *Ancient Israelite Religion: Essays in Honor of Frank Moore Cross* (ed. P. Miller et al.; Philadelphia: Fortress, 1987) 617–44. See also M. Tsevat, "Theology of the Old Testament—A Jewish View," *HBT* 8/2 (1986) 33–50; J. D. Levenson, "Why Jews Are Not Interested in Biblical Theology," in *Jewish Perspectives on Ancient Israel* (ed. J. Neusner; Philadelphia: Fortress, 1987) 281–307.

4. Cf. J. A. Fitzmyer, "Historical Criticism: Its Role in Biblical Interpretation and Church Life," *TS* 50 (1989) 244–59.

5. J. Barr issued this warning long ago; cf. *The Semantics of Biblical Language* (London: Oxford University Press, 1962).

6. The literature on the center of both the Old Testament and the New Testament has been voluminous, esp. among German scholars; cf. the studies of Reventlow (note 2 in this section) and also M. Oeming, *Gesamtbiblische Theologien der Gegenwart* (Stuttgart: Kohlhammer, 1985) 182–85. A recent attempt to systematize Old Testament theology was made by R. Knierim in *HBT* 6/1 (1984) 25–57, to which there was a reply by Roland E. Murphy in the same issue, pp. 65–71, and a counter-reply by Knierim in *HBT* 6/2 (1984) 91–128. The issue is not merely whether there is a "center," but the possibility of a systematic Old Testament theology.

7. The judgment of H. G. Reventlow should be noted: "The integration of wisdom into Old Testament theology is an unresolved task that remains for the future." Cf. his *Problems of Old Testament Theology,* 184.

8. J. Barr was among the first to object, and rightly so, to the imperialist and one-sided stance of history in the interpretation of the Old Testament text; see the summary presentation in *IDBSup,* 104–11, 746–49.

9. Gerhard von Rad, *Wisdom in Israel* (Nashville: Abingdon, 1972). The first mention of *Wirklichkeitsverständnis* occurs on p. 6 (p. 17 of the German edition of 1970). "Contemplation" is found at the end of the short foreword. For further (random) references to the understanding of reality (or to synonymous expressions such as *Weltvorstellung*), see pp. 6, 10, 59, 62–64, 287, 301–14 (in the English translation). In the spare indexes provided in both the German and English editions, there is the simple entry "Reality, as oriented towards humans." This single entry (esp. the word "oriented") speaks volumes in terms of von Rad's understanding of the wisdom enterprise. On von Rad's interpretation of the Old Testament worldview, see Chr. Link, *Die Welt als Gleichnis* (BevT 73; Munich: Kaiser, 1976) 268–85.

10. Cf. von Rad, *Wisdom in Israel*, 300–1, n. 16. Although the topic is not precisely the historical timeliness of the sayings, see also his treatment of "the doctrine of the proper time," pp. 138–43.

11. The need is shown by such statements as "It is a primary characteristic of wisdom literature that it formulates statements of timeless and universal validity"; so J. Høgenhaven, *Problems and Prospects of Old Testament Theology* (Sheffield: Almond Press, 1987) 99.

12. Von Rad, *Wisdom in Israel*, 301.

13. Von Rad, *Wisdom in Israel*, 62.

14. "Thus here, in proverbial wisdom, there is faith in the stability of the elementary relationships between man and man, faith in the similarity of men and of their reactions, faith in the reliability of the orders which support human life and thus, implicitly or explicitly, faith in God who put these orders in operation"; von Rad, *Wisdom in Israel*, 62–63. Von Rad is speaking here of trust (*Vertrauen*), not of theological faith (*Glaube*).

15. See the discussion in von Rad, *Wisdom in Israel*, 226–39, and also in his *Old Testament Theology* (New York: Harper & Row, 1962) I, 453–59. Cf. also Roland E. Murphy, "The Faith of Qoheleth," *Word & World* 7 (1987) 253–60.

16. The list of scholars would be a lengthy one: e.g., H. Gese, Hans H. Schmid, U. Skladny, W. Zimmerli, et al. So also von Rad, but not without some misgivings, it seems. In *Wisdom in Israel* he speaks of order innumerable times. Ultimately he identified order as a primeval order that addressed human beings and was the object of the sages' search (p. 157). But he also asked the tantalizing question "Is it faith in the orders or faith in Yahweh?" (p. 95). Even more explicitly, on p. 107: "Can one really say that the teachers were searching for a world order? . . . One can in no sense speak of a world order as really existing between God and man." Our concern here, however, is with the validity and application of the term "order" in wisdom research.

17. D. J. McCarthy made the point succinctly: "This fundamental conviction that there is an order in the world which can be discerned by experience and to which life should conform is a central doctrine of ancient wisdom literature." Cf. "Be Sober and Watch," *The Way* 14 (1974) 167–75, esp. 167.

18. Cf. Siegfried Morenz, *Egyptian Religion* (Ithaca: Cornell, 1973) 113.

19. See esp. Hans H. Schmid, *Wesen und Geschichte der Weisheit* (BZAW 101; Berlin: Töpelmann, 1966) 47–50, 156–66.

20. Cf. Elizabeth Huwiler, "Control of Reality in Israelite Wisdom" (Duke University dissertation, 1988). In chaps. 1 and 2 she questions the centrality of a fixed order of things underlying wisdom thought, and she concentrates on the sayings in Prov 10–29. She finds the sages preoccupied with the correspondences and distinctions that can be made out in reality. The goal of the sayings is to motivate rather than merely to convey meaning.

21. K. Koch first published his views in "Gibt es ein Vergeltungsdogma im Alten Testament," *ZTK* 52 (1955) 1–42. It is reproduced, along with essays that represent differing points of view, in a work he edited: *Um das Prinzip der Vergeltung in Religion und Recht des alten Testaments* (WF 125; Darmstadt: Wissenschaftliche Buchgesellschaft, 1972) 130–80. The article is almost completely translated into English in J. L. Crenshaw (ed.), *Theodicy in the Old Testament* (IRT 4; Philadelphia: Fortress, 1983) 57–87. For further reaction to Koch's view, see J. Barton, "Natural Law and Poetic Justice," *JTS* 30 (1979) 1–14.

  The importance of Koch's theory in German biblical scholarship can hardly be exaggerated. It is the basic reason why Horst D. Preuss, *Einführung in die alttestamentliche Weisheitsliteratur* (Urban-Taschenbücher 383; Stuttgart: Kohlhammer, 1987) considers the wisdom literature as theologically unsound if not invalid. Koch excepted Israel's election and covenant from the deed-consequence framework. Others, such as U. Luck, regard this deed-consequence mentality as a given human predisposition toward reality. For him the typical wisdom saying that expects prosperity from good conduct (e.g., Sir 7:1) is not a conclusion from experience but a wish, an expectation that humans should have toward life and the world if they have a will to live. He sees the verification of such sayings as hardly above 50 percent. Hence he concludes that they are witnesses of a trust in the world rather than conclusions drawn from observing deed and consequence. Cf. U. Luck, *Welterfahrung und Glaube als Grundproblem biblischer Theologie* (TEH 191; Munich: Kaiser, 1976) 25–29.

22. Cf. Hans H. Schmid, "Creation, Righteousness, and Salvation," in *Creation in the Old Testament* (IRT 6; ed. B. W. Anderson; Philadelphia: Fortress, 1984) 102–117, esp. 111. This article is a partial translation of an essay published in Schmid's *Altorientalische Welt in der alttestamentlichen Theologie* (Zurich: Theologicher Verlag, 1974) 9–30. That volume contains other essays in the same vein.

  We should note here an observation made by N. Lohfink in a description of the state of the art in Old Testament scholarship. He noted that the classic volumes on Old Testament theology by Gerhard von Rad remain to be read, even if not totally accepted. Indeed, von Rad himself had given the first signal insofar as he admitted that in his final work, *Wisdom in Israel*, he had not dealt sufficiently with knowledge of the world and creation theology. Lohfink goes on to say, "The broad views which arose in the meantime have been questioned—above all, those which derived from the prevailing ancient Near Eastern wisdom and which proposed its alleged world order concept as the broad framework of a biblical theology, based on detailed analysis of the oldest wisdom represented by the proverbial sayings"; cf. N. Lohfink, "Fortschritt oder Wachstumskrise?" *Evangelische Kommentare* 21/11 (November 1988) 638–41, esp. 638.

23. W. Zimmerli, "The Place and the Limit of the Wisdom in the Framework of the Old Testament Theology," in *SAIW*, 314–26; see p. 316.

24. This is the thesis of J. D. Levenson, *Creation and the Persistence of Evil* (San Francisco: Harper & Row, 1988) esp. 14–50. Contrary to Levenson, H.-J. Hermisson has argued that it is only in the wisdom texts that "the motif of the final limitation of the chaotic flood" occurs; cf. "Observations on the Creation Theology in Wisdom," in *Israelite Wisdom* (S. Terrien Festschrift; ed. J. G. Gammie et al.; Missoula: Scholars Press, 1978) 43–57, esp. 53. For Hermisson, the Lord's creative activity (conquering chaos) is "repeated" only in the cultic reenactment of the ancient event.

25. Cf. D. J. McCarthy, " 'Creation' Motifs in Ancient Hebrew Poetry," in *Creation in the Old Testament*, 74–89, esp. 80: "Early in its history Israel is so free from seeing any reality in the *Chaoskampf* theme that it has become a mere source for figures of speech. Its language can be used now one way, now another as seems useful in a given literary situation, something hardly possible if it were felt to be a description of reality, for then the use of the language would have to be controlled by the reality behind it." McCarthy points out how the mythic motifs become images of salvation (cf. Isa 51:9–11). See also R. J. Clifford, "The Hebrew Scriptures and the Theology of Creation," *TS* 46 (1985) 507–23.

26. Cf. Odil Hannes Steck, *World and Environment* (BES; Nashville: Abingdon, 1980) 167–68; see also R. Knierim, "Cosmos and History in Israel's Theology," *HBT* 3 (1981) 59–123.

27. Steck, *World and Environment*, 187.

28. So W. Dych, "The Achievement of Karl Rahner," *TD* 31 (1984) 325–33; the quotation is from p. 332.

29. Von Rad, *Wisdom in Israel*, 162.

30. See the essay by B. W. Anderson, "Creation and Ecology," in *Creation in the Old Testament*, 152–71.

31. See Preuss, *Einführung;* note his earlier studies indicated in p. 219, n. 300.

32. Preuss, *Einführung*, 60, 163.

33. Cf. G. E. Wright, *God Who Acts* (SBT 8; London: SCM, 1952) 103.

34. See W. Eichrodt, *Theology of the Old Testament* (Philadelphia: Westminster, 1967) II, 81ff.

35. See the summary discussion by Reventlow, *Problems of Old Testament Theology*, 172ff.

WISDOM LITERATURE AND THEOLOGY

36. This was noted emphatically by J. Barr, *Old and New in Interpretation* (London: SCM, 1966) 72–75.

37. Cf. Zimmerli, "The Place and Limit." This contrasts vividly with his earlier article on the structure of Old Testament wisdom in *SAIW*, 175–207.

38. Cf. W. Zimmerli, "Erwägungen zur Gestalt einer alttestamentlichen Theologie," in W. Zimmerli, *Studien zur alttestamentlichen Theologie und Prophetie* (Gesammelte Aufsätze II; TB 51; Munich: Kaiser, 1974) 27–54, esp. 46–51; the quotation is from p. 50.

39. Cf. C. Westermann, *Elements of Old Testament Theology* (Atlanta: Knox, 1978); the quotations are from pp. 72 and 100.

40. Contrast von Rad, *Old Testament Theology*, I, 355–455, esp. 355–56, with his *Wisdom in Israel*, 307.

41. Von Rad, *Old Testament Theology*, I, 135–39.

42. Gerhard von Rad, "Some Aspects of the Old Testament World-View," in *The Problem of the Hexateuch and Other Essays* (tr. E.W.T. Dicken; New York: McGraw-Hill, 1966) 146–65; the quotation is from p. 150.

43. Cf. B. Albrektson, *History and the Gods* (Lund: Gleerup, 1967).

44. As John J. Collins does in "The Biblical Precedent for Natural Theology," *JAAR* 45/1 (Supplement, March 1977) B: 35–67. But his position is sympathetic, as the words in his abstract indicate: "Wisdom is consistently presented as a revelation which is beyond human control and is experienced as a gift." In another study Collins has illustrated a basic trait that wisdom shares with Yahwism. Both "contained within themselves the seeds of a debunking tendency." Thus prophetic Yahwism, with its tendency to undermine established structures, cannot be legitimately contrasted with a supposedly rigid and dogmatic wisdom. Like prophecy, wisdom also raised questions (Job, Ecclesiastes). Cf. "Proverbial Wisdom and the Yahwist Vision," in *Gnomic Wisdom* (Semeia 17; ed. J. D. Crossan; Chico: Scholars Press, 1980) 1–17; the quotation is from p. 1. Contrast the rigidity of A. de Pury, "Sagesse et révélation dans l'Ancien Testament," *Revue de théologie et de philosophie* 27 (1977) 1–50, for whom wisdom is the realm of the rational, which excludes faith and any personal relationship with God.

45. See my "Israel's Wisdom: A Biblical Model of Salvation," *Studia Missionalia* 30 (1981) 1–43 for further articulation of these ideas, with specific references to Rahner's writings in pp. 2–3, n. 1.

46. This description of the wisdom experience is based on what I have written in *Studia Missionalia* (see n. 45). See also Roland E. Murphy, "Religious Dimensions of Israelite Wisdom," in *Ancient Israelite Religion*, 449–58.

47. Cf. Von Rad, *Wisdom in Israel*, 64.

48. Cf. J. Marböck, *Weisheit im Wandel* (BBB 37; Bonn: Hanstein, 1971) 104.

49. The terminology "above" and "below" is found in Marböck, *Weisheit im Wandel*, 127–28.

131

CHAPTER 9

LADY WISDOM

♦

Lady Wisdom is the most striking personification in the entire Bible. Personification as a literary device is not unknown in biblical literature. The justice or vindication (*ṣedeq*) of Israel will go before the Israelites when they leave from Babylon, and the glory of the Lord will be their rear guard (Isa 58:8). In Ps 85:11 kindness and truth meet; justice and peace kiss. The throne of the Lord has justice and judgment as the foundation, and the heralds that go before him are kindness and truth (Pss 89:15; 97:2; cf. 96:6).[1] In Prov 20:1 wine and strong drink are personified as proud and riotous figures; they impersonate the effects they produce. Indeed, wine has "eyes," as Prov 23:31 indicates: one is not to gaze upon wine in its redness, when it gives its "eye" (or sparkle) to the cup. Personification enlivens a text, and it fits well with the Israelite tendency toward anthropomorphism. In the case of biblical wisdom, however, the extent and the significance of the literary personification is so great that it has been questioned whether "personification" does justice to the figure of Wisdom. Are we dealing with more than a literary character— with a person or hypostasis, no less? A problem of terminology arises here. "Hypostasis," like "myth," is difficult to define, and it is subject to the various meanings that scholars have attached to it.[2] It has also acquired a technical meaning in Christian theological discussion of the three persons in the Trinity (e.g., "hypostatic" union). The word is used very broadly to refer to an extension of divine attributes, or to certain communications of God, such as spirit, word, or *Shekinah* (the divine presence in the world). In this respect it stands for a certain immanence of the transcendent one. But again, definitions can become arbitrary. It seems best to accept the term "personification" in our context in a literary sense, free from the baggage that philosophical thought came to attribute to the term "hypostasis." In the biblical context the figure of Wisdom cannot be conceived as hypostasis or person because of the strict monotheism of the postexilic period. Whatever associations Wisdom may have had in an earlier era, she is best understood in her biblical expression as a communication of God.

The approach of historians of religion has been to try to throw some light on the origins and development of the concept of Lady Wisdom. Such efforts are really dealing with the prehistory of the biblical figure, not with Wisdom as presented in the canonical text. They reveal the pedigree of Wisdom, rather than her identity. Nevertheless, such reconstructions are important, if hypothetical, and will be pointed out as we progress through the pertinent texts. The key passages in the wisdom literature that call for comment are Job 28, Prov 8, Sir 24, Bar 3:9–4:4, and Wis 7–9.[3] In fact, all of Prov 1–9 and many other passages in Sirach and Wisdom have a bearing on this theological development.

JOB 28

The poem in Job 28 proclaims that one can find all kinds of precious metals in the earth, but the most precious find of all is out of reach. Search as one might, the abyss announces that wisdom is not there; Abaddon and Death say that they have merely heard rumor of wisdom. Only God knows where wisdom is (cf. Bar 3:14–37):

God knows the way to it;
  it is he who is familiar with its place. . . .
When he made rules for the rain
  and a path for the thunderbolts,
Then he saw wisdom and appraised it,
  gave it its setting, knew it through and through. (28:23–27 NAB)

This is the definitive reply to the questions raised in vv 12 and 20 ("Where can wisdom be found? Whence does wisdom come?"). The female character of Wisdom is not highlighted here; indeed, wisdom might be interpreted simply as a divine attribute (as in Prov 3:19). But the verses just quoted suggest more than a divine attribute. God alone knows where wisdom is (Job 28:20–23). The reason given for this is that he sees "the ends of the earth"—wind, waters, rain, and thunderbolts are all God's doing. Then he "saw wisdom and appraised it, gave it its setting, knew it through and through" (28:27). The implication is that Wisdom is somewhere in this world, for God put her here. When God looked to the ends of the earth, he apparently saw Wisdom and gave her a setting. She seems distinct from the works of creation (such as the abyss or the seas, 28:14); she is somehow present and visible to God.

Here a comment of Ben Sira is helpful. He writes that God alone knows the subtleties of Wisdom, but also "he created her, has seen her and taken note of her. He has poured her forth upon all his works, upon every living thing according to his bounty; he has lavished her upon his friends" (Sir 1:9–10). According to Sir 1:9, Wisdom is something God has "numbered" (*exērithmēsen*, the Greek equivalent of *spr* in Job 28:27), and then "poured out" (*execheen*) on the works of creation. In the verses leading up to Sirach's statement there is mention of typical "works of creation" as things beyond human understanding: the sand of the seashore, the drops of rain (who can number these? Sir 1:2); heaven's height, earth's breadth (who can explore these? 1:3). Before all things wisdom was created (1:4). It appears then that wisdom is the peculiar quality of God that is manifest in creation because he has lavished it upon his works. Unless human beings have this perspective, they cannot find Wisdom. If they fail to recognize Wisdom's divine affiliation, they will not find her. She is the divine secret in the created world. One cannot predicate wisdom of an individual work of creation. The heavens are not wise, the earth is not wise, but wisdom is present in God's creation. Is this the glory of the Lord that fills the earth (Isa 6:1)? As we shall see, Ben Sira (chap. 24) clearly personifies Wisdom as a woman in the style of Prov 8; indeed, he is dependent upon the Book of Proverbs for his thought.

The poem in Job 28 is to be understood on several levels. As a poem, it claims that Wisdom belongs to God, who alone knows where she is. Because she is inaccessible to humans, the thrust of the poem is to underline the transcendence of this figure. However, although no human knows the "way" to her (28:13, LXX), God does know the "way" (28:23). The theme of the way to Wisdom, and the mystery of her location, will be taken up again, as we shall see, in Sirach and Baruch. Within the context of the Book of Job, the poem functions as an indicator of the futility of human probing into the divine mystery; neither Job nor the three friends can fathom the divine ways. Within the context of wisdom literature, one may say that a mysterious figure of a personified Wisdom has made her initial appearance.

PROVERBS 8

Proverbs 8 is the basic text for Lady Wisdom, because she speaks at length in her own name (as she also does more briefly in 1:22–33 and 9:4–6). In every instance, she is given a similar introduction; cf 8:1–3 with 1:20–21 and 9:3. Her address is public and universal (even to fools and simple ones). Her first claim is the honesty and integrity of her message—quite in contrast to the smooth talker, the "strange" woman of Prov 2:16; 5:3; 6:4; 7:21; Wisdom propounds *'ĕmet* and *ṣedeq*, truth and justice (8:7–8). This claim connotes more than simple honesty; these words are associated with the Lord, who is truthful (*'ĕmûnâ*) and just (*ṣaddîq*)—such is the way of wisdom and virtue. It is not surprising that her instruction is beyond price (8:10–11)—a claim many times repeated in wisdom literature (Prov 2:4; 3:14–16; Job 28:15–29; Wis 7:8; 8:5). Indeed, 8:11 repeats 3:15 and is apparently a gloss, for it is not in the style of the first-person address that Lady Wisdom is delivering.

In 8:12–16 she continues the description of the high qualities that she communicates (the Hebrew text emphasizes the "I" or ego throughout the next several verses): prudence, knowledge, and aversion to anything evil. Indeed, the qualities of counsel, strength, and understanding enable Wisdom to be the basis for royal rule (these qualities are divine, according to Job 12:13, and in Isa 11:2 they are gifts of the Lord's spirit to the messianic figure). Not only royalty, but anyone who will love her (vv 17–21) has the opportunity for riches. Then comes the remarkable passage about her origins, 8:22–31.

The Lord *begot* Wisdom as the firstborn ("begot" = "created" according to the LXX; others argue for "acquired," as though Wisdom had come from another area and was then used by the Lord).[4] The emphasis on divine origins continues in vv 24–25 ("brought forth," "born"). In about a half-dozen ways the origin of Wisdom *before* creation is affirmed (8:23–29). This enables the poet to give a description of the cosmos, above and below, leading into a statement of Wisdom's own place in creation:

I was beside him as an *'mwn,*
 I was delight day by day,
  playing before him all the time,
Playing on the surface of his earth,
  and my delight (was) with humankind. (8:30–31)

This literal translation respects the mystery of *'mwn,* whose meaning, as we have seen, is uncertain ("crafts [wo]man"? then Wisdom plays a role in the creative activity; "nursling"? then Wisdom's role is that of a child, simply playing). In any case, due attention should be given to the significant repetition of "delight" and "playing." The LXX interpreted the delight in v 30c as the Lord's delight, but the text simply says that Wisdom is (all) delight, and v 31 indicates that this delight is associated with humanity (as well as with God). The delight is further modified by her reference to "playing" before God on the face of his earth. We may conclude to the happy and joyful nature of Wisdom, which in some ways is connected with her association with humankind. The passage remains mysterious.

The conclusion of the speech (8:32–36) is very clear and direct. Commands to listen (three times in 32–34) and beatitudes are directed to those who will dedicate themselves to the pursuit of Wisdom. But v 35 is astonishing:

For the one who finds me finds life,
  and receives favor from the Lord.

This is the well-known association of wisdom and life, but made very personal ("who finds *me*"). There is an interesting overlap with Prov 18:22:

He who finds a wife finds happiness,
  and receives favor from the Lord.

The "finding" (i.e., attaining) of a good wife is viewed as a great gift in Proverbs (18:22; 31:10)—so also is the "finding" of Lady Wisdom (8:35; cf. 3:13; 8:17). The issue is one of life and death (8:36).

This remarkable speech of Lady Wisdom seems to have a very deliberate purpose within the book; if Prov 1–9 is the "introduction" to the collections of individual sayings that follow, this powerful motivating figure sweeps all the practical wisdom of Israel into the orbit of her activity. And yet this cannot exhaust the meaning of one who originates from God before creation, is a cause for joy, plays on the earth, and is involved with human beings. The functions of Lady Wisdom are manifold; they are as broad as life itself, in keeping with her eternal origins from the source of all life. As we shall see, this open-ended character of Lady Wisdom enabled future sages to make further additions and thus achieve a formidable description of her self and her activities. And even when she is specifically identified as Torah by Sirach and Baruch, she is not totally confined—she seems to transcend even the most noble limitations.

The question of Wisdom's identity in Prov 8 has been a particularly attractive challenge to historians of religion, and the issue remains unsettled still. B. Lang weighed carefully the various attempts to capture the elusive origins of this figure.[5] He rejected the proposed Canaanite/Assyrian influence that had been alleged on the basis of the uncertain text in Ahiqar (see Appendix). In Ahiqar there is no speech by a wisdom goddess, nor does Lady Wisdom have the traits of an Assyrian goddess. A stronger case for a relationship can be made between Wisdom and the Egyptian *maʿat* (recall that the abstract "justice" or *maʿat* was also personified as a goddess). The description of *maʿat* seems to have influenced the presentation of wisdom in Prov 1–9 (see Appendix), although this influence is less evident in Prov 8. Lang himself concluded that the figure was personified school wisdom: "a didactic reconstruction designed to make an impression on a student."[6] But when Lang returned to the topic in the English translation and adaptation of his study, he argued that Israel had a polytheistic past in which a goddess of wisdom was honored as the "divine patroness of scribal education and training."[7] He then hypothesized that she came to be understood as a simple personification of a poetic type, representing "wisdom teaching with its moral injunctions."[8]

Thus was she received into the biblical canon. The theorizing is ingenious but highly uncertain.

Gerhard von Rad claimed that, especially in Prov 8:22–29, "the style of a specific Egyptian divine proclamation has clearly been borrowed, and that in vv. 30f. the Egyptian idea of a deity caressing personified truth (ma'at) has somehow, though not without internal modifications, found its way into our didactic poem. . . . But what does all this prove? Only that ideas which had their roots elsewhere came to Israel's help when she needed them, in order [for her] to be able to progress in her thinking within her own domain."⁹ Von Rad viewed Lady Wisdom as a personification of the world order that he regarded as central to sapiential thinking. However, "the most interesting feature of what is new is that this world order turns, as a person, towards men, wooing them and encouraging them in direct address. What is objectified here, then, is not an attribute of God but an attribute of the world, namely that mysterious attribute, by virtue of which she turns towards men to give order to their lives."¹⁰ If one grants the primacy of order in wisdom thought, as so many scholars do, then von Rad's conclusion is logical. Personified Wisdom is for him "the self-revelation of creation," the title that he gives to his treatment of this topic in chap. 9 of *Wisdom in Israel.*

However, the very origins and the authority of Wisdom suggest more than a personified order of creation. Wisdom is somehow identified with the Lord. The call of Lady Wisdom is the voice of the Lord; she is the revelation of God, not merely the self-revelation of creation. She is the divine summons issued in and through creation, sounding through the vast realm of the created world, and heard on the level of human experience. This is the task that seems to be assigned to her in Prov 8:31. Von Rad's earlier description of Lady Wisdom is more accurate:

> None the less it is correct to say that wisdom is the form in which Jahweh's will and his accompanying of man (i.e. his salvation) approaches man. Wisdom is the essence of what man needs for a proper life, and of what God grants him. Still, the most important thing is that wisdom does not turn towards man in the shape of an "It," teaching, guidance, salvation or the like, but of a person, a summoning "I." So wisdom is truly the form in which Jahweh makes himself present and in which he wishes to be sought by man. "Whoso finds me, finds life" (Prov viii. 35). Only Jahweh can speak in this way. And yet, wisdom is not Jahweh himself; it is something separate from him: indeed, it once designates itself as Jahweh's creature, albeit the first-born of all creatures (Prov viii. 22), and identifies itself with the thoughts which God cherished in creating the world (Prov iii. 19).¹¹

One does not have to choose between God and creation in Lady Wisdom, as von Rad does. Ultimately the revelation of creation is the revelation of God. God speaks through wisdom/creation, which is turned to human beings and speaks in the accents of God. Such is the thrust of Prov 8.

SIRACH 24

In the time of Ben Sira (ca. 180 B.C.E.), the interpretation of Wisdom developed even further. She is very closely associated, as we have seen in chap. 5, with "fear of the Lord" (Sir 1:11–20), and she is "poured out" on creation. Then she is described and identified specifically in chap. 24. The question of the hidden abode (Job 28) and divine origin (Prov 8) of Wisdom is followed by a new development; where has she taken root? If in Job 28 she was not to be discovered in Sheol, much less on earth, the situation has now changed. In Sir 24 Wisdom describes her origins in a manner similar to that of Prov 8:22–31: "From the mouth of the Most High I came forth" (24:3). She is described as singing her own praises to her own people (24:1), but she does this from "the assembly of the Most High" (24:2)—that is, she is among the heavenly court. Her description of herself is very delicate: "mistlike" she covers the earth (24:3), much as the spirit or wind of God came over the waters of chaos (Gen 1:2). She is not confined to the earth: she is both on the heights (Sir 24:2, 4) and on a journey that will take her through the vault of heaven (24:5, just as God journeys through the vault of heaven in Job 22:14) as well as the abyss. Again like God, she has dominion over everything (24:6). Is this really God in the figure of traveling Wisdom?

In 24:7 her journey is seen as a search for a place to rest. The creator commands her to dwell in Jacob/Israel. She lays claim to eternity, forward and backward (24:9), and then settles in Jerusalem, where she leads the liturgical service (*eleitourgēsa*, v. 10) in the "Holy Tent." Here is her domain, in God's chosen city.

In a series of striking comparisons, all drawn from Palestinian life, Wisdom describes her gracious effects: tall cedars, fruitful olive trees, balm, and myrrh (vv 13–17). She issues her invitation to those who yearn for her: they are to come and be filled with her fruits. Paradoxically, however, partaking of her will only increase the appetite: a greater hunger and thirst for her will ensue. But she will always be present, and obedience to her will secure one against all evil.

At this point Ben Sira identifies Wisdom directly with the Torah:

All this is true of the book of the Most High's covenant,
  the law which Moses commanded us
    as an inheritance for the community of Jacob. (24:23)

139

This verse is an echo of Exod 24:7 ("the book of the covenant") and Deut 33:4 ("the law which Moses commanded"; cf. LXX). The identification had already been prepared for by Ps 19, which links creation with Law, and by Deut 4:6–9, which describes observance of the Law as giving evidence of wisdom to the nations. It is clear that Wisdom now includes far more than the insights of the sages, more even than the practical teachings with which Ben Sira fills his book. Yet there is a certain sapiential twist given to the Torah.[12] Sirach goes on to speak of the Torah as an ever rising flood (24:25–29), to which he can compare himself and his teachings (24:30–33). Although he himself is a modest stream in comparison, he has become a river, a sea, that pours out "instruction like prophecy." He surely understood his book as an extension of the Torah.

Ben Sira obviously wrote the twenty-fourth chapter under the influence of Prov 8,[13] but he has provided his unique development to the figure of Wisdom (e.g., her receiving the divine command to dwell in Jerusalem), and he has given an explicit definition. This narrows down, in a sense, the broad view of Wisdom that Prov 8 suggested. Both perspectives are valid. Lady Wisdom is adapted to the circumstances of the time (with Sirach, the Torah), but she also retains the mysterious identity of Prov 8.

BARUCH 3:9–4:4

The poem on Wisdom in Bar 3:9–4:4 stands out in a book that is otherwise concerned with the exile, repentance, and return.[14] This poem is linked to the prayer of confession in 1:15–3:8 by the opening verses, 3:9–13, which explain Israel's exilic punishment as the result of abandoning wisdom. There is a broad consensus that the opening and closing parts of the book are also independent pieces: (1) 1:1–3:8, which includes an introduction (1:1–14), a confession made by exiles to compatriots in Jerusalem (1:15–2:10; cf. Dan 9:4–19), and a prayer (2:11–3:8) to the Lord to save his people Israel; and (2) a prophetic address to the Diaspora and to Jerusalem that the exiles will return, spoken now by a prophet (4:5–9), by Jerusalem (4:10–29), and again by a prophet (to Jerusalem, 4:30–5:9). Against this background the Wisdom poem functions as a basis for the hope of restoration. It presents the Torah as Wisdom, abandoned by Israel in the past, but now the means to restoration and piety. The theme is the "way to wisdom/understanding" (vv 20, 23, 27, 31, 36). The poem is close in spirit to the identification of Wisdom and Torah made by Ben Sira (Sir 24:23; cf. Bar 4:1–2) and generally envisioned in the postexilic period (Deut 4:6; Ps 19:8; 119:97–98; Ezra 7:6, 14, 25).

The poem begins with a "shema" reminiscent of the "listen!" of Deut 5:1; 6:4—an exhortation that is also characteristic of the sage (Prov 1:8; 4:1;

etc.). The plight of the exiles is interpreted as the result of their abandoning "the spring of wisdom," the God from whom all wisdom comes (Sir 1:1). They must find where Wisdom and life are (Bar 3:14)—no mean task, for the ancient question of Job is echoed here: who has found the place of Wisdom (Bar 3:15; Job 28:12, 20)? Typically, Baruch answers this as Job did, indicating where she is *not* to be found (3:16–32). Some sources of ancient wisdom known to Israel are mentioned, only to be rejected: Canaan and Edom (v 22), the Ishmaelites ("sons of Hagar," v 23). Wisdom is not to be found there, nor among the giants (v 24; Gen 6:4). In short, no one knows the way to her (vv 20–21, 23, 27, 31). God alone knows her whereabouts (vv 32–37). The divine "knowledge" is associated in both Bar 3 and Job 28 with the divine control over the created world, which is guided by his intelligence and omniscience (v 32). The joyous response to creation by the host of heaven is noted in 4:34 (the stars shine joyfully for their creator, and they sing praise; cf. Job 38:7).

Baruch cleverly takes up the words of Deut 30:12–13 (the laws are not hidden somewhere in the sky or across the sea, but are clear and plain in the Torah) to show that it is only God who knows the way to Wisdom, and humans cannot find it (3:29–31). Whereas in Job 28 it is not clear just what God did with Wisdom, in Bar 3:37–4:2 it is obvious: Wisdom has been given to Jacob/Israel; indeed, she appeared upon earth and lived among men (v 37 is *not* to be eliminated as a Christian gloss!): "She is the book of the commandments of God, the Torah that stands forever" (4:1). Baruch's treatment of Wisdom is influenced by Job 28, but the identification of this mysterious being is foursquare with Sir 24: Wisdom is the Torah. Gerald T. Sheppard has summarized the path of Wisdom from Proverbs to Sirach and Baruch very neatly: "An older connection between the goals of Torah and the wisdom literature is fully exploited by the author. Traditionally, wisdom literature offered 'life' (e.g., Prov 3:18; 4:13, 22, 23; 13:14; 16:22), even 'the way of life' (e.g., 2:19; 5:6; 6:23; 10:17; 15:24), in a manner fully compatible with the same promise, based on obedience to the Torah (e.g., compare Deut 30:15 with Prov 3:1ff.). This symbiosis of Torah and wisdom, apparent already in Proverbs, has in the time of Sirach and Baruch led to a relatively more aggressive reunion of the different parts of the canon."[15]

The identification of Wisdom and Torah seems neat and clear; it gives an unambiguous answer to a question that always lurks in the mind of the reader. By the same token, one can fail to appreciate what a strange and, in a sense, forced identification this is. It is not a conclusion that a reader of Prov 1–9 and Job 28 would have anticipated. C. Larcher[16] has remarked of Sir 24 that "the entire movement of Wisdom's discourse depends more on a theology of presence than on a theology of revelation" (mistlike she covers the earth, and she roams the heavens and abyss with equal ease; Sir 24:3–5). But with Sir 24:23 Lady Wisdom has become the book of the Torah. Although

Wisdom's origins and existence had been closely associated with the Lord, there was always the nagging question "where?" (Job 28:12, 20; Bar 3:14; Eccl 7:23–24; Wis 6:22.) Now she is definitively located by Ben Sira. Mysterious and touching is the portrayal of Wisdom accepting the Lord's "order" in Sir 24:8, and then being involved in the divine "liturgy" before God in v 10. If the development and identification of Wisdom in Sirach is surprising, the author of the Book of Wisdom has even more surprises in store for those in quest of Lady Wisdom. Ultimately Prov 8 lies behind Sir 24 and Wis 7–9, but the elaboration of the figure of Lady Wisdom is unique in both cases: Torah for Sirach, and pneuma or spirit for the author of the Book of Wisdom.

WISDOM 7–9

The Book of Wisdom is well named, since wisdom pervades it all. It was described by the ancient Muratorian canon (ca. third century C.E.?) as a volume we would today call a "Festschrift": *sapientia ab amicis Salomonis in honorem ipsius scripta* (wisdom written in honor of Solomon by his friends). The most pertinent section describes the nature of Wisdom and pseudo-Solomon's quest for her (Wis 7:1–9:18). This magnificent portion is introduced by 6:22–25, which assures the reader that "Solomon" will hide no "mysteries" (*mystēria*) concerning Wisdom's nature and origin.

The author's emphasis on his purely human origins ("mortal") stands in contrast to Wisdom's godly character, but especially to the "kings" to whom the book is ostensibly addressed (recall 1:1; 6:1). Along with vv 5–6, v 1 leaves no opening for special claims of royal (divine) birth. No, one has to *pray* for Wisdom (7:7). Oddly enough, Wisdom is not explicitly prayed for in the wisdom literature (except here, and see Sir 37:15). But the model of the historical Solomon (1 Kgs 3:9) is being recalled here.

In response, there came to him a spirit of Wisdom (*pneuma sophias*), a relatively new way of conceiving Wisdom. Already in Job 32:8 it was stated that human understanding is due to the breath of Shaddai (*nišmat shadday*, parallel to the *ruah* that is in human beings). In its most general meaning, *pneuma sophias* designates the action of Wisdom upon pseudo-Solomon, but the Greek *pneuma* had acquired specific meanings in Hellenistic thought. It stood for the Platonic "soul" of the world, and in Stoicism it took on a particular nuance: "a universal divine principle which animated and penetrated the entire universe, giving it substance and unity."[17] This idea is already hinted at in Wis 1:7, "The spirit of the Lord fills the world, is all embracing. . . ." The cosmic function is specified further in 12:1, "Your imperishable spirit is in all things." This is a real presence of the divine spirit, not merely the dependence of creatures upon creator. In 9:17 Wisdom is parallel to "your holy spirit" sent from on high, and she is responsible for knowing the divine counsel.

The old clichés concerning the incomparable value of Wisdom are reiterated in 7:8–12; she surpasses all riches, gems, gold, and silver, for the treasure she brings is the friendship of God (7:14). But her gifts belong to the secular world as well, for an astonishing list of intellectual achievements are given in 7:15–21: a knowledge of the structure of the world, astronomical facts, beasts, flowers, and humans—the encyclopedic knowledge of the ancient Greek sage. In this case, Wisdom the *technitis* (7:22; cf. also 8:6—the author seems to understand the *ʾmwn* of Prov 8:30 as artisan or crafts [wo]man), or maker of all, was the teacher of pseudo-Solomon. Hence she is identified with God (cf. 7:25–26), and her remarkable qualities are detailed in the twenty-one attributes (seven times three, a triple perfection).

The personification of Lady Wisdom in 7:22–8:1 is one of the more famous and striking passages in the Bible, and perhaps the most mysterious.[18] The author never explains the difference between Lady Wisdom as spirit (Wis 7:7; 9:17) and Wisdom as *having* a spirit that is qualified in 7:22–23 as "holy, intelligent, unique," and the like. We would not be far from the mark if we conceived of Lady Wisdom as acting in the guise of a spirit, and not being merely the effect of the Lord's spirit (as, e.g., in Isa 11:2).[19] Here the cosmological ubiquity of Wisdom comes into play. She is active within human beings (1:4–6; cf. Prov 2:10) because she is a spirit that loves humans (1:6, literally, "philanthropic"); she is hardly distinct from the spirit of the Lord that observes the human heart and "fills the world" (1:6–7). In 1:1–15 spirit and Wisdom do not seem to be distinct from the divinity; they express the ways in which God is present to the world and to humans. The twenty-one qualities of 7:22–23 serve to elaborate the spiritual nature of Lady Wisdom, the kind of activity she engages in. Here the most telling attribute is the pervasive character she has: penetrating all spirits (v 23) and indeed all things because of her "purity" (v 24). This quality prepares us somewhat for the remarkable description of 7:25–26:

> For she is an aura of the might of God
>   and a pure effusion of the glory of the Almighty;
>   therefore nought that is sullied enters into her.
> For she is the refulgence of eternal light,
>   the spotless mirror of the power of God,
>   the image of his goodness. (*NAB*)

The passage leaves one rather breathless—it is impossible to convey more intimately the relationship of Lady Wisdom to God: breath, outpouring of divine glory, eternal light, mirror of divine activity, a divine image. The previous chapters highlighted Wisdom's pervasive activity in the world; now her divine character is articulated in a manner that goes beyond the traditional "begetting" in Prov 8:22–25 or "coming from the mouth of the Most High" in Sir 24:3. If previously she was the bond that cemented creation together, now her intimacy with the divine is celebrated.

As Addison Wright[20] observes of vv 25–26, "The author, enlarging on Prov 8 and Sir 24, seeks the most immaterial images possible to describe the origin of Wisdom," and, one might add, to describe the intimacy of her relationship with God. The general image is a sort of radiation from the divinity: vapor, effusion, reflection, mirror, image. As breath of the divine power, she is the outflowing of divine glory, which is usually conceived of as light or fire. The metaphor of light is continued in v 26, where she is the reflection of the "light that is forever." According to Isa 60:19–20, this light is the Lord, whose radiance will replace the sun in the eschatological era. This ties in with the divine glory of v 25, since such glory in the Old Testament seems to be conceived of in terms of light. We know whence the unsullied character of Wisdom comes; she is bathed in the eternal light. She is the mirror or reflection of the divine energy (v 26). God, as it were, pours self into her in the various divine operations. Finally she is the image of the divine goodness; she is the very icon of that goodness that was celebrated in creation (Gen 1:4, 10, 12, etc.).

After this really unfathomable description of Lady Wisdom, pseudo-Solomon returns to the narrative of his love affair. She led to a "sharing [*symbiōsis*] in the life of God," just as a spouse would, because God loves her (8:3) and even depends upon her for his own designs. Indeed, she is the mother (*genetis*) of all Solomon's benefits (7:12; cf. 8:5)—the artisan of all (7:22; 8:6), as God is termed in 13:1. The close relationship of Wisdom to creation is further spelled out in 9:9: Wisdom knows God's works and was present when he made the world. If the role of Wisdom in creation had remained ambiguous in the past (Prov 8:30), there is no longer any doubt. According to Wis 8:4 she even participates in the understanding of God, who defers to her selection in the process of creation. This is due to her common life with God, who loves her (8:3). He favors her so much that her decision is his in all his works! Larcher carefully notes that the author of Wisdom, thanks to Greek influence, goes far beyond his predecessors in the matter of continuous creation, and the reason is God's special presence to the world by reason of spirit and Wisdom.[21] Thus, "She renews everything, while perduring" (7:27), just as the breath of God creates and renews the face of the earth (Ps 104:30). She is mobile and all-pervasive by reason of her purity (7:24), and hence she "reaches from end to end mightily and governs all things well" (8:1). This means that she is in effect the providence of God, even if the term *pronoia* is used directly of God only in 14:3 and 17:2.

In view of all this, it is not surprising to read Solomon's impassioned prayer for Wisdom (9:1–12), because she "knows and understands all things," but particularly because she enables him to "know what is pleasing" to God (9:10–11). It is no surprise that he learned the four cardinal virtues from Wisdom the teacher (8:7).

CONCLUSION

There are many faces to Wisdom in the Old Testament, and it is well-nigh impossible to make a synthesis. Each book and each chapter in which she appears is conditioned by some authorial intention, some situation to which she was an appropriate response. Nonetheless, a certain profile seems desirable as a summary of the foregoing discussion.[22]

1. Wisdom has a divine origin: Prov 8:22; Sir 24:3, 9; Wis 7:25–26.

2. She existed before creation and seems to have had a role in creation: Prov 8:22–29; Sir 1:4; Wis 9:9; Prov 8:30?; 3:19 (cf. 24:3); Sir 1:9–10 (cf. 16:24–17:7); Wis 7:22; 8:4–6 (cf. 13:1); see also 9:2, 9.

3. Wisdom is identified with the (divine) spirit: Wis 1:7; 9:17; 12:1; and she is also immanent in the world: 7:24; 8:1.

4. Wisdom accounts for the coherence and permanence of the cosmos: Wis 1:7; 7:24, 27; 8:1; 11:25.

5. Wisdom has a particular mission to human beings: Prov 8:4, 31–36; Sir 24:7, 12, 19–22; Wis 7:27–28; 8:2–3.

   (a) She speaks to them in the world (Prov 1, 8, 9; Sir 24:19–22; Wis 6:12–16; 7:22a; 8:7–9; 9:10–16).

   (b) She promises her followers life and prosperity, every blessing (Prov 1:32; 3:13–18; 8:1–5, 35; 9:1–6; Sir 1:14–20; 6:18–31; 15:1–8; 24:19–33; Wis 7:7–14).

6. Wisdom is particularly associated with Israel:

   (a) She dwells in Israel, by divine command (Sir 24:8–12).

   (b) She can be identified with the Torah (Sir 24:23 and passim: 1:25–27; 6:37; 15:1; 19:20; 33:2–3; etc.; Bar 4:1).

   (c) She was at work in Israel's history (Wis 10:1–21).

7. Wisdom is a gift from God: Prov 2:6; Sir 1:9–10, 26; 6:37; Wis 7:7; 9:4). But at the same time she is associated with effort and "discipline" (mûsar, usually rendered paideia): Sir 4:17; 6:18–36; Prov 4:10–27; 6:6; Wis 1:5; 7:14.

8. A list of the passages (minimum) where Wisdom is found to be personified: Job 28; Prov 1, 8, 9; Sir 1:9–10; 4:11–19; 6:18–31; 14:20–15:8; 51:13–21; Bar 3:9–4:4; Wis 6:12–11:1.

What conclusions can be drawn from this exposition of the many traits of personified Wisdom? The description just enumerated has been as relatively complete as a chapter would allow, and in itself is more in the nature of an invitation to the reader to take up the challenge of identifying Lady Wisdom on his or her own initiative.

Various reasons have been put forward to explain why Wisdom is personified as female. There are no satisfactory answers (an indication that the question should not be raised in the first place?). It is simply not adequate to say that the Hebrew noun ḥokmāh is feminine gender, or that the female figure is an obvious one for literature that aims to educate young men, or that Lady Wisdom has been influenced by the description of goddesses. Some theologians have succeeded in reading Lady Wisdom in an oblique manner, seeking to correlate the biblical figure with the data that the Bible provides about women in Israelite society, both real and literary.[23] This surely says something about women in society, which biblical scholarship has passed over in the past. But many questions remain to be answered.

In the *biblical* quest for Lady Wisdom, we are limiting ourselves to the Old Testament. A discussion of Wisdom/Sophia as she appears in the New Testament and beyond is not within our compass. We merely wish to point out that the personification continues (cf. Luke 7:35; 11:49; Matt 11:19; and the Wisdom background to John 1:1–18). Sophia has also played a large role in the development of Gnosticism. Modern scholarship speaks of a "wisdom myth," a reconstruction based on biblical and extrabiblical data that portrays the descent and reascent of Wisdom to her heavenly home. The point to be made here is that the Bible provides only part of this alleged myth: Wisdom does come into the world (Sir 24; Bar 3:9–4:44), where she finds delight among humans (Prov 8:31) and, more specifically, dwells within Israel as the Law (Sir 24:23; Bar 4:1). But the idea of her reascending is not found in the Bible; it is expressed in 1 Enoch 42:2 (*APOT*, II, 212):

Wisdom went forth to make her dwelling among the children of men,
  and found no dwelling place;
Wisdom returned to her place,
  and took her seat among the angels.

Merely a glimpse at the figure of Lady Wisdom in both Jewish and Christian tradition bears out a characteristic of the biblical data: she seems to be essentially a changeable being—that is, to be defined anew in successive generations.

As with so many key biblical concepts, there is a temptation for us to choose, to limit ourselves to what impresses us as most important. The first significant observation to be made about Wisdom is this: Wisdom speaks with divine accents. Second, one should distinguish between her identity and her manifold descriptions. Her identity as Law is clearly enunciated, particularly by Ben Sira and Baruch. But she is a world principle, immanent and also divine, according to Wisdom. For Proverbs, she is an appeal to life, to live it fully. These various identifications are there in the Bible for us to take advantage of, to profit from. Obviously, the Christian can infer—and, in the person of Paul, has inferred—that Christ is the Wisdom of God (1 Cor 1:24). On the other hand, the Judaic tradition preserves the identification of Wisdom with Torah.[24] All these conclusions are possible and legitimate; the very fluctuation in the identity of Wisdom within the Bible justifies them. It is not really possible to reduce all these identities to a unity. The best one can say is that Lady Wisdom is a divine communication: God's communication, extension of self, to human beings. And that is no small insight the biblical wisdom literature bequeaths to us.

Notes to "Lady Wisdom"

1. H. Brunner has shown the Egyptian background to the idea of justice as the foundation of the throne; cf. "Gerechtigkeit als Fundament des Thrones," VT 8 (1958) 426–28, reproduced in Das hörende Herz (OBO 80; ed. W. Röllig; Fribourg: Universitätsverlag, 1988) 393–95.

2. The literature on this topic is voluminous. One should mention Wilhelm Schencke, Die Chokma (Sophia) in der jüdischen Hypostasenspekulation (Kristiania: Dybwad, 1913); H. Ringgren, Word and Wisdom: Studies in the Hypostatization of Divine Qualities and Functions in the Ancient Near East (Lund: H. Ohlssons, 1947) esp. 89–171; R. Marcus, "On Biblical Hypostases of Wisdom," HUCA 23 (1950–51) 57–71.

3. In addition to commentaries on these particular books, see also Schenke, Die Chokma; Gerhard von Rad, Wisdom in Israel (Nashville: Abingdon, 1972) 144–76; S. Terrien, "The Play of Wisdom: Turning Point in Biblical Theology," HBT 3 (1981) 1–22; Roland E. Murphy, "Wisdom and Creation," JBL 104 (1985) 3–11.

4. B. Vawter, "Prov. 8:22: Wisdom and Creation," JBL 99 (1980) 206–16 argues strenuously for the notion of "acquire."

5. Cf. B. Lang, Frau Weisheit (Düsseldorf: Patmos, 1975). This was translated and completely revised in Wisdom and the Book of Proverbs: An Israelite Goddess Redefined (New York: Pilgrim, 1986). Lang is dealing with Prov 8, but there has been considerable speculation concerning the goddess behind the figure of Lady Wisdom in Sir 24 and Wis 7–9. H. Conzelmann claimed that Isis influenced Sir 24; cf. "Die

Mutter der Weisheit," in *Zeit und Geschichte: Dankesgabe an R. Bultmann* (ed. E. Dinkler; Tübingen: Mohr, 1964) II, 225–34. J. Kloppenborg, building on the previous studies of Burton Mack and J. Reese, has made a strong case for Isis behind the figure of Sophia in Wis 7–9; cf. "Isis and Sophia in the Book of Wisdom," *HTR* 75 (1982) 57–84.

6. Lang, *Frau Weisheit*, 170.

7. See B. Lang, *Monotheism and the Prophetic Minority* (SWBAS 1; Sheffield: Almond Press, 1983) 51.

8. Lang, *Wisdom and the Book of Proverbs*, 135.

9. Von Rad, *Wisdom in Israel*, 153.

10. Von Rad, *Wisdom in Israel*, 156.

11. Gerhard von Rad, *Old Testament Theology* (New York: Harper & Row, 1962) I, 444.

12. Of chap. 24 von Rad remarks, "It is wisdom who speaks here, not Torah, and this is where Sirach's heart beats"; cf. *Wisdom in Israel*, 246. See also J. Marböck, *Weisheit im Wandel* (BBB 37; Bonn: Hanstein, 1971) 81–96. Gerald T. Sheppard, *Wisdom as a Hermeneutical Construct* (BZAW 151; Berlin: de Gruyter, 1980) 61 describes the song in Sir 24:1–22 as "plainly a recital of the history of Wisdom who resides in Israel as the Torah. . . . The center of attention is consistently on Wisdom who is or becomes the Torah in the possession of Israel. Therefore, the Song offers a selective application to Wisdom of some Torah traditions which can be associated with the divine presence in Israel."

13. This is clearly brought out by P. Skehan, "Structures in Poems on Wisdom: Proverbs 8 and Sirach 24," *CBQ* 41 (1979) 365–79, where he reconstructs the Hebrew original of Sir 24 on the basis of Prov 8.

14. Cf. D. G. Burke, *The Poetry of Baruch* (SBLSCS 10; Atlanta: Scholars Press, 1982) esp. 20–23. Skillful analysis of the Greek text (the earliest extant text of the work) shows that it is most likely a translation from a Hebrew original, now lost. This is effectively demonstrated by Burke for 3:9–5:9. His study indicates the characteristic anthological style of the postexilic period, in which earlier portions of the (Hebrew) Bible are reused, and a pastiche of biblical phrases results. Sheppard, *Wisdom as a Hermeneutical Construct*, 84–99 presents a careful analysis of the wisdom poem, pointing out its biblical antecedents (Genesis, Deuteronomy, Job, especially). See also Carey A. Moore, "I Baruch," in *Daniel, Esther and Jeremiah: The Additions* (AB 44; Garden City: Doubleday, 1977) 255–316.

15. Sheppard, *Wisdom as a Hermeneutical Construct*, 99.

16. Cf. C. Larcher, *Etudes sur le livre de la Sagesse* (EBib; Paris: Gabalda, 1969) 342.

17. Larcher, *Etudes*, 361.

18. I am indebted for the treatment of Wis 7–9 to Larcher, *Etudes*, 356–414; see esp. at this point pp. 367–76.

19. Larcher, *Etudes*, 365.

20. Addison Wright, "Wisdom," in *NJBC*, 516.

21. Larcher, *Etudes*, 391.

22. One should also compare the independent and helpful description of Lady Wisdom by Burton Mack, *Logos und Sophia* (SUNT 10; Göttingen: Vandenhoeck & Ruprecht, 1973): "She is a teacher, one who shows the way, a preacher and a disciplinarian. She seeks out human beings, meets them on the streets and invites them in for a meal. The bewildering sexual aspects include sister, lover, wife and mother. She is the tree of life, the water of life, the garment and crown of victory. She offers to human beings life, rest, knowledge and salvation." For all these characteristics Mack offers several biblical references. He prefers to use a different terminology for personified Wisdom: *verborgen*, or "hidden," for the remoteness of Wisdom in Job 28 and Bar 3:9–4:4; *nahe*, or "near," for the intimate presence of Prov 8:22–31. Both types are in Sirach (24:3–7 would be "near"). One may prefer the terminology used by Marböck, *Weisheit im Wandel*, 127–33, who speaks of wisdom "from above" and "from below" (categories seemingly derived from current christological discussion). Thus Sir 24 is "from above" and the table manners in 31:12–32:13 are "from below." See also Larcher, *Etudes*, 398–414.

23. Cf. Claudia Camp, *Wisdom and the Feminine in the Book of Proverbs* (BLS 11; Sheffield: Almond Press, 1985), and also the comment of Carole R. Fontaine on the personification of Wisdom in "Proverbs," in *HBC*, 501–3.

24. E. E. Urbach, *The Sages: Their Concepts and Beliefs* (Jerusalem: Magnes, 1975) 198ff., 286ff. A brief survey of the developments in rabbinical and patristic studies has been provided by H. Jaeger, "The Patristic Conception of Wisdom in the Light of Biblical and Rabbinical Research," in *Studia Patristica IV* (ed. F. L. Cross; Berlin: Akademie-Verlag, 1961) 90–106; see also E. Johnson, "Jesus, the Wisdom of God: A Biblical Basis for Non-Androcentric Theology," *ETL* 61 (1985) 261–94.

APPENDIX

♦

The primary reasons for this Appendix dealing with nonbiblical wisdom literature are the convenience of the reader and clarity of presentation. The debt of Israelite wisdom to its neighbors is unmistakable, and some details will be indicated in this Appendix, where they do not interfere with the exposition of the biblical books. The Appendix has also been correlated with the previous chapters by frequent references. Another reason for separate treatment is that both Mesopotamian and Egyptian literature deserve special attention for their own sake. They should be seen as wholes and not as mere appendages to some related ideas in the Bible.

No effort will be made to exactly define "wisdom literature" in the ancient Near East. It is simply a useful term designating an area within which the ancient cultures have something in common. Broadly, it refers to common topics and often common literary forms (sayings, admonitions, etc.). Precisely because of the humanistic concerns of wisdom literature, it is to be expected that "parallels" with the Bible will appear. Riches and poverty, justice and wickedness, speech and silence, relationships between individuals and the community, relationships between the sexes—these are the common coin of human existence, and similarities are not surprising.

PRIMARY SOURCES

The following anthologies will provide the reader with available (English) translations of the primary texts.

General Ancient Near East

James B. Pritchard (ed.), *Ancient Near Eastern Texts Relating to the Old Testament* (Princeton: Princeton University Press, 1950; 3rd ed. with supplement, 1978) (= *ANET*).

Mesopotamia

W. G. Lambert, *Babylonian Wisdom Literature* (Oxford: Clarendon, 1960) (= *BWL*).

Egypt

W. K. Simpson (ed.), *The Literature of Ancient Egypt* (2nd ed.; New Haven: Yale University, 1973) (= *LAE*).

Miriam Lichtheim, *Ancient Egyptian Literature* (Berkeley: University of California Press, 1975–80) 3 vols. (= *AEL*).

SECONDARY LITERATURE

JAOS 101/1 (1981) contains valuable summaries (with extensive bibliographies) of Hebrew, Egyptian, and Mesopotamian wisdom by Roland E. Murphy, R. J. Williams, and G. Buccellati.

H. Brunner, "Zentralbegriffe ägyptischer und israelitischer Weisheitslehren," *Saeculum* 35 (1984) 185–99.

E. I. Gordon, "A New Look at the Wisdom of Sumer and Akkad," *BO* 17 (1960) 122–52.

Michael V. Fox, "Two Decades of Research in Egyptian Wisdom Literature," *ZAS* 107 (1980) 120–35.

W. McKane, *Proverbs* (OTL; Philadelphia: Westminster, 1970) provides a summary introduction to "international wisdom," pp. 51–208.

See also the notes to this Appendix.

ANCIENT NEAR EASTERN WISDOM

The following sketch is limited to the pertinent texts of Mesopotamia and Egypt, concentrating on themes that are important for the background of biblical wisdom. Greek and Hellenistic documents are too diffuse and not easily available for comparison. Hence three books (Ecclesiastes, Sirach, Wisdom) will be only briefly discussed against the general background of Hellenism.

Mesopotamia

The Tigris-Euphrates basin was the home of two separate, if historically related, cultures and languages: non-Semitic (Sumerian) and Semitic (Babylonian and Assyrian). Sumerian domination can be dated from about 3000 B.C.E. down to the rise of Babylonian culture (especially under Hammurabi, eighteenth and seventeenth centuries); this latter culture was considerably influenced by the Sumerian. Thereafter Akkadian, as opposed to the Sumerian language, became the normal medium of communication, expressed in two principal dialects, Babylonian and Assyrian. Like Sumerian, Akkadian was also written in cuneiform signs (wedge-shaped writing, impressed upon clay tablets). In the first millennium B.C.E. Aramaic began to replace Akkadian, becoming the language of international communication.

The appropriateness of applying the term "wisdom literature" to the Mesopotamian heritage has been challenged by G. Buccellati. At the most he is willing to speak of wisdom "themes" that occur in various types of literature. One may agree with him that wisdom is not to be identified with a literary genre, or to be limited to a specific intellectual movement. He writes, "Wisdom should be viewed as an intellectual phenomenon in itself. It is the second degree reflective function as it begins to emerge in human culture; in Mesopotamia, it takes shape in a variety of realizations and institutions, from onomastics to literature, from religion to the school."[1] These reflections indicate the difficulty of definition, which of course cannot be our purpose here. Our intention is to provide the reader with specimens of ancient literature that are comparable to the biblical wisdom books, even if there is a different literary type or setting in question.

The inherent difficulties of the Sumerian (and also Akkadian) languages demanded sophisticated training. There were schools for this purpose: the Sumerian *edubba*, or "tablet house," was designed for the training of the scribes, who were ultimately responsible for whatever literary remains have come down to us. The existence of bilingual as well as unilingual texts should be noted. Presumably all these texts served many purposes: the learning of one or two languages, and also the inculcation of lessons about life and, especially, the inherited traditions of the people.

Lists (Onomastica)

Lists for the various cuneiform signs were composed as an aid to the learning of the language and vocabulary. Some lists came to be topically arranged, and word lists pertinent to plants, animals, stones, and other objects came to be formed. Thus the Akkadian Charra-Chubullu lists are some twenty-four cuneiform tablets that contain hundreds of names. Similar lists also exist in the so-called Egyptian Onomastica. More is made of these lists for their wisdom impact than they deserve. Some have interpreted them as an effort to establish "order" (which, as pointed out in chap. 8, has become a favorite concept with scholars of wisdom literature).[2]

Instructions

The Instructions of Shuruppak was originally written in Sumerian, and it has been published by Bendt Alster.[3] It is important for two reasons: because it approximates the royal instruction genre that is common in Egypt, and because Ziusudra, who receives the instruction, is the Sumerian counterpart to Utnapishtim, the hero or "Noah" of the ancient flood stories (found in the Atra-hasis and in the Gilgamesh epics). A sample of the instruction is provided in *BWL*, 92–94, and *ANET*, 594–96.

The Counsels of Wisdom is an Akkadian work (dated probably between 1500 and 1200), consisting of about 140 lines, which was once thought to be part of The Instructions of Shuruppak. As in Egypt and in the Bible, the addressee is called "my son," and the counsels deal with such topics as bad companions, disputes and marriage. Lines 131–34 would fit with the biblical warnings about control of the tongue:

Beware of careless talk, guard your lips;
Do not utter solemn oaths while alone,
For what you say in a moment will follow you afterwards.
But exert yourself to restrain your speech. (*BWL*, 105; *ANET*, 595)

The proverbial wisdom of ancient Mesopotamia is instructive for biblical readers by the mere fact that it exists. It illustrates a point that can be made about most collections of sayings throughout the world: they spring from the ordinary experiences of daily life. It is not to be expected from similarities between biblical and Mesopotamian sayings that a given proverb is necessarily the source of another. In separate times and places similar situations can generate similar proverbs. As collections, the Mesopotamian sayings provide a model (like the Egyptian) for the collections of biblical sayings.

Proverbs

Many collections of unilingual Sumerian proverbs were identified by E. I. Gordon, and some of these collections have been published.[4] His definition of "proverb" ranges far beyond a pithy saying, and he includes taunts, toasts, short fables, and other types.[5] His distinctions among "maxim," "adage," and "byword" may not suit everyone's taste, but he has had the merit of making the texts available. The number of collections is high, and in many of them it is to be noted that initial words formed the basis for gathering many proverbs together.

As is well known, the Sumerians influenced the Babylonians, and several proverbs in both languages have been preserved—the bilingual proverbs, as they are called (*BWL*, 222–75). A few examples can suffice:

> It is not wealth that is your support. It is (your) God.
> Be you small or great, it is (your) God who is your support.
> A people without a king (is like) sheep without a shepherd. . . .
> A house without an owner (is like) a woman without a husband.
> (*BWL*, 232)

Oddly, few Babylonian proverbs are extant, although there is some evidence that they existed in oral tradition. Lambert is of the opinion that cultivation of the bilingual proverbs created a certain level of sophistication that did not tolerate sayings from among the uneducated. An example of a Babylonian proverb from Nippur:

> And a man, so long as he does not toil,
> will have nothing. (*BWL*, 277; *ANET*, 593)

Other Writings

The Epic of Gilgamesh. This much copied and widely known story (of about 1600) is not wisdom literature.[6] But its dominant motif is akin to wisdom concerns. It is the story of Gilgamesh's quest for immortality, and biblical wisdom is preoccupied with life and death. The climax of the quest comes when Gilgamesh is about to confront Utnapishtim, the hero of the ancient flood story, who was granted immortality by the gods after escaping the waters. He is warned by a tavern keeper, Siduri, that his search is futile:

> Gilgamesh, whither rovest thou?
> The life thou pursuest thou shalt not find.
> When the gods created mankind,
> Death for mankind they set aside,
> Life in their own hands retaining.

She continues immediately, in a passage that is strikingly similar to Eccl 9:7–9:

Thou, Gilgamesh, let full be thy belly,
Make thou merry by day and by night.
Of each day make thou a feast of rejoicing,
Day and night dance thou and play!
Let thy garments be sparkling fresh,
Thy head be washed; bathe thou in water.
Pay heed to the little one that holds on to thy hand,
Let thy spouse delight in thy bosom!
For this is the task of [mankind]! (*ANET,* 90)

The interview with Utnapishtim ultimately fails. Gilgamesh is not able to avoid sleep (the mirror of death) for six full days (*ANET,* 95–96); the gift of the plant of life, which he receives from Utnapishtim, is lost to the serpent when Gilgamesh goes into water to bathe. Death weighed heavily upon human beings in Mesopotamia and in Palestine.

I Will Praise the Lord of Wisdom (*Ludlul bel nēmeqi; BWL,* 21–62, 343–45; *ANET,* 596–600). This piece, dated between 1500 and 1200, has long been compared to the Book of Job, because in tablet 2 there is a vivid description (and lament) of a suffering person who claims to be righteous. The comparison is inadequate. The poem is essentially a praise of Marduk (who is the "lord of wisdom") because he has delivered his servant—a kind of psalm of thanksgiving. W. G. Lambert has suggested "The Babylonian Pilgrim's Progress" as a better title (*BWL,* 27). H. Gese has found in it the literary form of the "paradigm of an answered complaint," and attempted to find here the literary form of the Book of Job.[7] This view fails to appreciate the depth of the problem of suffering in Job, where no definitive answer is given. The Akkadian work (really a monologue) exemplifies the innocent sufferer, but that is a tenuous basis for comparison with the full thrust of the Book of Job. One can catch some of the flavor of the Akkadian piece in the following lines:

What is good for oneself may be offense to one's god,
What in one's own heart seems despicable may be proper to one's
   god.
Who can know the will of the gods in heaven?
Who can understand the plans of the underworld gods?
Where have humans learned the way of a god? (*ANET,* 597; *BWL,*
   41; cf. p. 266)

However, the complaint of the Babylonian nobleman (named Šubši-mešre-Šakkan) is as old as suffering humanity in the face of divine mystery. The mood is closer to the acknowledgment of the rescuing god, which is found in the Old Testament psalms of thanksgiving (see tablets 3 and 4; *ANET*, 599–600; *BWL*, 47–62).

The Babylonian Theodicy (*BWL*, 63–91; *ANET*, 601–4). This work is also known as The Dialogue About Human Misery. It has been dated by Lambert on stylistic considerations to about 1000; broadly it fits between 1400 and 800. It is an acrostic poem with twenty-seven stanzas (nineteen of which are fairly well preserved) of eleven lines each. Like Ps 119, each of the lines in the stanza begins with the same letter, or sign. This is a dialogue between a sufferer and his friend, a relatively serene exchange in comparison to Job and his friends. The sufferer begins with his own situation: born the youngest in the family and then bereaved of his parents, and without a protector. The soft answer from the friend is the reminder that all must die, that a relationship with one's god brings prosperity. The topics that are covered are similar to those in Job: the inequities of life, which cannot be squared with divine justice. The friend consistently returns to the theme that wrongdoing will not prosper, that worship of god will bring success. In particular, the sufferer maintains that the privileged (such as the firstborn) and the rich prevail over the honest person. Then the friend makes an astonishing admission. When the gods made the human race, they gave them perverse speech: "With lies, and not truth, they endowed them forever" (stanza 26). Lambert (*BWL*, 65) astutely remarks that "this conclusion undermines the premises on which the two argued. Both sufferer and friend began by assuming that the gods were responsible for maintaining justice among men. They end by admitting that these very gods made men prone to injustice. In a sense the real problem has been shelved." In the final stanza the sufferer asks the gods for help. This is hardly theodicy; the case is argued in too serene a fashion, and sometimes with monotonous uniformity. The *agôn* of Job is lacking.

The Dialogue of Pessimism (*BWL*, 139–49; *ANET*, 600–1). This is another dialogue, a most unusual one between master and slave, perhaps from around 1300. The master proposes to do a certain thing (e.g., make a home, lead a revolution, make love), and the slave replies with reasons affirming his action, sometimes with proverbial sayings. Then the master abruptly changes his mind and embraces the opposite course. The servant moves with him and gives reason for the contrary decision. At the end, the master raises the question of what is good, and proposes death. The slave seems to accept this with a saying: "Who is so tall that he can reach to the heavens? Who is so broad that he can encompass the underworld?" This reply seems ambiguous, pointing out human limitations, and thus accepting the proposal of death somewhat stoically. But then the master proposes to kill the servant first—to which the versatile slave replies by saying that the master would not outlive the servant even by three days. This ending is tantalizing. Does it propose suicide, or does the slave question whether suicide is the answer (since the slave claims the master could not continue to live without him)? Scholars have disputed about the nature of the dialogue, whether it is intended seriously (W. G. Lambert) or as a farce (E. Speiser). There is no mistaking the satirical edge to the unsteadiness of human reasoning, shown in the flip-flop of the servant's replies.

The liveliness of the exchange can be illustrated by the following:

"Slave, listen to me." "Here I am, sir, here I am."
"I will perform a public benefit for my country."
"So perform, sir, perform.
The man who performs a public benefit for his country,
His deeds are placed in the *ring* of Marduk."
"No, slave, I will by no means perform a public benefit for my
   country."
"Do not perform, sir, do not perform.
Go up on to the ancient ruin heaps and walk about;
See the skulls of high and low.
Which is the malefactor, and which is the benefactor?"
                          (lines 70–78; *BWL*, 149; *ANET*, 601)

The work has been deservedly compared with the Book of Ecclesiastes. In both, extreme positions are taken. Qoheleth consistently rejects values if he can show even one disadvantage; the author of the Babylonian piece operates in a similar way—what seems to be a good has a negative side. There is no question but that Qoheleth's verdict is deadly serious: all things are vanity.

The Words of Ahiqar (*ANET*, 427–30).[8] The celebrated story of Ahiqar deserves to be considered here, insofar as it reflects an Assyrian background. More probably, it was written in Aramaic—not in Akkadian—in the sixth century. It has had an extraordinary history, being reproduced in many ancient languages (Syrian, Armenian, Arabic, etc.) and expanded in the process. The Aramaic text was discovered among the fifth century B.C.E. papyri found at the start of the twentieth century on the island of Elephantine in the Nile. One must distinguish between the story and the sayings. The story deals with the betrayal of Ahiqar by Nadin, a nephew he has raised, who frames him with a charge of treason. King Sennacherib of Assyria orders the death penalty, but the executioner, whose life had once been saved by Ahiqar, keeps him alive and has another killed in his place. Later, when the king is put in an impossible situation and yearns for the wise Ahiqar, the executioner comes forth and informs Sennacherib of his existence. The happy monarch dispatches Ahiqar on the mission to fulfill the impossible task, which Ahiqar successfully accomplishes. Upon his return, Ahiqar refuses all honors and merely wants to discipline Nadin. This he does, severely, and also with his "words" or sayings, and Nadin dies. The relationship between the sayings and the story is not clear, and many think that the proverb collection once existed independently. Ahiqar has also entered the Book of Tobit (1:22; 2:10; 11:17; 14:10; Greek numbering). But it is the sayings that are relevant to biblical wisdom.

The sayings of Ahiqar are in the mold typical of ancient Near Eastern wisdom. There are fables (rare in the Old Testament), numerical sayings, admonitions, a prayer, and popular sayings. Parallelism is frequent. The content is familiar to us from the Book of Proverbs: sayings about the king, control of speech, discipline for the young, diligence, retribution for good and evil deeds, riches, and honesty. J. M. Lindenberger concludes his study of Ahiqar by saying that the "genuinely close parallels between the Aramaic Proverbs and the Bible are few."⁹ He singles out two as being the most obvious: lines 81–82 about the disciplining of children (cf. Prov 23:13–14), and line 207 concerning the rich man glorying in his riches (cf. Jer 9:22 [23]). There is no way to establish the dependence of one source upon another, because these themes are so frequent in wisdom literature. Parental discipline is treated in other sayings of Ahiqar, as also in Prov 13:24; 19:18; 22:15; 29:15, 17; cf. Sir 30:1–13. Humility is likewise a frequent theme: cf. Sir 3:17; 4:8; and James 1:9–10. Other similarities between the two works can also be pointed out: the power of a soft tongue (lines 105–6; Prov 25:15; Sir 28:17); in case of hunger, the bitter is sweet (line 188; Prov 27:7). There is also a famous statement about personified Wisdom (lines 94b–95), but the text is uncertain: It is translated by H. L. Ginsberg (*ANET,* 428) as "To gods also she is dear. F[or all time] the kingdom is [hers]. In he[av]en is she established, for the lord of holy ones has exalted [her]." Wisdom is precious; she is associated with a kingdom (eternal?) and the "lord of holy ones." All this seems comparable with the personification of Wisdom in Prov 8 and elsewhere (see chap. 9). But it must be remembered that the term "wisdom" is partially restored in the text (although it occurs twice in the preceding lines, 92 and 94a).

Egypt

Since the publication of the Instruction of Amenemope by Sir E. A. Wallis Budge in 1923, it has become usual among Egyptologists to speak of Egyptian "wisdom literature," adopting the term from biblical studies. But the term is used broadly, since it embraces not only the ancient instructions but also laments, and even writings of political propaganda. Almost all the progress made in this area has occurred in the twentieth century. Particularly pertinent are the many texts of instructions or teachings (*Sebayit*), which have come down to us from various sources.

The Instructions

The Egyptian word *Sebayit* is not an indication of literary genre; it occurs as a heading for various types of literature (didactic treatise, tomb autobiography, etc.), and it designates the purpose, to instruct.[10] About a dozen extant works are usually considered to be "instruction," and many more are known only by title. The following characteristics of the *Sebayit* deserve mention:[11] First, there is usually a title, often phrased as "the beginning of the instruction," with identification of the writer by name (only a few of the instructions are anonymous). Some scholars (Miriam Lichtheim in *AEL*, I, 6–7) are inclined to regard many of these indications as untrustworthy; we are really dealing with pseudepigrapha. The title usually describes the teaching that X has composed for his son (i.e., student) Y.

Second, often an introduction or prologue explains the purpose of the work. Thus for Amenemope: "The beginning of the teaching of life, the testimony for prosperity, all precepts for intercourse with elders, the rules for courtiers, to know how to return an answer to him who said it, and to direct a report to one who has sent him, in order to direct him to the ways of life, to make him prosper on the earth . . ." (*ANET*, 421; *AEL*, II, 148; *LAE*, 242). This can be compared to Prov 1:1–6; 22:21. Already a certain class ethic appears that is relatively absent from the Bible: an emphasis on training courtiers. Moreover, tradition plays an important role: the teaching has been handed down and is now given to the student. Tradition is not absent in the Old Testament wisdom books, but experience is much more to the fore. It is difficult to speculate about the oral tradition that may be behind the Egyptian treatises. The extant works are very much the product of the writing exercises in the scribal schools, where they were copied in successive generations.

In style, the body of the instruction consists of admonitions or imperatives, and it resembles the wisdom poems in Prov 1–9, in contrast to the discrete sayings in Prov 10ff. The instruction develops a theme in a logical and consecutive way; some sayings will appear, but they are integrated into a larger whole. It is only when one arrives at the late demotic works (Ankhsheshonq or Papyrus Insinger; see later) that short one-line sayings become the vehicle for the instruction. The *Sebayit* is marked by plays on words, parallelism, and certain admonitions that will ensure the "way" (as also in the Book of Proverbs, a common term) of life: self-control (appetite, tongue), kindness, proper attitude toward riches and poverty, honesty, and other typical values. The admonitions frequently have a motive clause (as also in Hebrew admonitions) designed to persuade the student. Very often these clauses will strike the modern reader as merely oriented to personal profit. Many scholars scored this self-serving type of ethic as "eudaemonism." However, others have rightly pointed to the religious thrust of this "reward" ethic. By following the teaching, the student is obeying and also establishing the *ma'at* ("justice," "order"), which is ordained by the divinity. A classical description of *ma'at* is given by Ptah-hotep (*ANET,* 412; *AEL,* II, 64; *LAE,* 162): "Justice is great, and its appropriateness is lasting; it has not been disturbed since the time of him who made it. . . . It is the (right) path before him who knows nothing. . . . The strength of justice is that it lasts. . . ." *Ma'at,* and not wisdom (*rḥw*), is recognized as the keystone of Egyptian didactic teaching.[12] If humans abide by this divinely established order, everything will turn out well. *Ma'at* was divinized as a goddess, daughter of the sun-god, and the necessary guide for the reigning monarch.

In the *Eloquent Peasant* (*AEL,* I, 169ff.) the peasant describes *ma'at* ("justice") in these words:

> For justice is for eternity:
> It enters the graveyard with its doer.
> When he is buried and earth enfolds him,
> His name does not pass from the earth;
> He is remembered because of goodness,
> That is the rule of god's command. (*AEL,* I, 181; 8th petition)

The role of *ma'at* is portrayed in a papyrus drawing[13] in which the god Anubis leads the deceased toward a scale in a judgment scene. One side of the balance carries an image of *ma'at.* This is weighed against the heart of the deceased to determine the judgment. A life lived according to *ma'at* weighs only a feather (a symbol of truth, which *ma'at* carries on her head in her images[14]). But a wicked life will pull the scale the other way.

The evaluation of *ma'at* has given rise to several important biblical issues. Is the Israelite understanding of wisdom to be identified with the Egyptian mind-set concerning *ma'at?* It was indicated earlier (chap. 8) that many scholars have adopted this view: a kind of "ma'atizing" of biblical wisdom has taken place.[15] Such an interpretation is very tempting, since it is clear that Israel was influenced by Egyptian wisdom (Prov 22:17ff. and Amenemope being the outstanding example). In both cultures, the right "way," similar values, and an emphasis on the good "life" are cultivated. And this is to be transmitted by teaching. But the transfer of a mind-set from one culture to another calls for careful scrutiny.

There seems to be reason to claim that the figure of *ma'at* had some influence on the description of Wisdom in Prov 1–9. Christa Kayatz has pointed out a number of ideas held in common between Egypt and Israel.[16] The "I-style" of speech is perhaps not striking, because frequently the Lord speaks in the first person throughout the Old Testament (especially in the

Prophets). But within the wisdom literature, it is Lady Wisdom who speaks thus, in Prov 1, 8, 9, and with a certain divine accent, as we have noted earlier (chap. 9). In both Israel and Egypt there is self-predication ("I am the Lord, that is my name; my glory I give to no other . . . ," Isa 42:8). But *ma'at* gives no such speeches; she is rather talked about, not talking, in the Egyptian literature. However, other divinities, such as Isis, deliver addresses that are comparable to those of Lady Wisdom, because they consist of a summons, a promise (such as life), and a self-description or self-recommendation.[17]

The association of Wisdom and royalty is clear in Prov 8:15–16 ("By me kings reign . . ." and cf. the figure of Solomon). In a similar way, *ma'at* is the foundation of royal rule in Egypt, and the "beloved of Re." Life is the gift of Wisdom (Prov 1:33; 3:16, 18; 8:35). Similarly, *ma'at* is life, the giver of life, as shown by representations of her: holding the *ankh* sign, the symbol of life, in one hand, and a scepter, symbol of power, in the other. These symbols are found with divine kings and other divinities, as well as with the goddess *ma'at*.[18] In Prov 6:21 (cf. 1:9) the student is ordered to bind the teaching of his parents about his neck, over the heart. In 1:9 this teaching is called a necklace and in 3:22, a grace. Similarly, high officials in the Egyptian court would wear an amulet of *ma'at* about the neck. Finally, the reciprocity formula for love (Prov 8:17, "I love those who love me") is found in several Egyptian scarabs.[19]

The study of Kayatz surely suggests that there are common themes associated with *ma'at* and Hebrew wisdom, and the probability is in favor of Egyptian influence. Whether the adoption of these motifs can serve to date Prov 1–9 to the so-called Solomonic "enlightenment," when Israel seemed to turn to Egyptian style and culture, is debatable, since the same motifs could have been as readily operative in the postexilic period. But the use of the motifs associated with *ma'at*, and thus evidence of the influence of Egyptian wisdom, seems most tangible in Prov 1–9.

The Egyptian ideal was that of the strong, silent man who has self-control. He has achieved harmonious integration with the divine order and is master of any situation. He is described more by contrast with the "heated man," the rash and impetuous person who constantly brings trouble upon himself and others. This contrast, which is very frequent in Amenemope, is found also in Proverbs (15:18, "A hot-tempered man stirs up strife, but a patient man allays discord"; cf. 14:17, 29; 22:24–25; 29:22). .

Although Egypt was a land of many gods, only a general reference to "god" (*ntr*) is usually found in the instructions.[20] The divinity is characterized by power, omniscience, and justice (*ma'at*), and the god stands ready to help those who pursue the divine order. There are a few references to the cultic worship of god, but the concern is with living in the here and now, without much attention to the next life. According to Hans H. Schmid (and many others), this divinity is an *Urhebergott*, who created and also sustains his creation through the establishment of *ma'at*.[21]

The Egyptian Sages

It will be recalled that some (R. N. Whybray) have argued that the Israelite sages did not constitute a particular professional class. They were simply a relatively small group of men of superior intelligence. It must be admitted that it is difficult to draw their sociological profile. In the case of the Egyptian sage a much clearer picture emerges.[22] They are scribes, described as "men of knowledge," whose words are sayings or, more literally, "knots" (tight, pithy thoughts?). Because they are students of *ma'at*, they know the order of the world (and hence prophecies, e.g., Neferti, could come within their expertise). Unlike the biblical wisdom writers, they deal specifically with history (the writings of Merikare, Amenemhet). Although it is possible that Israelite sages may have been involved in the writing of various parts of the Old Testament, there is little evidence to show that they were (see chap. 7). For the Bible we speak of "the wise," who authored and transmitted the wisdom literature. But there is no strictly comparable class in Egypt, as Michael V. Fox has pointed out:

> There is no special term to designate the authors or speakers of wisdom texts. They were educated men—called scribes—whose education and literary activity included various areas of study, among them gnomic wisdom. Wisdom literature is the product of the scribal class, i.e., the educated class, but so are most other forms of Egyptian literature. There is no point in calling the scribal class the "wisdom school." We could just as well label the scribal class the "magical school" because some of its members produced magical texts. This is not to deny the distinctive style and content of wisdom literature, but to stress that this distinctive character was determined by the function of the genre, just as the distinctive character of epistolic literature and even magic was determined by their function, not by the group from which they derived.

The earliest sage appears to be *Imhotep*, the architect for King Djoser's famous step pyramid, of the third dynasty (ca. 2600). His repute is established, but there is no trace of any of his writings. He and Hardedef are commemorated for their wisdom in one of the Harper's songs (*ANET*, 467; *AEL*, I, 196; *LAE*, 306).

Hardedef (also written Hardjedef or Djedef-Hor) was son of King Khufu (Cheops) of the fourth dynasty, and only fragments of his work have come down. They deal with founding a family and concern for one's grave (*AEL*, I, 58–59; *LAE*, 340).

Also fragmentary is the teaching (by an unknown writer) for *Kagemni*, a vizier under King Snefru of the fourth dynasty (*AEL*, I, 59–61; *LAE*, 177–79). Restraint in eating, conduct at the table, and modesty are the topics treated.

The Instruction of *Ptah-hotep* (*ANET*, 412–14; *AEL*, I, 61–80; *LAE*, 159–76) purports to be the teaching of a vizier under King Izezi of the fifth dynasty (ca. 2450). Miriam Lichtheim (*AEL*, I, 61) counts thirty-seven "maxims" that are set in the framework of a prologue and epilogue. The prologue has an interesting description of old age given by Ptah-hotep, to which the king replies concerning instruction "in the sayings of the past" that are to be communicated; "hearing" (greatly emphasized in the epilogue) is to enter into the student, because "no one is born wise." Ptah-hotep covers a wide range of topics, for example, proper speech, self-control in dealing with disputants, blameless conduct, table etiquette, responsibility as a messenger, justice (*ma'at*), honesty, attitude toward riches (greed) and poverty, how to deal with honors and with litigation, friendship, and generosity. The style is primarily admonitory; commands and prohibitions are directed to the situations the teacher explicitly indicates (if . . . then . . .). In some cases there are also lines that appear to be proverbial: "He who steps gently, his path is paved. He who frets all day has no happy moment" (*AEL*, I, 70). The emphasis on hearing (i.e., docility, obedience) in the rather lengthy epilogue is extraordinary ("He who hears is beloved of god. He whom god hates does not hear," *AEL*, I, 74). W. McKane characterizes the work as establishing "the conditions of effective and successful statesmanship in ancient Egypt."[23] He points out that the concept of power (not arbitrary, but regulated by *ma'at*) is central to the way in which one is to exercise statesmanship. At the same time, Ptah-hotep warns, "Do not put trust in your wealth which came to you as gift of god; so that you will not fall behind one like you, to whom the same has happened" (*AEL*, I, 71).

The statesmanship emphasized by Ptah-hotep continues in the Instruction for King *Merikare* (*ANET*, 414–18; *AEL*, I, 97–109; *LAE*, 180–92), who reputedly was the son of an unnamed Pharaoh (perhaps one of the Khetys in the ninth and tenth dynasties). Miriam Lichtheim (*AEL*, I, 97) defines the work as a royal testament. Indeed the work is primarily concerned with the problems of ruling a nation (some history appears here) and dealing with situations in the life of the court. It ends with a hymn in honor of the sun-god. In addition to the political advice there are many familiar themes: justice, care for the weak, importance of speech (the tongue is a "sword"). At least one saying is close to the biblical thought: "More acceptable is one upright of heart than the ox of the evildoer" (lines 128–29; *ANET*, 417; cf. Prov 15:8; Sir 34:21ff.; 1 Sam 15:22).

The Instruction of King *Amenemhet* (*ANET*, 418–19; *AEL*, I, 135–39; *LAE*, 193–97) is another royal testament, destined for his son, Sesostris (twelfth dynasty, twentieth century B.C.E.). It is important as a source for history more than as a wisdom document. The royal advice is rather curt: don't trust anyone. The king was apparently assassinated. The initial glories of his reign are "prophesied" (after the fact) in the *Prophecies of Neferti* (*ANET*, 444–46; *AEL*, I, 139–45; *LAE*, 234–40). W. K. Simpson calls this latter writing "a blatant political pamphlet designed to support the new regime" (*LAE*, 234).

The Instruction of *Khety*, son of Duauf (or Dua-Khety), dated ca. 2000 in the Middle Kingdom, is known also as the Satire on Trades (*ANET*, 432–34; *AEL*, I, 184–92; *LAE*, 329–36). Satire it is, as the father ridicules various trades (goldsmith, carpenter, barber, reed-cutter [?], potter, mason, gardener, farmer, weaver, arrow-maker, courier, cobbler, bird-catcher, fisherman) in order to enhance the vocation of the scribe: "See, there's no profession without a boss, except for the scribe; he is the boss" (*AEL*, I, 189). He concludes with some general recommendations about caution, right speech, moderation, and hearing. Miriam Lichtheim has characterized the work thus: "In short, the unrelievedly negative descriptions of the laboring professions are examples of humor in the service of literary satire. The result is obtained through unflattering comparisons and through exaggerations that rise to out-right fabrications. What if not a fabrication for the sake of caricature is a bird-catcher who does not have a net—the very tool of his trade?" (*AEL*, I, 184). Needless to say, Ben Sira's description of worker and scribe in 38:24–39:11 is cut from very different cloth.

The Instruction of *Ani*, also spelled Any (*ANET*, 420–21; but more complete in *AEL*, II, 135–46) is dated ca. 1500. It is the work of a simple scribe, who offers far-ranging advice to his son, Khonshotep, about marriage, the "strange woman" (cf. Prov 1–9), silence, moderation in drink, wealth and self-sufficiency, study, care for one's mother, generosity to the poor, and other topics. The style is generally admonitory, with an occasional saying ("Wealth accrues to him who guards it"). The admonition about sincere prayer in the temple (*ANET*, 420; *AEL*, II, 137) is reminiscent of Qoheleth in Eccl 4:17–5:1. The charm of this work lies in the reaction of Ani's son. In the epilogue he expresses his admiration for his father; he would want to be like him, but he feels that he cannot understand and obey him. Ani replies vigorously and gives him several examples of obedience (interestingly, from animals! Cf. Prov 6:6ff.). The son still remonstrates with his father, but to no avail. The rather terse ending suggests that he is worn down by the scribe, his father. Encapsulated in this little dialogue is a testing of the Egyptian style of education: the scribe insists on study and memorization and "hearing" or obedience; the son is contesting this, unsuccessfully.

Because of the relationship to Prov 22:17ff., the Instruction of

Amenemope (*ANET*, 421–25; *AEL*, II, 146–63; *LAE*, 241–65) is familiar to many readers of the Bible. It seems indisputable that there is some literary connection between the two (see the discussion in chap. 2), and the instruction is certainly older (ca. 1200) than Proverbs. The text has been arranged stichometrically in some copies, enabling one to see more clearly the connection of thought and especially the parallelism. The author deliberately numbers the thirty chapters (cf. "thirty" in the emended text of Prov 22:20).

The topics treated by Amenemope are those traditional in many instructions: kindness and moderation, poverty and riches, self-control (the "heated man" is mentioned many times and the "silent" one is his opposite), honesty, respect for others, and modesty. Twice (chaps. 21, 22; *AEL*, II, 159) there is the refrain: "Indeed you do not know the plans of god and should not weep for tomorrow; settle in the arms of the god." The god is the giver of *ma'at*, but humans should be aware of the divine mystery: "The words men say are one thing, the deeds of the god are another" (chap. 18; *AEL*, II, 157; cf. Prov 16:1, 9; 19:21). The writer lays out "the paths of life" (prologue), but one must also pray to the Aton (sun-god) for well-being, and it will be granted. The style is admonitory, but there are many sayings to be found, notably "better" sayings such as "Better is poverty in the hand of the god, than wealth in the storehouse; better is bread with a happy heart than wealth with vexation" (chap. 6; cf. chap. 12; Prov 15:16–17). The divine determinaism that is characteristic of the Bible (1 Sam 2:6–7; Prov 16:33; 22:2) appears in chap. 25: "Man is clay and straw, the god is his builder. He tears down, he builds up daily, he makes a thousand poor by his will, he makes a thousand men into chiefs" (*AEL*, II, 160).

Although Amenemope and Prov 22:17ff. have been the principal object of discussion among biblical scholars (see chap. 2), there are sayings in other collections of Proverbs (e.g., Prov 18:1 and chap. 18; cf. *AEL*, II, 157) that are similar to those in the Egyptian work. In those instances there is no need to postulate a dependency of one on the other; these sayings merely illustrate the international, humanistic character of ancient Near Eastern wisdom.

The life of the Egyptian instruction form is extraordinarily long (three millennia!), since it reaches down into the Ptolemaic period (last two centuries B.C.E.), which has yielded two lengthy works written in demotic script (a cursive Egyptian hand that arose in the seventh century). The first is the Instruction of *Ankhsheshonq* (*AEL*, III, 159–84). The prologue describes the deplorable situation of the priest Ankhsheshonq. He tried unsuccessfully to dissuade a friend from killing the Pharaoh. When the plot was foiled, the priest was implicated as an accomplice (because he did not tell the king) and imprisoned. Here he wrote his instruction for his son "on the sherds of the jars that were brought into him containing mixed wine" (4:18). This fictional introduction (cf. the story of Ahiqar) sets the stage for a teaching that covers about twenty-eight columns. Sayings (many of them doubtless proverbial) mingle with commands and admonitions almost equally. There is no logical ordering of the material, although several times a given topic is repeated in successive sentences (wealth, 8:17–23; borrowing, 16:9–12). The aura of the court, which could be detected in the older instructions, is absent; Ankhsheshonq is writing for ordinary people, not for officials.

The following examples will convey a flavor of this instruction:

7:24—"Do not say right away what comes out of your heart."

8:23—"The wealth of a wise man is his speech."

11:19—"Do not laugh at your son in front of his mother, lest you learn the size of his father."

14:14—"He who is bitten of the bite of a snake is afraid of a coil of rope."

19:10—"Do a good deed and throw it in the water; when it dries you will find it."

23:8—"It is better to dwell in your own small house than to dwell in the large house of another."

26:14—"The plans of the god are one thing, the thoughts of men are another." (cf. Prov 16:1, 9.)

In 26:5–8 are a series of paradoxes: "There is imprisonment for giving life. There is release for killing. There is he who saves and does not profit. All are in the hand of the fate and the god."

The second demotic instruction is the *Papyrus Insinger* (*AEL*, III, 184–217), so called after the Dutchman who purchased the papyrus for the Leiden royal museum in 1895. Written in demotic script and dating from the Ptolemaic period, it is lacking the usual title and prologue, and the first five and a half units. It consists of some twenty-seven units in all, and these are so labeled and numbered. They are provided with headings that describe the general theme of the specific teaching—thus betraying a careful organization of the material on the part of the author. It may be, as with the collections in the biblical Book of Proverbs, that many of the sayings have come from various sources. But there is no denying the fact that the unknown author has put his stamp upon them by the arrangement, and he could very well be the true author in many cases. Like the Instruction of Ankhsheshonq, this papyrus consists of sayings that are more or less one line long. There are several commands and prohibitions, but maxims or aphorisms are by far in the majority. What is unique, as Miriam Lichtheim has pointed out, are the paradoxes and conclusions that mark the end of the various teachings.[24] When the text is not disturbed one can detect a pattern: seven sentences made up of two pairs of paradoxes, followed by two conclusions and a refrain. This device serves to qualify the teaching: things may not turn out as expected. "Fate and fortune" is a phrase appearing regularly in these conclusions, a refrain that indicates that the god can modify the order one naturally expects. This is clearly portrayed in the ending of the eighth teaching, which begins, "Do not be a glutton, lest you become the companion of poverty" (*AEL*, III, 189; 5:12). Many reflections on gluttony and its ill effects follow until we reach the stylized ending:

> 7:13—"There is one who lives on little so as to save, yet he becomes poor.
> 7:14—There is one who does not know, yet the fate gives (him) wealth.
> 7:15—It is not the wise man who saves who finds a surplus.
> 7:16—Nor is it the one who spends who becomes poor.
> 7:17—The god gives a wealth of supplies without an income.
> 7:18—He also gives poverty in the purse without spending.
> 7:19—The fate and the fortune that come, it is the god who sends them." (*AEL*, III, 191)

Even though the ambiguities of life are thus pointed out, retribution remains intact: "A lifetime is given to the impious man in order to make him encounter retaliation" (*AEL*, III, 209; 30:23).

Other Relevant Egyptian Writings

This survey of the Egyptian instructions witnesses to the high premium that Egyptian civilization set upon writing and education. An important factor in all this was the office of scribe. The instructions served a double purpose: their doctrine educated the scribe into a way of life, and their transmission over the centuries gave him the wherewithal for his scribal expertise. The instructions (not to mention the other types of Egyptian literature, which are not our concern here) were copied and recopied, and fragments recorded on writing tablets are to be found throughout the Western world. Scribal art succeeded in ancient Egypt in an unparalleled fashion. It is no wonder that we find a regular schoolbook in *Papyrus Lansing* (*AEL*, II, 167–75; *LAE*, 343–47), which is a paean of praise to the art of being a scribe and a teacher of scribes. No occupation can compare with the scribal profession (as we saw earlier in the Satire on Trades), and the teacher is praised as no other educator: he possess all virtues and abilities. The Lansing concludes, "You are a man of choice words, who is skilled in saying them; all you say is right, you abhor falsehood . . . you serve your lord, you nourish your people; whatever you say soothes the heart" (*AEL*, II, 174).

Nothing less than immortality is claimed for a scribe. The *Chester Beatty Papyrus IV* (*AEL*, II, 175–78; *ANET*, 431–32) claims immortality of name (note that not all of the instructions have names that have been preserved, and few of the names of other writers were ever given). The scribe's tools are his family: the reed-pen, the child; the stone surface, the wife:

> Man decays, his corpse is dust,
> All his kin have perished;
> But a book makes him remembered
> Through the mouth of its reciter.
> Better is a book than a well-built house,
> Than tomb-chapels in the west. . . .

The writer goes on to ask about the famous sages of old, such as Ptah-hotep and others, and he concludes:

> Death made their names forgotten
> But books made them remembered! (*AEL* II, 177; *ANET* 432)

Both the schoolbook of *Papyrus Lansing* and the praise of the Chester Beatty Papyrus are relatively old, going back to the thirteenth and twelfth centuries.

The *Songs of the Harper*, twenty-four of which have been preserved, provide a sharp contrast to these schoolbooks. Perhaps the most famous is the Harper's song from the tomb of King Intef (one of the Intefs of the eleventh dynasty, ca. 2000). Originally they were written in praise of death and the life after death, hence they were funerary texts. But they developed a certain skepticism, and a hedonism: live it up in the here and now and forget about death (carpe diem). Not all the songs gave into skepticism (cf. *AEL*, II, 115–16; *ANET*, 33–34). One copy of the Intef song is inscribed on a tomb wall, on which a blind harpist is depicted directing four musicians. The song begins with a reflection on the disappearance of great people of the past, and continues:

> Their walls have crumbled,
> Their places are gone,
> As though they had never been!
> None comes from there,
> To tell of their state,
> To tell of their needs,
> To calm our hearts,
> Until we go where they have gone!
> Hence rejoice in your heart!
> Forgetfulness profits you,
> Follow your heart as long as you live!
> Put myrrh on your head,
> Dress in fine linen, . . .

Lo, none is allowed to take his goods with him,
Lo, none who departs comes back again! (*AEL*, I, 196–97; *ANET*,
  467; *LAE*, 306–7)

Echoes of this mentality can also be found, even if in a very different context
and thrust, in Ps 49; but Eccl 9:7–10 is akin to the spirit of such a song (see
also the treatment of the Gilgamesh epic earlier).

No one has ever equaled ancient Egypt for the extent and excellence of
its instructions, but they are only a small portion of the extant works, which
include autobiographies, monument inscriptions, tales, hymns, and prayers. A
few more literary items should be singled out here for comparison with biblical wisdom literature.

Because the Song of Songs has been possibly transmitted by the sages,
although it is not wisdom literature, brief notice should be taken of the
Egyptian love songs, which constitute the closest parallels that the ancient
Near East has provided for the Song. The Egyptian songs are translated in
AEL, II, 181–93; *LAE*, 296–306; 308–25; and there are excerpts in *ANET*,
467–69. The sensuality, the imagery (flowers, exotic scents, animals), and the
yearning of lovers are expressed in language that is akin to the language of the
biblical Canticle. They are independent poems (each is written from the
point of view of one gender only), dating from various periods, but they are
not orchestrated in the form of a dialogue—in contrast to the Song of Songs.
The language and the spirit are remarkably similar. For translations and
analysis, see J. B. White, *A Study of the Language of Love in the Song of
Songs and Ancient Egyptian Poetry* (SBLDS 38; Missoula: Scholars Press,
1978) and especially Michael V. Fox, *The Song of Songs and Ancient Egyptian Love Songs* (Madison: University of Wisconsin Press, 1985), which com-
bines translation and analysis with a sound commentary on the biblical Song.

Akin to the problem literature of the Old Testament is the *Dispute
Between a Man and His Ba* (*AEL*, I, 163–69), also designated as The Man
Who Was Tired of Life (*LAE*, 201–9) and Dispute over Suicide (*ANET*,
405–7). The various titles suggest the wide range of interpretations given to
this difficult work, whose only manuscript dates from the twelfth dynasty.
The basic facts are the sufferings of a man who wants to die. But his *Ba* (his
"soul") will not hear of this and will instead leave him, depriving him of the
happiness beyond the grave. The man counters the *Ba* by portraying death as
a natural result (even if he desires it). But the *Ba* concentrates on life, which
is to be enjoyed, and not on death such as the man envisions. To make his
point the *Ba* relates two stories that are not very clear. The reply of the man
consists in four poems with steady refrains (e.g., "Death is before me today,"
in the third poem), the third and fourth dealing with death and the next life
("yonder"). Finally, the *Ba* replies, to the effect that they will stay together
(in suicide, according to the interpretation in *ANET*; but this is not at all

certain).[25] Ultimately it is not clear whether the issue is suicide or simply the desirability of death in view of life's adversities. As far as the theme is concerned, this work has obvious parallels in the Book of Job, which brings up death (as a respite) several times (3:11–19; 7:21; 10:21–22). But there is no thought of suicide in Job (if even there is in the Egyptian work), nor of any real life in the "yonder" world. The complaints about life are simply common coin for the human condition.

The role of onomastica or lists (*Listenwissenschaft*) in ancient Egypt and Israel has been seriously questioned. The Egyptian onomastica published by A. H. Gardiner contain lists that have organized individual items in various realms, for example, offices, tribes, cities, plants, and animals.[26] It has been conjectured that they served as textbooks, and from this Gerhard von Rad moved to the influence of a particular work—the *Satirical Letter* of Hori, preserved in the *Papyrus Anastasi I* of the thirteenth century B.C.E. (*ANET,* 475–79)—on the speeches in Job 38–39.[27] But the interpretation of the Satirical Letter is not clear. Michael V. Fox has pointed out that most of the relevant questions (interpreted as satirical) are really negative statements. Hori is asking for information, whereas the Lord's questions in Job 38–39 are largely rhetorical.[28]

There is clear evidence that lists existed, but the issue here is how they functioned. Doubtless they helped a scribe to learn names and spellings; the cataloguing of names, places, and other items is a natural development. But one should not read more into this than was intended. There are "lists" in ancient Egypt, but no "science of lists."

Hellenism

Sophia, or "wisdom," played a large role in the thought of ancient Hellas, and there is an extensive Greek gnomic and ethical wisdom with which the Bible might be and has been compared. Hesiod (ca. 700, the author of *Works and Days*) may be considered the father of didactic poetry in Greece. Phocylides of Miletus (ca. 550), "the wisest of men," was imitated in the pseudepigraphical *Sentences of Pseudo-Phocylides,* a Jewish wisdom collection of the Hellenistic period (*OTP* II, 565–82). Menander (ca. 300), the great representative of the "new comedy," was similarly honored later by the Jewish-Hellenistic sentences of pseudo-Menander (or Syriac Menander; *OTP,* II, 583–607). This is not the place for a description of this abundant and far-flung literature. Our purpose here is quite modest, merely to indicate the state of the question as regards the relationship of Hellenism to Qoheleth, Sirach, and the Wisdom of Solomon. All three books are clearly Jewish, but also the product of the Hellenistic age. In his valuable study of the encounter of Judaism and Hellenism in the early Hellenistic period (fourth through second centuries), Martin Hengel wisely states that it is "extraordinarily difficult" to demonstrate direct "Hellenistic influences" in the Jewish (Hebrew and Aramaic) literature of the period.[29] He has recourse to the Hellenistic *Zeitgeist*, or "spirit of the times," as a factor in the literature under consideration. This would be preeminently true of these three works.

Qoheleth

It is well to eliminate at the outset two extreme views concerning Qoheleth: the Phoenician background urged by M. Dahood, and a dating after Ben Sira, with Epicurean influence, advocated by C. F. Whitley.[30] Neither view has rallied support. The real options are Mesopotamian, Egyptian, and Greek or Hellenistic. Mesopotamian influence, urged emphatically by O. Loretz,[31] is remote and does not really explain the novelty or the peculiar emphases of Qoheleth on the wisdom scene of ca. 300. We have already indicated a certain "similarity" between Qoheleth and the Dialogue of Pessimism, and also between Eccl 9:7-9 and the advice given to Gilgamesh. Loretz adds many other considerations, such as the importance attached to name and memory in both cultures, and the relationship between *hebel* (breath, wind, vanity) and Akkadian *šāru*. His arguments show that Qoheleth remains a genuine Semite and a Hebrew thinker; they do not eliminate the question of Hellenistic influence.

Egyptian influence upon Ecclesiastes was strenuously argued by P. Humbert and to a certain extent by K. Galling.[32] It is not seriously considered today, except for the possible influence of demotic literature (Ankhsheshonq and Papyrus Insinger, treated earlier), which is rather to be classified with Hellenistic Egypt (reign of the Ptolemies). The real issue remains that of Greek influence upon Qoheleth.

In his erudite study *Judaism and Hellenism*, Martin Hengel wrote, "Influence from the Greek world of ideas is seen [this is stronger than the original German, which has only *vermutet*] in Koheleth more than in any other Old Testament work."[33] He seems to agree that the alleged Grecisms and parallels between Qoheleth and Greek philosophy—arguments that flourished at the beginning of the twentieth century—are not on target, but he also regards the criticisms of O. Loretz as too one-sided. For various reasons (and these are highly inferential) he is inclined to date Ecclesiastes between 270 and 220 B.C.E. He is not interested in "direct dependence," but rather in illustrating the *Zeitgeist und Lebensgefühl* (the spirit and the feeling for life) of early Hellenism. The first evidence of this *Zeitgeist* is "the personally engaged, *critical individuality* of an acute and independent thinker." Secondly, there is Qoheleth's universalism, expressed among other ways by his use of the generic *hā'ĕlōhîm* (eight out of forty times without the article), by the use of "under the sun" (twenty-seven times)—which indicates the breadth of his observations—and by the broad use of "man" and "children of men." Hengel concludes with enumerating several aspects of Qoheleth's thought "in which contacts with the spirit of early Hellenism might be visible": (1) individuality of personality; (2) detached observations and rational thought in his attack on the traditional doctrine of retribution; (3) the distancing of God, eliminating a trustful relationship; (4) arbitrariness of human existence, governed by fate; (5) the resulting necessity of humans to be resigned, exercising a middle way in life's course, with the possibility of carpe diem, however fleeting; (6) a certain "bourgeois ethic" in Qoheleth, who belonged to the upper class of society. All in all, Hengel's arguments remain impressionistic, and dependent for the most part on secondary sources.

R. Braun has tried a different approach, adducing an astonishing number of parallels between Ecclesiastes and Greek thought from Homer to Menander.[34] But therein lies the difficulty. Few have taken the time to evaluate these examples. O. Kaiser cuts down Braun's list to a third, and he also points out that the similarities may not be due to a literary knowledge, but merely reflect common themes and problems of life.[35] In sum, he agrees with the judgment of J. Loader that the question is really "how" Greek thought functions within the book. In other words, elements of Greek thought can be found, but how are they used by Qoheleth?[36]

In his commentary on Ecclesiastes, N. Lohfink has made some debatable inferences about the author and the book. Lohfink states that the work is basically a compromise, attempting to preserve biblical wisdom but with liberal inspiration from Greek writers, and that it was written for a Jerusalem Temple school in the third century (before Sirach).[37] This rather detailed reconstruction of Qoheleth and his activity remains very hypothetical.

At the present time the verdict on Qoheleth and Hellenism is still out.[38] The general judgment is that he was a Jewish sage who was influenced by the Hellenistic spirit of his time, but the precise details for this position are difficult to establish.

Sirach

Martin Hengel entitles his treatment of Sirach "Ben Sira and the controversy with hellenistic liberalism in Jerusalem."[39] This reflects the fact that we can pinpoint his active period—in the first quarter of the second century. The process of Hellenization was being vigorously mounted in Jerusalem (1 Macc 1:11–15; 2 Macc 4:7–17) under Jason the high priest (174–171 B.C.E.). This was clearly a Hellenistic world, and the question arises: What was

APPENDIX

Sirach's relation to this culture? Can it be said that he was in "controversy" with it?

As we have seen in discussing Sirach, he is very much a conservative and traditionalist, relying strongly on the Book of Proverbs, emphasizing the Torah and Jewish fidelity. He does not appear as an "apostle to the Gentiles," or even as speaking to Jews in the Diaspora. Hengel concludes that his "controversy is with those groups of the Jerusalem upper classes who as a result of their assimilation to foreign culture had become almost completely alienated from the belief of their ancestors." If "controversy" there was, it was positive, not negative (but cf. Sir 41:8–9), because Sirach believed that the tradition is its own best argument.

Did Sirach incorporate Greek ideas to this end? The most extensive study of "parallels" between Sirach and Hellenism is that of Th. Middendorp, who lists "about one hundred" examples.[40] In his view, these wide-ranging sources (especially Theognis, Euripides, and even Homer) were probably available to Sirach in a chrestomathy, and he read Theognis directly. But one may question if such a hypothesis really explains the alleged parallels. J. T. Sanders[41] agrees with several of Middendorp's conclusions about Sirach and Theognis, and he also discusses the relationship that authors have made between Sirach and the Isis texts (H. Conzelmann), Stoicism (R. Pautrel), and other Greek sources. But Sanders's main concern is to show an even greater dependence of Sirach upon the Papyrus Insinger, which he calls Phibis, the name of the apparent author that Lichtheim renders as Phebhor (*AEL*, III, 213). He reviews the work of previous scholars (P. Humbert, W. Fuss) on this question, and he offers some new examples of dependence. But this remains very hypothetical; how could Sirach have known of this work, which so far has been transmitted only in its original demotic? This entire matter of parallels with Ben Sira is a difficult area. Is the alleged dependence a literary one, or due to the common cultural legacy (e.g., attitude toward women), or to commonsense attitudes of daily experience (e.g., judgment on friends and friendship)? The picture seems too complex to be settled by lines of simple dependence. This can be best illustrated by Miriam Lichtheim's study of the Egyptian demotic literature roughly contemporary with Ben Sira.[42] She concludes that the Instruction of Ankhsheshonq draws on "widely shared international sapiential topics, treated in the prevailing modes of aphoristic gnomologia." This work reflects the sayings of Ahiqar as well as Hellenistic themes and concerns. Similarly for the Papyrus Insinger, which has many themes in common with Ben Sira: both have "reworked traditional sapiential topics in a modern spirit, one which reveals acquaintance with the internal culture of Hellenism." In short, much more study is needed to detect the lines of dependence.

Wisdom of Solomon

It is clear from the discussion of the Wisdom of Solomon (chap. 6) that the writer was considerably influenced by Greek thought, and hence there is little need to rehearse the material laid out by the studies of C. Larcher, J. Reese, D. Winston, and Burton Mack, which have already been indicated. It should be noted, however, that the dependence of the writer on Greek ideas is not mechanical. The author remained intensely Jewish, while writing in a Hellenistic milieu and borrowing freely from it.[43]

Conclusion: Israel and Her Neighbors

Biblical scholarship has been marked frequently by exciting discoveries of artifacts and texts from the ancient Near East. Perhaps the Dead Sea Scrolls come to mind as the most dramatic of the recent discoveries. Drama usually involves exaggeration and fanfare, but it takes several years of patient analysis of texts before one can come to sound conclusions. The comparison between Israel and her neighbors in the area of wisdom has been fruitful, and that is the whole purpose of this Appendix. We want to see the broad picture, to establish some relationships, without necessarily claiming dependence of one upon the other. One may readily grant dependence in the specific case of Prov 22:17ff. and the wisdom of Amenemope. But the broader issue is to situate Israelite wisdom in its historical milieu. What general conclusions can be drawn?

First, it is important to recognize that a precedent for this kind of literature existed long before Israel. Second, although the precise life setting varies from one area to another, a great similarity lies in the didactic situation that is common to all. The similarity can be more or less outstanding from culture to culture, but a certain common basis is provided. The hard question is the determination of the influence of one upon another (e.g., Hellenism and Qoheleth). However, one can point to remarkable similarities between the Book of Proverbs and the Egyptian wisdom—for example, common features such as "my son" and "hear!" There are common themes (e.g., discipline—control as opposed to lack of control, the "silent" one as opposed to the rash or "heated" person). There are virtues shared in common: speaking well; table manners; diligence; honesty; one's attitude toward the divinity; and so forth. In both there is reliance upon experience and tradition. Finally, the comparative approach has not been limited in biblical studies to one type of literature, as the comparison of the covenant with ancient treaties has shown. Careful comparisons have illustrated the entire range of biblical literature, and they enable us to understand more clearly the issues in the Bible itself.

Notes to Appendix

1. Cf. G. Buccellati, "Wisdom and Not: The Case of Mesopotamia," *JAOS* 101/1 (1981) 35–47; the quotation is from p. 44. W. G. Lambert points out that the Babylonian term for "wisdom" is quite unlike the Hebrew *ḥokmāh*. It generally refers to skill in cult and magic. However, "wisdom" has been used "for a group of texts which correspond in subject-matter with the Hebrew Wisdom books, and may be retained as a convenient short description." See *BWL*, 1.

2. On the Mesopotamian lists, see A. L. Oppenheim, *Ancient Mesopotamia* (Chicago: University of Chicago Press, 1964) 244–49. He resolutely refuses to see here "such a quasi-mythological concept as *Ordnungswille*, according to which the scribes who made these lists aimed at 'organizing' the universe around them by listing what they saw of it in word signs" (p. 248). The Egyptian Onomastica will be treated later; see n. 26.

3. Cf. Bendt Alster, *The Instructions of Suruppak* (Mesopotamica 2; Copenhagen: Akademisk Forlag, 1974).

4. Cf. E. I. Gordon, *Sumerian Proverbs* (Philadelphia: University of Pennsylvania Museum, 1959).

5. E. I. Gordon, "A New Look at the Wisdom of Sumer and Akkad," *BO* 17 (1960) 122–52.

6. There is a huge literature about this personage. See the illuminating interpretation of Thorkild Jacobsen, *The Treasures of Darkness* (New Haven: Yale University, 1976) 195–219.

7. Cf. H. Gese, *Lehre und Wirklichkeit in der alten Weisheit* (Tübingen: Mohr/ Siebeck, 1958). Essential to this form is the complaint, fully expressed, and the recourse to God by the one lamenting; cf. p. 63. Gese further thinks that the Book of Job breaks through the old deed-consequence mentality (cf. the discussion in chap. 8 concerning K. Koch) because of Yahwistic religion (pp. 70–78).

8. A new translation from the Aramaic, with detailed notes and introduction, has been presented by J. M. Lindenberger, *The Aramaic Proverbs of Ahiqar* (Baltimore: Johns Hopkins University Press, 1983). See also his translation in the *OTP*, II, 479–93.

9. Lindenberger, *The Proverbs of Ahiqar*, 25.

10. R. J. Williams, "The Sages of Ancient Egypt in the Light of Recent Scholarship," *JAOS* 101-1 (1981) 7.

11. Cf. H. Brunner, "Die Lehren," in *Handbuch der Orientalistik* (ed. H. Spuler; Leiden: Brill, 1970) 1st Abt., I/II, 113–39. See also K. A. Kitchen, "Egypt and Israel During the First Millennium B.C.," in *Congress Volume Jerusalem 1986* (VTSup 40; Leiden: Brill, 1988) 107–23, esp. 119ff.

12.   The literature on *ma'at* is enormous. Cf. W. H[elck], "Maat," in *Lexikon der Ägyptologie* (ed. W. Helck et al.; Wiesbaden: Harrassowitz, 1980) III, 1110–19; A. Volten, "Der Begriff der Maat in den ägyptischen Weisheitstexten," in *Les Sagesses du proche-orient ancien* (ed. J. Leclant; Paris: Presses universitaires, 1963) 73–101.

13.   See item 639 in James B. Pritchard (ed.), *The Ancient Near East in Pictures Relating to the Old Testament* (Princeton: Princeton University Press, 1964) 210 and 326.

14.   For such an image, see item 561 in Pritchard, *Ancient Near East in Pictures*, 188 and 317.

15.   Cf. Roland E. Murphy, "Religious Dimensions of Israelite Wisdom," in *Ancient Israelite Religion: Essays in Honor of Frank Moore Cross* (ed. P. Miller et al.; Philadelphia: Fortress, 1987) 449–58.

16.   Cf. Christa Kayatz, *Studien zu Proverbien 1–9* (WMANT 22; Neukirchen-Vluyn: Neukirchener, 1966) esp. 86–119.

17.   See the analysis in Kayatz, *Studien zu Proverbien 1–9*, 86–92, and also the treatment of *ma'at* that follows in the Appendix.

18.   An excellent drawing of the goddess *ma'at* is found in Kayatz, *Studien zu Proverbien 1–9*, opposite 105. See also the many representations in O. Keel, *Die Weisheit spielt vor Gott* (Fribourg: Universitätsverlag, 1974), beginning with figure 20; note the insignia of *ma'at* around the necks of officials in figures 23, 24. Even in a crowd, *ma'at* is always recognizable by the feather.

19.   See Kayatz, *Studien zu Proverbien 1–9*, 98–102 for the evidence.

20.   Michael V. Fox describes the religion of wisdom literature as "best designated as polytheism with a monistic perspective"; see his discussion in "Two Decades of Research in Egyptian Wisdom Literature," *ZÄS* 107 (1980) 120–35, esp. 125. Cf. also B. Couroyer, " 'Le Dieu des sages' en Egypte," *RB* 94 (1987) 574–603; 95 (1988) 70–91 and 195–210. For Couroyer, Egyptian "monotheism" is in fact henotheism: the worship of Thot, patron of scribes and the supreme god.

21.   Cf. Hans H. Schmid, *Wesen und Geschichte der Weisheit* (BZAW 101; Berlin: Töpelmann, 1966) 26–27; Horst D. Preuss, *Einführung in die alttestamentliche Weisheitsliteratur* (Urban-Taschenbücher 383; Stuttgart: Kohlhammer, 1987) 50–60.

22.   This description is based on the comments of Fox, "Two Decades," 127–28, with the quotation taken from p. 128.

23.   W. McKane, *Proverbs* (OTL; Philadelphia: Westminster, 1970) 56.

24.   See *AEL* III, 185, and esp. Miriam Lichtheim, "Observations on Papyrus Insinger," in *Studien zu altägyptischen Lebenslehren* (OBO 28; ed. E. Horning and O. Keel; Fribourg: Universitätsverlag, 1979) 283–305, and also Miriam Lichtheim, *Late Egyptian Wisdom Literature in the International Context* (OBO 52; Fribourg: Universitätsverlag, 1983).

25. Various interpretations of the work are summarized by Fox, "Two Decades," 134.

26. Cf. A. H. Gardiner, *Ancient Egyptian Onomastica* (London: Oxford University Press, 1947).

27. Gerhard von Rad, "Job and Ancient Egyptian Wisdom," in *SAIW*, 267–77.

28. Cf. Michael V. Fox, "Egyptian Onomastica and Biblical Wisdom," *VT* 36 (1986) 302–10, and also D. Hillers, "A Study of Psalm 148," *CBQ* 40 (1978) 323–34. See also A. L. Oppenheim, *Ancient Mesopotamia*, 244–49.

29. Cf. Martin Hengel, *Judaism and Hellenism* (Philadelphia: Fortress, 1974) I, 107. For a fuller orientation to wisdom in this period, see Max Küchler, *Frühjüdische Weisheitstraditionen* (OBO 26; Fribourg: Universitätsverlag, 1979).

30. Cf. initially M. Dahood, "Canaanite-Phoenician Influence in Qoheleth," *Bib* 33 (1952) 30–52, 191–221, followed by several later studies; C. F. Whitley, *Koheleth* (BZAW 148; Berlin: de Gruyter, 1979) 165–75, argues for Epicurean influence on Qoheleth.

31. Cf. O. Loretz, *Qohelet und der alte Orient* (Freiburg: Herder, 1964) 90–134. His list of seventy-one topoi that Qoheleth shares with other biblical works is particularly valuable (pp. 197–200). Loretz also answers effectively the older arguments (from the turn of the century) about Greek influence.

32. Cf. P. Humbert, *Recherches sur les sources égyptiennes sur la littérature sapientiale d'Israël* (Neuchâtel: Delachaux & Niestlé, 1929); K. Galling, "Der Prediger," in *Die fünf Megilloth* (HAT 18; Tübingen: Mohr/Siebeck, 1969) 77.

33. Hengel, *Judaism and Hellenism*, I, 115–26.

34. Cf. R. Braun, *Kohelet und die frühhellenistische Populärphilosophie* (BZAW 130; Berlin: de Gruyter, 1973) esp. 156–59 for a list of Hellenistic parallels.

35. Cf. O. Kaiser, "Judentum und Hellenismus," in O. Kaiser, *Der Mensch unter dem Schicksal* (BZAW 161; Berlin: de Gruyter, 1985) 138–40.

36. This is the question of J. Loader, who grants that Ecclesiastes contains "elements from early Hellenistic philosophy"; Cf. J. Loader, *Polar Structures in the Book of Qohelet* (BZAW 152; Berlin: de Gruyter, 1979) 129.

37. N. Lohfink, *Kohelet* (Die Neue Echter Bibel; Würzburg: Echter, 1980) 11–13.

38. Diethelm Michel observes that for the moment the pendulum has swung toward acceptance of Hellenistic influence; cf. *Qohelet* (EF 258; Darmstadt: Wissenschaftliche Buchgesellschaft, 1988) 52; see his discussion on pp. 58–65.

39. Cf. Hengel, *Judaism and Hellenism*, I, 131. His conclusion, quoted in the next paragraph, is from p. 249.

40. Th. Middendorp, *Die Stellung Jesu Ben Siras zwischen Judentum und Hellenismus* (Leiden: Brill, 1973) 8–24. Middendorp characterizes Sirach as a schoolbook executed according to Hellenistic standards. However, there is only one such school-

book that can be dated approximately from this period (ca. 225); it is an anthology of selections from Euripides, Homer, and other Greek writers. From such a work, Middendorp thinks, Ben Sira would presumably have drawn some of his knowledge of Hellenistic culture (he already knew Theognis). See the conclusions on pp. 32–34, 48–49. As a balance, see the moderate conclusions of J. Marböck, *Weisheit im Wandel* (BBB 37; Bonn: Hanstein, 1971) 160–73. Lichtheim, *Late Egyptian Wisdom Literature*, 185 describes the situation thus: "Ben Sira's knowledge of Hellenistic culture is beyond dispute; only its extent and the attitude in which he responded to Hellenism have been variously interpreted."

41. J. T. Sanders, *Ben Sira and Demotic Wisdom* (SBLMS 28; Chico: Scholars Press, 1983).

42. Lichtheim, *Late Egyptian Wisdom Literature;* the quotations are from pp. 65 and 185.

43. The writer's relationship to Hellenism has been described by M. Gilbert:

> The originality of Wisdom may be seen from the way it assimilates Hellenistic culture. Not only does the author write in Greek, use a Greek literary genre and take over, with due modifications, the Stoic doctrine of *pneuma*, but closely akin to the Bible though he is, he adopts the imagery, vocabulary and theories of contemporary Stoicism, a component of Middle Platonism. But he shows no mastery of these philosophies. His knowledge, indirect, seems to derive only from his general education. This may be illustrated by two points. In Wis 13:1–9, the author seems clearly to be discussing a doctrine coming from the lost works of Aristotle, according to which the nature of the divine can be known from the world as a starting-point. But he eliminates the pantheistic tendencies of this doctrine by stating that recourse must also be made to the analogy of proportionality. Then, he adopts the Hellenistic doctrine of "philanthropia". This virtue, composed of goodness, kindness and mercy, is found, he says, in God (12:8) and in wisdom (1:6; 7:23). And Israel should imitate its God by practising it towards its enemies (12:19). The universalism of the author of Wisdom goes beyond that of his predecessors in the Bible.

Cf. M. Gilbert, "Wisdom Literature," in *Jewish Writings of the Second Temple Period* (CRJNT 2; ed. M. E. Stone; Philadelphia: Fortress, 1984) 283–324, esp. 312.

ABBREVIATIONS

◆

AB	Anchor Bible
AEL	Miriam Lichtheim, *Ancient Egyptian Literature* (Berkeley: University of California Press, 1975–80) 3 vols.
AnBib	Analecta Biblica
ANET	James B. Pritchard (ed.), *Ancient Near Eastern Texts Relating to the Old Testament* (Princeton: Princeton University Press, 1950; 3rd ed. with supplement, 1978)
AnGreg	Analecta Gregoriana
AOAT	Alter Orient und Altes Testament
APOT	R. H. Charles (ed.), *Apocrypha and Pseudepigrapha of the Old Testament* (Oxford: Clarendon Press, 1913)
ATD	Altes Testament Deutsch
AzTh	Arbeiten zur Theologie
BASOR	*Bulletin of the American Schools of Oriental Research*
BBB	Bonner Biblische Beiträge
BEATAJ	Beiträge zur Erforschung des Alten Testaments und des antiken Judentums
BES	Biblical Encounter Series
BET	Beiträge zur biblischen Exegese und Theologie
BETL	Bibliotheca ephemeridum theologicarum lovaniensium
BevT	Beiträge zur evangelischen Theologie
Bib	*Biblica*
BibInt	*Biblical Interpretation*
Bij	*Bijdragen*
BKAT	Biblischer Kommentar: Altes Testament
BLS	Bible and Literature Series
BN	*Biblische Notizen*
BO	*Bibliotheca Orientalis*
BRev	*Biblical Review*
BTB	*Biblical Theology Bulletin*

BWANT	Beiträge zur Wissenschaft vom Alten und Neuen Testament
BWL	W. G. Lambert, *Babylonian Wisdom Literature* (Oxford: Clarendon Press, 1960)
BZAW	Beihefte zur *Zeitschrift für die alttestamentliche Wissenschaft*
BZNW	Beihefte zur *Zeitschrift für die neutestamentliche Wissenschaft*
CB	Coniectanea Biblica
CBQ	*Catholic Biblical Quarterly*
CBQMS	Catholic Biblical Quarterly — Monograph Series
CCSL	Corpus Christianorum — Series Latina
CRJNT	Compendia Rerum Judaicarum ad Novum Testamentum
CSBS	*Currents in Research, Biblical Studies*
CTM	Calwer theologische Monographien
DBSup	*Dictionnaire de la Bible, Supplement*
DNEB	Die Neue Echter Bibel
EBib	Etudes Bibliques
EF	Erträge der Forschung
Eng. ·	English translation
ETL	*Ephemerides theologicae lovanienses*
FAT	Forschungen zum Alten Testament
FOTL	Forms of the Old Testament Literature
GHAT	Göttingen Handkommentar zum Alten Testament
HAR	*Hebrew Annual Review*
HAT	Handbuch zum Alten Testament
HBC	J. L. Mays (ed.), *Harper's Bible Commentary* (San Francisco: Harper & Row, 1988)
HBIS	History of Biblical Interpretation Series
HBMI	D. Knight and G. Tucker (eds.), *The Hebrew Bible and Its Modem Interpreters* (Philadelphia: Fortress, 1985)
HBS	Herder Biblische Studien
HBT	*Horizons in Biblical Theology*
HS	*Hebrew Studies*
HTR	*Harvard Theological Review*
HUCA	*Hebrew Union College Annual*
ICC	International Critical Commentary
IDBSup	Supplementary volume to *The Interpreter's Dictionary of the Bible*
Int	*Interpretation*
IRT	Issues in Religion and Theology
ISBE	*International Standard Bible Encyclopedia*
JAAR	*Journal of the American Academy of Religion*

JANES	*Journal of the Ancient Near Eastern Society*
JAOS	*Journal of the American Oriental Society*
JBL	*Journal of Biblical Literature*
JSOT	*Journal for the Study of the Old Testament*
JSOTSup	Journal for the Study of the Old Testament — Supplementary Series
JTS	*Journal of Theological Studies*
KAT	Kommentar zum Alten Testament
KBW	Katholisches Bibelwerk
LAE	W. K. Simpson (ed.), *The Literature of Ancient Egypt* (2nd ed.; New Haven: Yale University Press, 1973)
LSB	La Sacra Bibbia
LUA	Lunds universitets årsskrift
LXX	Septuagint
MT	Masoretic text
NAB	*New American Bible*
NBl	*New Blackfriars*
NEB	*New English Bible*
NJB	*New Jerusalem Bible*
NJBC	R. E. Brown, J. A. Fitzmyer, and Roland E. Murphy (eds.), *The New Jerome Biblical Commentary* (Englewood Cliffs: Prentice-Hall, 1990)
NJV	*New Jewish Version (Tanakh — The Holy Scriptures)*
NRSV	*New Revised Standard Version*
OBO	Orbis biblicus et orientalis
OTA	*Old Testament Abstracts*
OTG	Old Testament Guides
OTL	Old Testament Library
OTP	J. Charlesworth (ed.), *The Old Testament Pseudepigrapha* (Garden City: Doubleday, 1983–85) 2 vols.
QD	Quaestiones Disputatae
RB	*Revue Biblique*
RivBibSup	Supplementi alla Rivista Biblica
RSV	*Revised Standard Version*
SAIW	J. L. Crenshaw (ed.), *Studies in Ancient Israelite Wisdom* (New York: KTAV, 1976)
SANT	Studien zum Alten und Neuen Testament
SB	Sources Bibliques
SBL	Society of Biblical Literature
SBLEJL	Society of Biblical Literature Early Judaism and Its Literature
SBLDS	SBL Dissertation Series

ABBREVIATIONS

SBLMS	SBL Monograph Series
SBLSCS	SBL Septuagint and Cognate Studies
SBS	Stuttgarter Bibelstudien
SBT	Studies in Biblical Theology
SPCK	Society for Promoting Christian Knowledge
SOR	Studies in Oriental Religions
S.T.	*Summa Theologica*
SUNT	Studien zur Umwelt des Neuen Testaments
SWBAS	The Social World of Biblical Antiquity Series
TB	Theologische Bücherei
TD	*Theology Digest*
TDNT	*Theological Dictionary of the New Testament*
TDOT	*Theological Dictionary of the Old Testament*
TEH	Theologische Existenz heute
THAT	*Theologisches Handwörterbuch zum Alten Testament*
ThRu	*Theologische Rundschau*
TOTC	Tyndale Old Testament Commentary
TQ	*Theologische Quartalschrift*
TS	*Theological Studies*
TTS	Trierer theologische Studien
VF	*Verkündigung und Forschung*
VSAT	Verbum Salutis Ancien Testament
VT	*Vetus Testamentum*
VTSup	Vetus Testamentum Supplements
WF	Wege der Forschung
WBC	Word Biblical Commentary
WMANT	Wissenschaftliche Monographien zum Alten und Neuen Testament
ZAS	*Zeitschrift für ägyptische Sprache und Altertumskunde*
ZAW	*Zeitschrift für die alttestamentliche Wissenschaft*
ZB	Zürcher Bibelkommentare
ZTK	*Zeitschrift für Theologie und Kirche*

SELECTED AND ANNOTATED BIBLIOGRAPHY

◆

The notes in this work cover a wide range of pertinent studies, but an annotated bibliography will be more serviceable to the general reader. Previous bibliographical reports can be found in *JAOS* 101-1 (1981) 21–34 (Roland E. Murphy) and in *HBMI*, 369–407 (J. L. Crenshaw). It is possible to keep up to date by perusing the entries in the Elenchus of *Biblica*, and the surveys in *OTA*.

I. *Encyclopedia Articles*
   These are very helpful for a general orientation to the field, and they are usually written by experts.
   IDBSup, 949–52 (R. J. Williams and J. L. Crenshaw). Williams was a specialist in Egyptian literature; see also his contribution in *JAOS* 101-1 (1981) 3–20.
   TDNT, VIII, 476–96 (G. Fohrer), reproduced in *SAIW*, 63–83.
   TDOT, IV, 364–85 (H.-P. Müller, M. Krause).
   ISBE, IV, 1074–82 (Gerald T. Sheppard).
   THAT, I, 557–67 (M. Saebo).
   DBSup, XI, 4–58 (A. Vanel).

II. *Anthologies*
   J. L. Crenshaw (ed.), *Studies in Ancient Israelite Wisdom* (New York: KTAV, 1976). These articles, by various authors here and abroad, illustrate the growth of scholarly interest in the wisdom books.
   P. Skehan, *Studies in Israelite Poetry and Wisdom* (CBQMS 1; Washington: Catholic Biblical Association, 1971). A valuable collection of the perceptive articles (updated) by an outstanding scholar.
   M. Gilbert (ed.), *La Sagesse de l'Ancien Testament* (BETL 51; Leuven: University Press, 1979). A collection of papers read (in several languages) at the Nineteenth Louvain Biblical Colloquium (1978).
   J. Leclant (ed.), *Les Sagesses du proche-orient ancien* (Paris: Presses universitaires, 1963). A collection of papers concerning ancient Near Eastern wisdom, given at the Strasbourg Colloquium, 1962.
   M. Noth and D. Thomas (eds.), *Wisdom in Israel and in the Ancient Near East* (VTSup 3; Leiden: Brill, 1955). A Festschrift in honor of H. H. Rowley that illustrates where wisdom studies were ca. 1950.

J. G. Gammie et al. (eds.), *Israelite Wisdom* (Missoula: Scholars Press, 1978). Festschrift in honor of S. Terrien. A wide coverage, from Ugarit to Qumran.

J. G. Gammie and L. Perdue (eds.), *The Sage in Israel and the Ancient Near East* (Winona Lake, Ind.: Eisenbrauns, 1990).

III. *General Works*

A. M. Dubarle, *Les Sages d'Israël* (Paris: du cerf, 1946). Still valuable for its careful analysis of individual books.

H. Duesberg and I. Fransen, *Les Scribes inspirés* (Paris: Desclée, 1939) 2 vols. Strong emphasis on courtly ties of early wisdom. Extensive summaries of content, but somewhat prolix.

Horst D. Preuss, *Einführung in die alttestamentliche Weisheitsliteratur* (Urban-Taschenbücher 383; Stuttgart: Kohlhammer, 1987). An excellent introduction, but marred by several presuppositions, among them the notion that wisdom is foreign to the "Yahwistic" doctrine known from the rest of the Old Testament.

Gerhard von Rad, *Wisdom in Israel* (Nashville: Abingdon, 1972). Without equal (see the Introduction).

J. Fichtner, *Die altorientalische Weisheit in ihrer israelitisch-jüdischen Ausprägung* (BZAW 62; Giessen: Töpelmann, 1933). At one time the standard reference work on wisdom, and it still has some value.

Max Küchler, *Frühjüdische Weisheitstraditionen* (OBO 26; Fribourg: Universitäts-verlag, 1979). This work carries forward the studies by Fichtner and Schmid, offering a view of wisdom in writers of the intertestamental period, and in rabbinical and Christian sources.

Hans H. Schmid, *Wesen und Geschichte der Weisheit* (BZAW 101; Berlin: Töpelmann, 1966). This work replaced Fichtner as a standard reference. It treats of Mesopotamian, Egyptian, and Israelite wisdom according to the author's view of the evolution of thought (similar in all three); it is provided with selections from extrabib-lical wisdom books.

Roland E. Murphy, *Wisdom Literature* (FOTL 13; Grand Rapids: Eerdmans, 1981). An analysis of the various literary forms found in wisdom literature.

Gerald T. Sheppard, *Wisdom as a Hermeneutical Construct* (BZAW 151; Berlin: de Gruyter, 1980). The author analyzes several "test" cases in late wisdom, showing how the Old Testament was viewed through the lens of wisdom.

R. N. Whybray, *The Intellectual Tradition in the Old Testament* (BZAW 135; Berlin: de Gruyter, 1974). The writer argues in favor of an intellectual tradition formed by men of superior intelligence who passed on their insights, as opposed to such a tradition conceived by a professional class of sages.

IV. *Textbooks*

R. E. Brown, J. A. Fitzmyer, and Roland E. Murphy (eds.), *The New Jerome Biblical Commentary* (Englewood Cliffs: Prentice-Hall, 1990). This contains a general article on the wisdom literature and specific succinct commentaries on the five wisdom books.

J. Blenkinsopp, *Wisdom and Law in the Old Testament* (New York: Oxford, 1983). Oriented more to law than to wisdom.

J. L. Crenshaw, *Old Testament Wisdom* (Atlanta: Knox, 1981). A general survey of all the wisdom books, including deuterocanonicals.

V. *Proverbs*

a. Commentaries:

B. Gemser, *Sprüche* (HAT 10; 2nd ed.; Tübingen: Mohr/Siebeck, 1963). Succinct comments on chaps. 1–9; essay style for chaps. 10ff.

A. Barucq, *Le Livre des Proverbes* (SB; Paris: Gabalda, 1964). Particular attention given to the LXX. After chaps. 1–9, the commentary is topical. See also his valuable entry in *DBSup*, VIII, 1395–1476.

L. Alonso Schökel, *Proverbios* (Madrid: Ediciones cristiandad, 1984). A very original commentary, with special attention to literary aspects.

W. McKane, *Proverbs* (OTL; Philadelphia: Westminster, 1970). Learned and acute, but marred by presuppositions in the classification of three levels of sayings. There is also an extensive introduction to ancient Near Eastern wisdom literature.

O. Plöger, *Sprüche Salomos* (*Proverbia*) (BKAT 13; Neukirchen-Vluyn: Neukirchener, 1984). Scholarly and clear, with an attempt to find context for the disparate sayings.

Two older commentaries in English are still quite valuable: C. H. Toy in ICC series (1899, and reprinted) and F. Delitzsch in the Keil & Delitzsch Commentary (German original 1872, and translation reprinted).

b. Studies:

G. Bryce, *A Legacy of Wisdom* (Lewisburg: Bucknell, 1979). The most recent study of the Instruction of Amenemope and Proverbs 22:17ff.

Claudia Camp, *Wisdom and the Feminine in the Book of Proverbs* (BLS 11; Sheffield: Almond Press, 1985). An original study that demonstrates the pertinence of the title.

J. D. Crossan (ed.), *Gnomic Wisdom* (Semeia 17; Chico: Scholars Press, 1980). A collection of valuable essays, especially those of John J. Collins and J. G. Williams.

Carole R. Fontaine, *Traditional Sayings in the Old Testament* (BLS 5; Sheffield: Almond Press, 1982). An approach to Old Testament wisdom sayings by way of modern paroemiology.

H.-J. Hermisson, *Studien zur israelitischen Spruchweisheit* (WMANT 28; Neukirchen-Vluyn: Neukirchener, 1968). A historical and literary analysis of the sayings in Prov 10ff.

Elizabeth Huwiler, "Control of Reality in Israelite Wisdom" (Duke University dissertation, 1988). A perceptive study of the mentality of Israel's sages. Forthcoming in a *JSOT* series.

B. Lang, *Die weisheitliche Lehrrede* (SBS 54; Stuttgart: KBW, 1972). An analysis of the poems in Prov 1–9.

B. Lang, *Frau Weisheit* (Düsseldorf: Patmos, 1975), revised and translated as *Wisdom and the Book of Proverbs: An Israelite Goddess Redefined* (New York: Pilgrim, 1986). An erudite and penetrating analysis of Lady Wisdom in Prov 1, 8, 9, dependent upon the author's hypothetical reconstruction of Israelite religion.

J. G. Williams, *Those Who Ponder Proverbs* (BLS 2; Sheffield: Almond Press, 1981). A provocative study of the aphorisms in Proverbs as both poetic and philosophical.

SELECTED AND ANNOTATED BIBLIOGRAPHY

VI. *Job*

a. Commentaries: out of the many that could be mentioned, the following can be noted:

F. Andersen, *Job* (TOTC; Downers Grove: Intervarsity, 1976). Cautious but informed treatment of MT.

E. Dhorme, *A Commentary on the Book of Job* (Nashville: Nelson, 1967). Learned and detailed.

G. Fohrer, *Das Buch Hiob* (KAT 16; Gütersloh: Mohn, 1963). Erudite, with excellent treatment of form-critical problems.

N. Habel, *The Book of Job* (OTL; Philadelphia: Westminster, 1985). Careful, learned, and clear.

J. G. Janzen, *Job* (Interpretation; Atlanta: Knox, 1985). Creative and stimulating.

M. Pope, *Job* (AB 15; 3rd ed.; Garden City: Doubleday, 1979). Insightful, and strong on Ugaritic connection.

H. H. Rowley, *Job* (repr. Grand Rapids: Eerdmans, 1980). Solid and clear comment.

L. Alonso Schökel, *Job* (Madrid: Ediciones cristiandad, 1983). A literary and theological commentary.

b. Studies:

D. Cox, *The Triumph of Impotence* (AnGreg 212; Rome: Gregorian, 1978). An interpretation of Job's "victory."

J. Lévêque, *Job et son Dieu* (EBib; Paris: Gabalda, 1970) 2 vols. Very complete, but prolix.

M. Tsevat, "The Meaning of the Book of Job," *HUCA* 37 (1966) 73–106.

R. Polzin and D. Robertson, *Studies in the Book of Job* (Semeia 7; Missoula: Scholars Press, 1977). Challenging interpretations.

Gustavo Gutiérrez, *On Job* (Maryknoll: Orbis, 1987). Reading Job as a lesson in how to speak of God from the viewpoint of the suffering of the innocent.

VII. *Qoheleth*

a. Commentaries:

E. Podechard, *L'Ecclésiaste* (EBib; Paris: Gabalda, 1912). Still one of the best, despite his theory of later glosses.

A. Barucq, *Ecclésiaste* (VSAT 3; Paris: Beauchesne, 1967). Succinct and insightful. See also his entry in *DBSup*, IX, 609–74.

W. Zimmerli, "Das Buch des Predigers Salomo," in *Sprüche/Prediger* (ATD 16/1; Gottingen: Vandenhoeck & Ruprecht, 1962). A solid theological commentary.

K. Galling, "Der Prediger," in *Die fünf Megilloth* (HAT 18; 2nd ed.; Tubingen: Mohr/Siebeck, 1969). Succinct, but on target.

A. Lauha, *Kohelet* (BKAT 19; Neukirchen-Vluyn: Neukirchener, 1978). A disappointment.

N. Lohfink, *Kohelet* (Die Neue Echter Bibel; Würzburg: Echter, 1980). Very original and stimulating—commenting on the *Einheitsübersetzung* (the ecumenical version of the Bible for German-speaking areas), but going beyond it.

R. Gordis, *Koheleth—The Man and His World* (New York: Schocken, 1968). A solid and clear commentary.

J. L. Crenshaw, *Ecclesiastes* (OTL; Philadelphia: Westminster, 1987). An introduction, a new translation, and appropriate commentary.

Addison Wright, "Ecclesiastes," in *NJBC*, 489–95. Succinct and to the point; particularly valuable for his comments on the structure of the book.

b. Studies:

O. Loretz, *Qohelet und der alte Orient* (Freiburg: Herder, 1964). A valuable presentation of the literary style and theological themes in the light of ancient Near Eastern parallels.

Diethelm Michel, *Qohelet* (EF 258; Darmstadt: Wissenschaftliche Buchgesellschaft, 1988). An up-to-date and clear summary of the usual introductory questions, with a brief exposition of the author's own interpretations. More details are to be found in his *Untersuchungen zur Eigenart des Buches Qohelet* (BZAW 183; Berlin: de Gruyter, 1989).

Michael V. Fox, *Qohelet and His Contradictions* (JSOTSup 18; Sheffield: Almond Press, 1989). A presentation of Qoheleth as a philosopher of the absurd, with a succinct but meaty commentary; the best available study in English at the present time.

VIII. *Sirach*

a. Commentaries:

P. Skehan and A. Di Lella, *The Wisdom of Ben Sira* (AB 39; Garden City: Doubleday, 1987). Outstanding for its textual and literary analysis. Particular attention needs to be given to *any* translation of this book; is it merely from the Greek, or from a critically established text?

b. Studies:

J. Haspecker, *Gottesfurcht bei Jesus Sirach* (AnBib 30; Rome: Biblical Institute, 1967). Shows how "fear of the Lord" is a dominant theme in Sirach.

J. Marböck, *Weisheit im Wandel* (BBB 37; Bonn: Hanstein, 1971). A study of the theology of Sirach.

Burton Mack, *Wisdom and the Hebrew Epic* (Chicago: University of Chicago Press, 1985). A provocative study of Sir 44–50.

IX. *Wisdom of Solomon*

a. Commentaries:

Many of the older commentaries (A. Goodrick, J. Gregg, P. Heinisch, J. Fichtner, etc.) are still of value. See the very complete bibliography of M. Gilbert in C. Larcher, *Salomon*, I, 11–48 (see below).

C. Larcher, *Etudes sur le livre de la Sagesse* (EBib; Paris: Gabalda, 1969). An excellent study of the theology of the book and its relationship to Hellenistic thought.

C. Larcher, *Le Livre de la Sagesse ou La Sagesse de Salomon* (EBib; Paris: Gabalda, 1983–85) 3 vols. The best and most complete commentary, if somewhat prolix at times.

D. Winston, *The Wisdom of Solomon* (AB 43; Garden City: Doubleday, 1979). Strong on Hellenistic contacts, especially with Philo.

Addison Wright, "Wisdom," in the *NJBC*, 510–22. The best short commentary there is on this book.

b. Studies:

J. Reese, *Hellenistic Influence on the Book of Wisdom and Its Consequences* (AnBib 41; Rome: Biblical Institute, 1970). It lives up to its title.

M. Gilbert, "Sagesse de Salomon," *DBSup*, XI, 58–119. A splendid survey of introductory questions and the outstanding theological themes.

SUPPLEMENT

◆

The purpose of this Supplement is twofold: to make some helpful additions to the contents of each of the chapters in this book, and also to take into account some of the literature that has appeared since its initial publication several years ago. I am told that it has been used as a textbook in various colleges and seminaries. Such use would make an updating desirable. I see no reason for any major change in the main text, and the additions and modifications in this Supplement can be easily correlated with the discussions in each of the nine chapters. Another select and annotated bibliography is not necessary. Instead, it seems advisable to use the social science method of references in this Supplement. This makes for smoother reading, without the interruption of references to footnotes, and it provides a list of pertinent literature published in the last seven years. It will be obvious from the recent publications that research in the so-called wisdom books is steadily increasing. In addition to the general bibliographical aids indicated on **p. 185** above, the following deserve notice: The *Book List* of the Society for Old Testament Study (an annual from Britain); *Internationale Zeitschriftenschau für Bibel-wissenschaft und Grenzgebiete* (an annual, with very many entries in English), and of course the perennial *Elenchus of Biblica*.

Among the recent bibliographical treatments of wisdom literature, the following should be noted: H. Delkurt, "Grundprobleme alttestamentlicher Weisheit," *VF* 36 (1991) 38–72; C. Westermann, *Forschungsgeschichte zur Weisheitsliteratur 1950–90* (AzTh; Stuttgart: Calwer, 1991). As regards specific books, Proverbs has fared best; see the survey of the twentieth century by R. N. Whybray, *The Book of Proverbs* (HBIS 1; Leiden: Brill, 1995); cf. also R. E. Murphy, "Recent Research on Proverbs and Qoheleth," *CSBS* 1 (1993) 119–40; C. Newsom, "Considering Job," *CSBS* 1 (1993) 187–218; O. Kaiser, "Beiträge zur Kohelet-Forschung," *ThRu* 60 (1995) 1–31 (with a continuation in a forthcoming issue). On Ben Sira, see D. J. Harrington, "Sirach Research since 1965: Progress and Questions," in *Pursuing the Test* (B. Wacholder Festschrift; ed. J. Reeves and J. Kampen; JSOTSup 186; Sheffield: JSOT Press, 1995) 164–76.

CHAPTER 1:
INTRODUCTION

Page 3. Who were the sages? The answer to this question seems to become more and more problematic. To see this one need only peruse the answers presented for the various books and countries in *The Sage in Israel and the Ancient Near East*, edited by J. G. Gammie and L. G. Perdue (1990). Despite the efforts of scholars, there is no clear answer. Each book poses its own difficulties, and much depends upon the assumptions of the writers concerning wisdom literature and its development. One is tempted to adopt the position enunciated by R. N. Whybray (1974), who denied that there was a *class* of sages in Israel, proposing instead that those responsible for books classified as "wisdom" were intellectuals of various types. This point of view stands at one extreme, and it has some truth to it. But one must also try to deal with the royal associations of wisdom (e.g., what is the meaning of the association with Solomon, despite the historical uncertainty? See Prov 25:1 for the men of King Hezekiah). There is also the family or clan background that is maintained by C. Westermann (1995), and also by R. E. Murphy (1994: 199–212). One must keep in mind that we are dealing in this book with two different expressions of wisdom: proverbial wisdom or the wisdom of sayings, and didactic wisdom, the type found in the exhortatory poems in Prov 1–9, which are urgent in tone and also heavily weighted toward moral conduct.

The Egyptian "instructions" (see Appendix above, **pp. 160–62**) are usually considered to have influenced Prov 1–9, but this influence is not easy to measure. Surely there was a basic stratum of exhortations and prohibitions among Israelite folk. The problem becomes more complicated when one investigates the life setting of the various proverbial sayings and their collections. Who were the tradents? Ecclesiastes seems to find an easy answer; Qoheleth is described as a *ḥakam*, a wise man (Eccl 12:9), who taught the people. The situation seems to be the same about a century and a half later in the case of Ben Sira, whose work can be characterized as that of a scribe and teacher (Sir 51:23), well acquainted with both the Torah and traditional wisdom. The book of Job seems to be a tour de force in its final form, accomplished by one writer, even if it is judged to have been supplemented. In the end, we are woefully ignorant about the many writers who contributed to the wisdom corpus. Their skill in handling language has been graphically illustrated by T. McCreesh's study (1991) of the poetic sound patterns in Prov 10–31. But the concrete life situations of the wisdom writers escape us. M. Sneed (1994) has taken biblical scholars to task for failing to use social theory, especially sociology of knowledge ("modern sociological method"), to identify the class(es) of sages. But we really lack enough historical sociological data to pursue that path with security. At the present time, the study of M. Fox (1996) presents the most sober picture of the "social location" for Prov 10–29.

References

Fox, M. V.
1996   "The Social Location of the Book of Proverbs," in *Texts, Temples, and Traditions* (M. Haran Festschrift; ed. M. Fox et al.; Winona Lake, IN: Eisenbrauns). Pp. 227–39.

Gammie, J. G., and L. G. Perdue
1990   *The Sage in Israel and the Ancient Near East* (Winona Lake, IN: Eisenbrauns).

McCreesh, T.
1991   *Biblical Sound and Sense* (Sheffield: JSOT Press).

Murphy, R. E.
1994   "Israelite Wisdom and the Home," in *Où demeures-tu? La maison depuis le monde biblique* (Guy Couturier Festschrift; ed. J.-C. Petit et al.; Montreal: Fides). Pp. 199–212.

Sneed, M.
1994   "Wisdom and Class," *JAAR* 62/3: 651–71.

Westermann, C.
1995   *Roots of Wisdom* (Louisville: Westminster/John Knox).

Whybray, R. N.
1974   *The Intellectual Tradition in the Old Testament* (BZAW 135; Berlin: de Gruyter).

CHAPTER 2:
PROVERBS — THE WISDOM OF WORDS

Page 15. The list of collections. There is no denying that the book of Proverbs is ultimately the result of collections. But the description on this page is only a general framework. It is not misleading, but it is too broad in the judgment of the many scholars who have attempted a more detailed analysis of the composition of the book: D. C. Snell (1993: 80–81), T. A. Perry (1993), R. N. Whybray (1994), and R. Scoralick (1995: 238–43).

These studies are probably more profitable in their methodology than in their results. That is to say, any restoration of collections within collections remains hypothetical, but the close reading of the texts yields new insights into the sayings themselves. Snell's approach is by way of analysis of "twice-told proverbs," which many readers of the book might tend to overlook. He lays them out neatly and forces a reader to come to terms with such repetitiveness. One comes to realize that what seem to be boring repetitions are in fact interesting variations that lead to new insights. The study of Perry analyzes a saying from the point of view of its quadripartite structure, which he defines as "A *valuational topic* or its *opposite* in a series of *binary propositions* until the *(four)* logical possibilities have been exhausted" (p. 23). Whybray (1994: 159–65) finds Prov 1–9 and 31:10–31 to be the "framework" of the book, but he concludes on a modest note "that there is insufficient evidence to uncover the whole process by which the different sections of the book came to be arranged in their present order" (p. 165). Scoralick limits herself to Prov 10–15 and finds that another division begins at 15:33 (cf. the key word, *yhwh*, in 15:33 and 16:7). Within the six chapters she maintains that five units can be detected, with the middle being 12:14–13:2, a "nodal point," and it is itself an inclusion that unites the preceding with the following units. Whatever be the reception given to these studies of the structure of the book, they reward the reader by calling attention to deeper ties that unite what seems at first sight to be a haphazard collection. All these observations make for a more careful reading of the book (see my remarks on **p. 20** above).

Page 16. The vision of Prov 1–9. I think this vision is properly centered, even if what we see leaves us with several unanswered questions. It is filled with encouragement to the moral life; it has the urgent tone of Deuteronomy. But the detailed treatment of the "strange woman" remains a problem, as indicated on **pp. 17–18.** C. Newsom (1989) has written a challenging feminist analysis of these chapters that brings out their unmistakable patriarchalism. The symbolic structure of these chapters, she claims, indicates a phallocentric understanding of the world. The opposition between Woman Wisdom (chap. 8) and the strange woman is compared to the "gate of Heaven" and "the gate of Sheol" (p. 157), "the boundaries of the symbolic order of patriarchal wisdom." This may be one way of reading the material, but it gives short shrift to a broader and neutral reading that chaps. 1–9 would suggest. This is not the place to enlarge on the problem of patriarchalism in the Bible, but the discovery of it and the ensuing blame for the subjection of women should not blind one to the biblical message. That message is time-conditioned, but it is not a hopeless morass of patriarchalism. It would be a drastic mistake to think that Prov 1–9 (as well as most of the patriarchal Bible) has nothing to say to half of the human race. R. Clifford (1995: 7–8) openly admits the difficulty that the male world of Proverbs poses to the modern reader, but he points out that the book does not envision young men as the sole audience: "The introduction (1:1–7) states the intention explicitly, and the *intention* overrides implicit *assumptions.*" The individual who is being instructed by the sayings is a type, "further reducing the importance of the author's culture-bound assumption of a young man as subject. The major point of chapters 1–9 is the analogy between choosing a life partner and choosing wisdom. And that analogy transcends the original ancient Near Eastern social model."

Pages 19–29. The other collections. Only a few scholars would consider the collections of sayings to be preexilic. N. Shupak (1993) is one of these, and she has marshalled strong evidence for the relationship between the language of wisdom literature in Israel and in Egypt. The linguistic evidence is formidable, but does it support the claim that the "Egyptian connection" began with the reign of Solomon (pp. 14, 352–54)? There can be no doubt about the similarity (and the dependence on the part of Israel) between Prov 22–24 and the teaching of Amenemope (see **pp. 23–25** above). But the time and manner of this undoubted Egyptian influence is not easy to determine. Even though there are echoes of Egyptian wisdom elsewhere in chaps. 10–31, it is difficult to draw secure conclusions. S. Weeks has argued convincingly against "any supposed imitation of the Egyptian administration as evidence for the nature of Israelite wisdom" (1994: 131). Apropos of this, John Day (1995: 62–70) has pointed to West Semitic wisdom tradition as a source for Israelite wisdom, especially the Book of Proverbs, without denying Egyptian influence.

The above discussion is tied in with the problem of schools and education in Israel, and also with the orality of the proverbial sayings. The school question is still bitterly contested (see **pp. 3–4** and also **p. 13, n. 9**). A recent survey of the state of the question has been presented by G. I. Davies (1995: 199–211); he concludes, on the basis of direct and indirect evidence, that schools did exist, but this conclusion "must be qualified in several ways." Further, "much of Proverbs will have been drawn from traditional popular wisdom, which was disseminated in ways that remain unclear" (pp. 209–10). At the other end of the spectrum is the recent study of C. Westermann, who insists on the oral transmission of the proverbial sayings (1995). This does not of itself preclude a setting in schools, especially when sayings were reduced to writing, but there are many uncertainties. For Westermann the transition from oral to written form is very important, for it coincides with a transition from short saying to didactic poem, from experiential observation to more abstract thinking about wisdom (pp. 108–10, 133–34).

One of the striking characteristics of the book is the frequency of the righteous/wicked contrast, especially in Prov 10–15 (according to Scoralick [1995: 86], in 49 of the 184 verses). Almost all of Prov 10–15 is expressed in the so-called antithetic parallelism (according to Scoralick, p. 55, about half of those that are not antithetic occur in 15:9ff.). There is a tendency to equate righteous with wise and wicked with foolish, but Scoralick (pp. 67–73) points out that the textual evidence for this synonymous understanding is very slim (some texts are problematical, such as 11:30 and 14:9; but there are a few that support this understanding: 9:9; 23:24). This lack of textual evidence contradicts the identification of wisdom with righteousness and folly with wickedness, which is expressed above on **p. 15** and elsewhere. Yet the frequency of the contrast and the often implicit identification of wisdom with righteousness cannot simply be waved aside; it must have some implications. One question arises immediately: why were so many righteous/wicked sayings incorporated into the wisdom corpus? Some connection between wisdom and virtue must have been recognized. The thrust of the opening chapters surely suggests this. When "fear of the Lord" can be touted as the beginning of wisdom, the orientation to virtue is unmistakable. The preoccupation of the sages with moral conduct is clear, and this seems to be the basis for the identification of wisdom and virtue, despite the lack of explicit parallelisms in the text.

A far-reaching concern of C. Westermann (1995: 76–77) is his contrast of truly oral experiential sayings with the conceptual and schematic statements about the just and the wicked. He concludes that the latter "are artificially constructed. Their purpose is to propound a teaching or theory" (p. 76). Whatever their origin, he notes that the contrast itself is found also in Psalms and Job, especially. The statistics he lists for the term "wicked" (rāšā‛) are striking: "out of 203 occurrences in the Old Testament, 78 are found in Proverbs . . . 82 in the Psalms and 26 in Job" (p. 81). This emphasis on the wicked is balanced by a study of C. Levin (1993) that bears the significant title, "The Prayer of the Righteous." It is a study of the psalter in terms of references to the righteous. He finds that 42 of the 150 psalms portray the contrast between the righteous and the wicked. If synonyms of the term "righteous" are included, then 89 of the 150 psalms deal with the contrast. A certain reinterpretation of wisdom is postulated in the late period, and he gives Prov 29:15–17 as an example (pp. 373–74). The parade example, of course, is the introductory Psalm 1. But despite these studies, there is no easy explanation of the frequency and nature of the just/wicked sayings in chaps. 10–15 of Proverbs.

There can be no denying the clearly religious tone of postexilic wisdom compositions. Indeed, it was in this period that most of the wisdom heritage became literature. But I am unwilling to conclude that it was not religious in the preexilic period as well, in agreement with L. Boström (1990: 31–45). The influential study of R. Albertz (1994) has reinforced the assumption of "personal religion" in the postexilic period (2:493–522; German ed., 2:536–76). In his view there is a sharp division between the upper and lower classes in Judean society. A social crisis appeared already in the eighth and seventh centuries (the Deuteronomic reform?), but in the postexilic period there is a cleft in the upper class, some of whom are in sympathy with the poor lower class and some of whom are not. It is this split that Albertz purports to find in Job and Psalms, and it dominates the background of his understanding of the righteous/wicked cleavage in Proverbs (see pp. 512–13). He describes the "piety of the poor" thus: "In all probability, the social split in the community of Judah in the second half of the fifth century, after first beginning in the late pre-exilic period, also led to the formation of a special personal piety in the impoverished lower class, to the so-called 'piety of the poor'" (p. 518). He becomes very detailed in describing the situation (p. 501). The upper class who accepted the social obligations of their religion

> began with school education: they inserted into the collections of prov-erbs used above all by the children of the upper class in learning to read and write a whole series of proverbs about the wicked and the pious, in order to give adolescents a black-and-white picture of the two social alternatives between which they had to choose. . . . It has already frequently been noted that the proverbs about the wicked and the pious, which occur over and over again, keep stating in an almost incantatory undertone how evil the wicked man is and what a fearful fate he is going to meet. This can be explained from the purpose of the pious upper class to immunize the children of the well-to-do as early as possible against the option of not showing solidarity which was presented to them by many of their parents. (P. 501)

This description of postexilic society, with its implications for Proverbs, is terribly hypothetical, and only time will tell if it will gain a consensus. There is much circular reasoning at work in this reconstruction. There is no gain-saying the frequency of the topic of the rich and the poor (cf. R. N. Whybray, 1990: 60–63; R. C. van Leeuwen, 1992), but the sociological picture remains vague.

A balanced analysis of the proverbial sayings, because it is more synchronic than diachronic, is the study of the description of men and women (Men-schenbild) by J. Hausmann (1995). It is limited to Prov 10–31, and it embraces descriptions of the various groups (e.g., lazy/diligent) and the concrete situa-tions of the wise and their ideals. Although Hausmann acknowledges that the wisdom sayings are in the first instance directed toward males, she deems them capable of referring to women in most cases; it is the "openness" of the proverbs that makes this possible (p. 348). The adaptability of the sayings comes from their loose and often unattainable original setting, the original "proverb performance" that gave rise to the saying. Their very ambiguity and mystery is the source of their charm. What may seem merely to be a neutral observation, "telling it the way it is," is influenced by the educational and value-laden context in which it occurs (see also my remarks on **pp. 20–21** above). Hausmann recognizes that the description of the various types of the "wise" is ideal, but it is also realistic; wisdom knows its limitations. Training and discipline form the wise; the fools, *qua* fools, because of their perverse refusal to listen, cannot be changed, even though they were not born foolish.

The emphasis on language and the right word has as its corollary the relationship of people, one to another, and also the ethical implications of this fact. Hausmann does not fail to call "life" the goal of human existence, as far as Prov 10–31 is concerned (see my remarks above on **pp. 28–29** and **104**). It is here that she finds a close relationship between wisdom and virtue as the sapiential ideals of living (pp. 344–46, 358). In effect, proper conduct itself is the goal; with this come all the gifts of life: joy, satisfaction, well-being, and so forth. The ethical implications of the wisdom literature have yet to be properly explored. The material that is dealt with is the stuff that comes to be codified, especially in the decalogue and law codes.

The issue of ethics in the Old Testament is a difficult one, as the recent volume of essays in Semeia, edited by D. Knight (1994), amply illustrates. There is little agreement on the methodological questions that arise when one attempts to shape ethical policy on the basis of the Hebrew Bible. Is the wisdom literature considered in these essays? Only tangentially, since the various law codes, and also historical narratives describing events pregnant with moral considerations, form the bulk of the material. J. Barton makes a very important point when he writes that "in Proverbs, ethical reflections originally based on observation and 'natural' reasoning appear, in the final form of the text, as essentially divine revelation about the will of God" (p. 16). B. Birch emphasizes that the law codes are not static and authoritative; rather, they function to form community and identity. He agrees with Barton that the wisdom sayings are akin to the natural law, but this is not seen as part of "revealed morality" (p. 32). E. Davies suggests tentatively that a natural law type of ethic in the Bible may lead to a reconsideration of biblical ethics as "exclusively revelational" (p. 49). Obviously several issues concerning the Bible — its inspiration and authority, and the manner of utilizing it — are the important presuppositions in this discussion. Perhaps the issue of revelation is uppermost, and we will return to it later for a consideration of the way wisdom and theology are to be understood (thus commenting on **pp. 111–13** above).

For the moment I would offer three observations. First, the exhortations and sayings, and also other materials in the wisdom literature, form the basic material that comes to be codified in the laws, with the exception of the cultic codes. They are not to be separated out of the biblical legacy simply because they are not delivered by a prophet or a Moses. The decalogue is mostly a reflection of conclusions that derive from a familial and societal base of agreement. Second, the great part of wisdom "teachings" is presented in a persuasive and experiential manner; they are not apodictic in form, but they are not any the less authoritative. They are presented in terms of life and death. Third, as a rule they aim at the formation of character — what kind of person is one to be? This kind of goal transcends the casuistry that is too often associated with ethics. The mixture of command and observation in the wisdom literature, along with wide-ranging topics, is truly remarkable. It is not surprising that Ecclesiasticus (or Sirach) became early on a kind of vade mecum or moral guide for the early Christians. This is one explanation given for the name "Ecclesiasticus" — it became a "church" book.

A more delicate as well as more accurate way of referring to the moral standards of wisdom is reflected in the title of a book by H. Delkurt, *Ethische Einsichten in der alttestamentlichen Spruchweisheit* (Ethical insights in the proverbial wisdom of the Old Testament [1933]). He limits himself to the sayings in Prov 10:1–22:16 and chaps. 25–29, and he chooses to analyze parents and children, man and woman, the diligent and lazy, and the rich and poor, thus covering a wide area. He wisely claims the teachings as "insights," for that is what they are. They are insights for the modern reader, even if in Israelite society they enjoyed the authority of the family and the sage. His last quotation (p. 161, n. 67) is from a recent commentator on the Book of Proverbs, A. Meinhold (1991: 1:39), and it deserves to be recorded here:

> What is characteristic of *yhwh* faith in the book of Proverbs is expressed in the indissolubility of the two aspects of piety — the one towards *yhwh* and the other at the same time towards one's human companions . . . , as this also forms the basis of the Decalogue with its two "tablets" . . . , and this was to be expected from the beginning and ever afterward. . . . Faith, knowledge and action, in the every day world of ancient Israel, are to form a truly self-evident unity.

By far the most perceptive study of biblical wisdom is the work of William P. Brown (1996). While his study is broader than Proverbs (even including the epistle of James), his focus deserves attention here. He concentrates on the formation of moral character, a fundamental issue in ethical discourse, and the proper focus of biblical wisdom. It is not a matter of drawing up particular texts as if they were probative of something. Rather, "the appeal of positing character formation as the central framework and goal of biblical wisdom lies in the literature's focus on the developing self in relation to the perceived world" (p. 4). Ethics generally projects a picture of moral dos and don'ts, but for Brown moral rules "cannot operate independently of the formation of character in traditions transmitted and shaped by the community" (p. 14). The attractiveness of Brown's study is that he succeeds in capturing the development of moral character within the three traditional wisdom books. He analyzes the various personalities — parents, Wisdom herself, Job, Elihu, and even the Lord — for the values and virtues they embody in the narratives in which they appear. He is also concerned with the interrelationship between the individual and the community, and the way in which the self relates to the world and to God (p. 21).

The climax of the development within the three books comes with the eventual return of a changed and renewed self (p. 154). The "silent son" of Proverbs is united with the marvelous woman of Prov 31:10–31, a family but also a community context. Perhaps the greatest metamorphosis is in the Book of Job. Job returns, after the severe trials that also include a loss of family, to gain a new family and also true friends who come to console him. He is a different person, thanks to the experiences and especially the vision he has received. Brown's translation of 42:6 deserves notice here: "I hereby reject [my life], and am comforted concerning dust and ashes" (p. 108). The "return" of Qoheleth is not as spectacular as that of Job. It is manifested by a resigned attitude toward a life marked by toil, vexation, and death — by "vanity." He has no answers, but his well-known recommendations (seven times) to enjoy what God "gives" mark a turn. "Qoheleth's call is to relish each and every moment in gratitude, however sparse they may be. These redemptive moments cannot be had or made. . . . They are rather extended serendipitously, as 'providential chances'" (p. 157). Brown's work has set the path for a more trustworthy and profitable analysis of biblical ethics.

References

Albertz, R.
1994   A History of Israelite Religion in the Old Testament Period (OTLA; Louisville: Westminster/John Knox, 1994; 2 vols.).

Boström, L.
1990   The God of the Sages: The Portrayal of God in the Book of Proverbs (CB; Almquist & Wiksell).

Brown W. P.
1996   Character in Crisis: A Fresh Approach to the Wisdom Literature of the Old Testament (Grand Rapids: Eerdmans).

Clifford, R.
1995   The Book of Proverbs and Our Search for Wisdom (Père Marquette Lecture in Theology; Milwaukee: Marquette University Press).

Davies, G. I.
1995   "Were There Schools in Ancient Israel?" in Wisdom in Ancient Israel (Emerton Festschrift; ed. J. Day et al.; Cambridge: Cambridge University Press). Pp. 199–211.

Day, J.
1995   "Foreign Semitic Influence on the Wisdom of Israel and Its Appropriation in the Book of Proverbs," in Wisdom in Ancient Israel. Pp. 55–70. (See Davies entry above.)

Delkurt, H.
1933 *Ethische Einsichten in der alttestamentlichen Spruchweisheit* (Biblisch-theologische Studien 21; Neukirchen-Vluyn: Neukirchen).

Hausmann, J.
1995 *Studien zum Menschenbild der älteren Weisheit (Spr 10ff.).* (Tübingen: Mohr [Siebeck]).

Knight, D. (ed.)
1994 *Ethics and Politics in the Hebrew Bible* (Semeia 66; Atlanta: Scholars Press).

Levin, C.
1993 "The Prayer of the Righteous," *ZTK* 90:355–81.

Meinhold, A.
1991 *Die Sprüche* (2 vols; ZB, AT16; Zürich: Theologischer Verlag).

Newsom, C.
1989 "Woman and the Discourse of Patriarchal Wisdom: A Study of Proverbs 1–9," in *Gender and Difference in Ancient Israel* (ed. P. L. Day; Minneapolis: Fortress). Pp. 142–60.

Perry, T. A.
1993 *Wisdom Literature and the Structure of Proverbs* (University Park, PA: Pennsylvania State University Press).

Scoralick, R.
1995 *Einzelspruch und Sammlung. Komposition im Buch der Sprichwörter Kapitel 10–15* (BZAW 232; Berlin: de Gruyter).

Shupak, N.
1993 *Where Can Wisdom Be Found?* (OBO 130; Fribourg: University Press).

Snell, D.
1993 *Twice-Told Proverbs and the Composition of the Book of Proverbs* (Winona Lake, IN: Eisenbrauns).

Van Leeuwen, R. C.
1992 "Wealth and Poverty: System and Contradiction in Proverbs," *HS* 33:25–36.

Weeks, S.
1994 *Early Israelite Wisdom* (Oxford: Clarendon).

Westermann, C.
1995 *Roots of Wisdom* (Louisville: Westminster/John Knox).

Whybray, R. N.
1990 *Wealth and Poverty in the Book of Proverbs* (JSOTSup 99: Sheffield: JSOT).
1995 *The Composition of the Book of Proverbs* (JSOTSup 168; Sheffield: JSOT).

1995   *The Book of Proverbs: A Survey of Modern Study* (HBIS 1; Leiden: Brill).

CHAPTER THREE:
JOB THE STEADFAST

In the chapter on Job every effort was made to be "fair" to the many sides, even contradictions, to be found in this puzzling book.

Perhaps there is a strong tendency to make sense of the book as it stands, and to allow disparate views to be present without cancelling each other out (see **pp. 44–45** above). More recent studies live comfortably with the tensions and instabilities within the Job story. They provide a practical lesson in hermeneutics. Modern hermeneutical theory has made everyone aware of the inevitable role of presuppositions in biblical interpretation. The history of exegesis has illustrated this from the patristic period through to modern times. In the case of the Book of Job one can point to two recent studies, one by Susan Schreiner (1994) and the other by Oliver Leamann (1995).

Representative characters, from Philo to Aquinas to Buber, have matched the Book of Job against their understanding of God and the world, and especially their personal philosophy and experience. Perhaps this has never been better exemplified than by the challenging book of Jack Miles, entitled simply *God* (1995). The fact that many of his assumptions are clearly stated is an aid for us in examining our own prejudgments. His work follows rigorously the sequence of the books that Jewish tradition finally settled on as the Hebrew Scriptures. He attempts to mediate "knowledge of God as a literary character" (p. 4), and more than once he speaks of this as a "biography." Indeed, he speaks of two "key premises": first, presentation of an "interpersonal appraisal" of the Lord on the basis of biblical data, and second, that the order of books in the Hebrew "canon" is "a crucial artistic considera-tion" (p. 15). But of course many other premises or presuppositions appear in his treatment of Job. Thus, he plays off Elohim (= God; *eloah* or *el shaddai* in various places) in the dialogue against *yhwh* (the sacred name, rendered Lord in English Bibles), the positive God against the destructive God. This doubtful distinction is imposed on the Job narrative to heighten the wager with the Satan who is "legitimately" called the devil (p. 308). Instead of the Lord dominating the scene, it is the Satan who manipulates the divinity. Miles does not entertain the thought that the Satan is an agent of the Lord who looks out for the divine interests, who seems to be skeptical of human faithfulness and is anxious to prove his point. Neither does he take up a key question: What if the Lord had refused the challenge of Satan? Would this not be interpreted as a sign of uncertainty, of weakness, of fear that perhaps the Satan was right? Much effort is expended (pp. 425–30) on the translation and meaning of the difficult 42:6 (cf. C. Newsom, 1993a: 111–12). Whatever be the solution to this problem, one may readily grant with Miles that it does not describe Job repenting for his "sin(s)." His translation, "I shudder with sorrow for mortal clay," is a brave effort to make sense of the verse, and it is probably in the right direction. But it still does not justify the kind of psychoanalysis of God that Miles finds here: God discovers an inner ambiguity and recognizes a fiendish side. As I see it, Miles fails to exploit the distinction between the figure of God and the designs of the Job-poet (although he makes this distinction) in the narrative. It is not the Satan who manipulates *yhwh*, but the poet who draws together conflicting aspects of God in order to make his points.

Although D. Clines has not completed his commentary on Job, he has published a sophisticated deconstruction of the book (1995) that may be an augur of the second volume. The deconstruction is less clear in presuppositions than in the implications he finds in the text. As he reads Job (and there is a great emphasis on "reader-response"), it implies a very literate body of readers, who also enjoy the leisure appropriate to the class of the rich. He obtains these "implications" by reading across the grain of the text, describing the attitude toward the poor, the easy acceptance of wealth (when was acceptance ever hard?) — in short, a patriarchal society. Some of his inferences are arguments from silence; Job did not *say* something, but those moments of silence are pregnant with Clines's implications. This approach is questionable; one cannot expect the Job author to have pronounced on all social questions. More serious is an assumption derived from F. Jameson that texts exist because they aim to "repress social conflict." In the case of Job there is an effort to ease the conscience of the rich and to console the oppressed. The focus on Job is a focus upon an extreme case, and by this strategy the author supposedly diverts attention from a more basic question, the relationship between piety and prosperity. That is difficult to concede to Clines; the problem of retribution (the role of prosperity, suffering, sinfulness, and justice) is central to the book. Clines is an advocate of "reader-response," which leaves great creativity to the interpretation of a reader. Perhaps that makes it easier for others to disagree with his views.

Not unlike the deconstruction of Job by Clines is a "reading of Job" by E. M. Good. He describes the book as an "open" text that is to be played with (1990: 177–88). This mutual play between text and reader leads to many surprising views, as "reader-response" inevitably does. Good's final word is this: "There is no single correct understanding of the Book of Job" (p. 178). This may very well be true in the sense that the book is multifaceted and readers will emphasize one aspect more than another; the meaning of "correct" is doubtless an ambiguity here.

The interpretation of Job by Gustavo Gutiérrez has already been noted (**p. 45** above), but I mention it again because it is the best example of "reader-response" that I know of. The basic presupposition of his approach is indicated frequently in his work and is already contained in the subtitle to his book, "God-talk and the Suffering of the Innocent." His presupposition is clearly stated: "How are human beings to speak of God in the midst of poverty and suffering? This is the question the Book of Job raises for us" (1987: 12). I do not think that Job grows into an awareness of his solidarity with the poor, as Gutiérrez claims, nor can the last part of the book be classified as "the language of contemplation" (pp. 53–92). But one can see here an interpretation that rises genuinely from the Latin American experience, for and from readers who are poor and oppressed.

The later commentary of W. Vogels deals with a similar question, "How to speak of God in time of suffering" (1995: 26–27, 249). This is the question posed by the book, not the problem of suffering, for which there is no explanation. Vogels pays particular attention to the language in the Book of Job: that of popular faith, of silence, of doubt, of prayer, and even of mysticism (Job "sees" God). He interprets the book holistically or synchronically, building his interpretation around the idea of the type of language being used. This language, he argues, is in remarkable correspondence to the five steps that E. Kübler-Ross detected in the reactions of patients afflicted with terminal illness.

In a dense article (1993) B. Green argues forcefully for a holistic reading, keeping together the framework (prologue and epilogue) in tune with the rest of the work. She finds five key issues raised in the prologue that call for some kind of resolution in the dialogue that is played out: (1) who is God (of what sort)? (2) who is Job (wonderful yet wondrous)? (3) the relationship between God and Job (fluctuating); (4) the issue of good and evil, the beneficent and maleficent (is Job better off for it all?); (5) how does the book test the reader?

We raised the question on **p. 45** above whether it was really possible to understand the Book of Job. C. Newsom has described the work in terms of the well-known Gestalt drawing: is it a duck or a rabbit, a goblet or profiles facing each other (1993b: 137)? She proposes two readings, one of which hinges on the mysterious chapter 28 about the place of Wisdom. After the frantic and hectic back-and-forth between Job and his friends, where are we? The serene tone of chap. 28 reverts to Job's resignation in the prose tale of chaps. 1–2. In 28:28 there is the reassuring advice that the fear of the Lord is wisdom (and certainly *not* the inconclusive speeches of the friends and Job), and one is thus reminded of the description of Job's virtue (1:1, seconded by the Lord in 1:8). Newsom would consider this a "neo-traditionalist" reading that yields moral coherence to the story. It is supported by 42:7, where the Lord points out that Job has spoken rightly (referring to Job's acquiescence in chaps. 1–2?). From another point of view, however, one must seek the meaning of the speeches of the Lord. Although *yhwh* invites Job to speak (38:3), no opportunity is given to him to make a true reply; 40:2–5 is ambiguous, to say the least, and only gives time for the Lord to draw a breath. Even Job's final "reply" in 42:2–6 consists chiefly in quoting the authoritative words of the Lord. There can be no doubt that he yields to God in 42:5, whatever be the meaning of the enigmatic words of 42:6. Newsom closes on a note of puzzlement that deserves to be heard. In 42:7–8 does not God "endorse what God has just rebuked" (p. 136), namely the views of the three friends? And why does the Lord go back to the old line of retributive justice by the twofold restoration of Job? What is the result? The authoritative stance of the prologue is not affirmed, nor the critical position issuing from the dialogue; "now the decisive place is paradoxically in the gaps and the margins and the breaks in meaning. This discourse is truly plurivocal" (p. 136).

The study of K. Dell (1991) argues that the book should be classified as "sceptical literature," rather than as wisdom literature. The scepticism is indicated by a "misuse of forms," a kind of parody and irony that is to be seen by the juxtaposition of contradictory sections. Thus 7:7–8 is a parody of Ps 8:4; or 10:2–13 is a misuse of the kind of form found in Ps 139 (p. 139). This manner of argument is rather delicate. It depends greatly on one's definition of "sceptical," and on the way in which one construes the speeches and their meaning. From the point of view of traditional form criticism, I find the Book of Job *sui generis*, simply unique. It borrows certain established forms such as the lament, as many authors have claimed, but it cannot be classified as a lament. I have entitled chapter 4 above (**p. 49**) as "Qoheleth the Sceptic?" Even with the question mark, this may not be appropriate; sceptical literature is not a genre.

Subdivisions of the Book

The treatment in chap. 3 above (**pp. 33–46**) separated out the commonly accepted "parts" of the Book of Job. Whether or not we date one part differently from another or even eliminate a part as not "belonging" to the alleged "original" (these, too, are presuppositions) is not our concern here. Rather, we wish to review some of the several studies that treat these parts in some depth, and thus contribute to a broader understanding of the book.

The first two chapters seem so straightforward that many simply accept them as a given, and go on from there to interpret the book. In his 1989 Word commentary D. Clines points out that "the simple and repetitive structure of the prologue may be termed one of its falsely naive features" (p. 6). Indeed, it is a subtle description of a dialogue in heaven and on earth. One may instance the (only apparently) naive conversation between the Lord and the Satan (1:7) that sets up the question about Job. The question (v 9) is not lacking in guile; it goes beyond personalities and brings up the highly theological issue of the connection between piety and prosperity and eventually sin and suffering. The description of the calamities that ensue (1:13–19) is exceedingly repetitive and formal, almost formulaic. The "false naiveté" of the narrative continues down to the silence of seven days and seven nights on the part of the friends. Are they really condoling with him, or mourning for a dead person? At any rate, it is Job who breaks the silence with his violent outbreak in chap. 3.

A treatment of the dialogue (chaps. 3–31) between Job and the friends inevitably calls for taking a position about chaps. 25–27, where the difficulties in the flow of the dialogue (e.g., the absence of Zophar) occur. The solutions have led to redrawing the sequence of verses, and the result remains too hypothetical and complicated to attempt to summarize here. Instead we may note an unusual development affecting the dialogue. Scholars who have devoted studies to the Elihu narrative (chaps. 32–37), and have judged them to be later additions to the book, have also made changes in the dialogue at various places. This trend is noticeable in the latest monographs about Elihu (Mende, 1990, cf. CBQ 54 [1992] 55–56; H.-M. Wahl, 1993). Both Wahl and Mende regard Elihu as a later addition, and they advance serious reasons (Wahl, 1993: 204–7), but their approach also involves modifications of the dialogue in chaps. 3–31. This development is all the more noteworthy in view of recent authors (e.g., J. Janzen, N. Habel, E. M. Good) who consider Elihu an integral part of the book, or at least associate these chapters in a holistic way with the dialogue. A very complete summary of the fortunes of Elihu at the hands of commentators is presented in the historical survey of Wahl (1993: 1–35, 189–207).

God has not lacked for defenders in the discussion of this book. After his 1985 commentary, N. Habel wrote an article entitled "In Defense of God the Sage" (1992: 21–38, with a bibliography of previous studies on p. 232). He plays "God the Sage" off against the various other characterizations of God in the book. What does it mean to characterize God as sage? He has wisdom, exercises it, and also achieves the success that it assures. The first act is to "acquire" wisdom (Prov 8:22), and God works with wisdom in the construction of the universe (Prov 3:19). But the God who intervenes arbitrarily in the treatment of Job in chaps. 1–2 calls into question the characterization of God the sage. The three friends attempt to defend God by *their* notion of a just world, portraying God as a God who simply reacts. The description of God by Job is quite simple: he is God the Warrior, who hounds Job and indeed all of humanity in totally unjust ways. Then, in Job 28, God discovers wisdom, just as a sage does — by looking, by observation. In 28:23–27 God sees the ends of the earth and everything under heaven. This is a portrayal of God as the "First Sage," but as very remote. Thus far, then, God appears to be arbitrary in intervention, rigid in morality, violent in dealing with creatures, and inaccessible. So God must put forth an apologia — God speaking about God in chaps. 38–41. But God speaks more about creatures, and especially about the *design* in creation. "The speeches of God are the defense of a sage to a community of critics who would be wise in the ways of God. God offers a defense by challenging Job, and any who would listen, to discern God as a sage who designed a world of rhythms and paradoxes, of balanced opposites and controlled extremes, of mysterious order and ever-changing patterns, of freedom and limits, of life and death" (p. 38). The whirlwind is not a consolation for Job; it is a challenge.

Other general studies (apart from commentaries, of course) relate to the Book of Job in its entirety. Three of these underscore the influence of the thought world of Israel's neighbors, the myths of Canaan, Mesopotamia, and Egypt. The most general work is the study by D. Sitzler (1995) of the "reproach" of God as a religious motif in Mesopotamia and Egypt. She analyzes the well-known texts from both areas (adding to the Egyptian works the Coffin Text 1130 and "the Words of Heliopolis"). Most interesting are her conclusions: (1) there is no assumption in the Mesopotamian and Egyptian texts that the sufferer or complainer is a just person; rather, the sufferer serves as a type of loyalty to the god; (2) it is not to be presumed that the complaint represents a personal experience of crisis; (3) in fact, complaint incorporates an acknowledgment *(Bekenntnis)* of the god, so that loyalty (of both the sufferer and god) is the issue. This study is a warning to us not to impose the Joban mentality on these documents, or to import them into the Joban situation.

The second study (G. Fuchs, 1993) points out the way elements of ancient Near Eastern myths are picked up and reinterpreted in the Book of Job (with the exception of the chapter on wisdom, chap. 28, and the intervention of Elihu). This investigation does not deal merely with the obvious references such as Leviathan in 3:8 or *Yam* and *Tannin* (Sea, Monster) in 7:12. It succeeds also in showing how the *Chaoskampf* (the battle with chaos) motif pervades many other passages that may not seem obviously to link up with mythic ideas. It is helpful to set down here the more or less explicit references: 1:3; 7:12; 9:13; 15:7–8, 15; 18:13; 26:11–13. But there are other passages where mythic ideas seem to lie just under the surface: e.g., 5:2–7; 8:8–19; 11:20; 18:21 (n.b. 18:15); 20:1–29. A battle in heaven seems to be the background for chaps. 22–27; cf. 22:12; 24:13–17; 15:2–6. And there are several motifs (the *Urmensch*, or primeval human, and lost paradise) in chaps. 29–31. In the Lord's speeches the motifs appear in the descriptions of the heavens and the animals, and especially of the mythical powers, Behemoth and Leviathan. There is no universal agreement on a definition of myth, but one cannot read Job with full understanding without sensing the "mythical" background, as is well illustrated by the 1965 commentary of M. Pope.

Leo Perdue (1991) has investigated the "metaphorical theology" in Job, with particular attention to the mythic themes or paradigms: the battle with chaos, the revolt against the gods. He draws especially on the Enuma Elish and Atrahasis narratives from Mesopotamia and the Baal cycle from Ugarit. Unlike Fuchs, he treats chaps. 28 and 32–37 at the end of his book, although he considers them insertions. He begins by emphasizing wisdom theology as being a cosmology and anthropology that draws its metaphors from the ancient myths. Then he pursues a broad description of these ideas according to the sequence of the chapters in the book. This is another way of reading Job, bringing us closer to the worldview of the author.

References

Clines, D.
1989   *Job 1–20* (WBC 17; Dallas: Word).
1995   "Deconstructing the Book of Job," *BRev* 11/2: 30–35, 43–44.

Dell, K.
1991   *The Book of Job as Sceptical Literature* (BZAW 197; Berlin: de Gruyter).

Fuchs, G.
1993   *Mythos und Hiobdichtung* (Stuttgart: Kohlhammer).

Good, E. M.
1990   *In Turns of Tempest* (Stanford, CA: Stanford University Press).

Green, B.
1993   "Recasting a Classic: A Reconsideration of Meaning in the Book of Job," *NBl* 74/870: 213–22.

Gutiérrez, G.
1987   *On Job* (Maryknoll, NY: Orbis).

Habel, N.
1992   "In Defense of God the Sage," in *The Voice from the Whirlwind* (ed. L. Perdue and W. C. Gilpin; Nashville: Abingdon). Pp. 21–38.

Leamann, O.
1995   *Evil and Suffering in Jewish Philosophy* (Cambridge: Cambridge University Press).

Mende, T.
1990   *Durch Leiden zur Vollendung* (TTS 49; Trier: Paulinus).

Miles, J.
1995   *God* (New York: Knopf).

Newsom, C.
1993a   "Considering Job," *CSBS* 1: 89–120.
1993b   "Cultural Politics and the Reading of Job," *BibInt* 1/2: 119–38.

Perdue, L. G.
1991   *Wisdom in Revolt: Metaphorical Theology in the Book of Job* (BLS 29; Sheffield: Almond).

Schreiner, S.
1994   *Where Shall Wisdom Be Found?* (Chicago: University of Chicago Press).

Sitzler, D.
1995   *Vorwurf gegen Gott* (SOR 32; Wiesbaden: Harrassowitz).

Vogels, W.
1995   *Job, l'homme qui a bien parlé de Dieu* (Lire la Bible 104; Paris: du Cerf).

Wahl, H.-M.
1993   *Der gerechte Schöpfer* (BZAW 207; Berlin: de Gruyter).

CHAPTER FOUR:
QOHELETH THE SKEPTIC?

Pp. 49–52. Introductory data. The nagging questions about the date and name of Qoheleth, the problems of style, and especially the structure of the book still remain. The most difficult and important of these issues is that of structure; considerable attention has been given to it in recent commentaries and monographs. My commentary (1992: xxxii–xli) surveys many views and elects to follow the suggestion of A. G. Wright (1990: 489–95), who had pointed to the significant repetition of certain key phrases (*hebel*, or "vanity"; the alternation of find/not find and know/not know). A. Bonora (1992: 16) also adopts the occurrence of "vanity" as a divider. There is no consensus for the overall structure of Qoheleth. T. A. Perry (1993) presents a radical departure from the usual patterns. He divides the text between P (the optimistic Presenter) and K (the pessimistic Koheleth). The dialogue between these two covers nineteen sections, but in detail the encounter can be between one verse and another. V. D'Alario (1992: 19–58) gives a summary of recent views, and she adopts a rhetorical approach, guided by repetitions and refrains (pp. 183–234). But in general it can be said that no conclusion about structure dominates the field. There is agreement only on the epilogue (12:9–14) and on the introductory verses (1:1–2).

However, there is a growing tendency to emphasize the central importance of the first three chapters. This unity was recognized as long ago as C. Siegfried's 1898 commentary, and it has been widely accepted in recent studies: D. Michel (1989: 1–83), J. Vilchez Lindez (1994: 147), F. J. Backhaus (1993: 87, 143), A. Fischer (1991; 1:3–3:15 is a "ring" composition), L. Schwien-

horst-Schönberger (1994), and O. Kaiser (1995a: 84–85). There are differences of opinion as to the precise ending, 3:15 or 3:22, depending on the way
the material is interpreted. But these chapters are seen to be a sort of key to
the rest of the work (so Michel; for Kaiser, they are a presupposition for the
following chapters). One may very well grant the unity of these chapters, but
it is not easy to see their central importance. For one thing, chap. 3 is far
more important than the "king fiction" in chap. 2, and together they are not
in clear synchronism with the following deliberations.

Structure is not easily separated from form-critical considerations. The
most significant recent study on forms in Qoheleth has been done by C. Klein
(1994), and it fills out the sparse remarks in Murphy (1992: xxx–xxxii). Klein
follows the definition of *māšāl* (customarily translated as "proverb" or "saying") of T. Polk: one may not be able to say what it means, but one must
see what it does. This serves better than the theoretical definition of a
comparative speech or a saying that convinces (Klein, 1994: 37). Klein then
analyzes twelve "artistic" sayings (e.g., 2:14a), twenty-nine proverbial sayings
(e.g., 11:7), twenty-five "better"-sayings, and thirty-two rhetorical questions
(pp. 158–59). He arrives at the unusual conclusion (p. 167) that Qoheleth
himself is a *māšāl* for the reader because he is not satisfied with traditional
wisdom and instead forges a new understanding of himself and of reality.

Structure, form, and meaning go together, and it is also difficult to pin
down the meaning of Qoheleth's work. On **pp. 52–59** above (see also Murphy,
1992: lvi–lxix) I have tried to present his thought adequately by commenting
on the themes that are continually repeated in the book. This has the advantage of illustrating the range and complexities of his thought. At the same
time, it is difficult to fasten upon any one or more themes as *the* message of
Qoheleth. This difficulty is due not merely to his "contradictions" but also
to the fact that he ultimately does not furnish a scale of values. On the one
hand, he affirms time after time the vanity or futility of human life (see **pp.
52–53** above). On the other hand, he affirms zest for life, and he makes several
recommendations to "eat and drink" (notice that these are gifts of God).
This latter emphasis persuades some interpreters to find here the "true"
Qoheleth. I continue to regard the seven statements about enjoying life (*carpe
diem* style) as merely concessions to any who would find life otherwise un-
bearable. They do not penetrate the mysterious inscrutability of God, whose
"gifts" remain arbitrary. Qoheleth accepted all the tensions that he found in
life; they were inevitable but bearable, and also inexplicable.

Qoheleth's thought is too complex to yield a "theology" that could be
called his own. He was not a "theologian," but he shared in many of the ideas
in the Israelite tradition. Thus he could say that God made everything
beautiful or appropriate in its time (3:11), affirming the creation doctrine.
M. Schubert (1989) can state that creation theology is without question the
theological basis of Qoheleth (p. 125), but at the same time it is in conflict

with the vanity he sees in the world (p. 189). There is a tension between knowledge and belief. Schubert has located one source of the problematic that Qoheleth is concerned with. He calls this a crisis that Qoheleth was not able to reconcile: the contradiction between his creation theology and the sapiential knowledge that the world was impenetrable. The human beings who were given rule over creation, according to Genesis, found that the world was incomprehensible and God was distant (p. 192). R. N. Whybray (1989: 81–82) writes of "Qoheleth as theologian" that he was trying to prepare his students for a new and different world of religious thought, but he was also seeking truth for himself. Although his work contains many apparent contradictions, it is "perhaps the most fascinating book in the Old Testament." O. Kaiser (1995a: 92–93) admits that Qoheleth is "the messenger of the futility of all human action," but his invitations to enjoy life "are the real conclusion which Qoheleth draws from his cryptic reflections, and this is why the advice in xi 9–xii 7, to enjoy one's youth, provides such a fitting ending to his teaching." In another article (1995c) Kaiser analyzes the two views expressed in the epilogue (12:9–14), which he judges to be contradictory. For him the "summa" of Qoheleth's teaching would be *carpe diem* (cf. 9:7–10). On the one hand, Qoheleth says: remember death. On the other, he also claims: forget your mortality. These two views supposedly complement each other; life is short, but the only possible joy is not to be neglected (p. 69). The emphasis on joy is also shared by N. Lohfink (1990) in a (problematical) translation. He understands 5:19[20] to mean that God reveals himself by the joy of the heart. Grammatically this is possible, although I do not think it is the obvious sense of the passage (Murphy, 1992: 53, 56). This brings up the problem of translation. One would think that grammar might answer all the problems, but much depends upon the construal of a book, upon the translator's understanding of the total message of the author.

In my article "On Translating Ecclesiastes" (1991) I underlined the fact that the difficulties in translating Ecclesiastes were not caused by textual problems but rather by our ignorance of the meaning of certain words and phrases, and by ambiguities. At times the text (not to mention the mind) of Qoheleth is quite obscure. This is particularly true of the famous passage on women that is generally deemed to be an example of misogynism (7:25–29) and typical of Hellenistic culture. The heart of the passage is 7:28, concerning one man in a thousand and no woman. This has been widely taken to indicate Qoheleth's dour outlook on the integrity of women (and he has not much to say here in favor of men). It is remarkable that several recent studies now adopt a translation that would reverse this understanding, so that one should read (cf. Murphy, 1992: 74–78): "what my soul has always sought without finding (is this): One man in a thousand I have found, but a woman among all of these I have not found." Thus Qoheleth is denying that the saying about women in v 28 is true. So he does not disparage women — a view that has been attributed to him in virtue of the customary translation (cf. NRSV) and by commentators. This understanding (represented by only a minority among previous scholars) is adopted by Backhaus (1993: 239–41) and Schwienhorst-Schönberger (1994: 175–80). A. Schoors (1993: 121–40) likewise absolves Qoheleth from misogynism in 7:26–29; Bonora (1992: 123–27) is uncertain about v 28, but concludes that Qoheleth cannot be accused of misogynism.

  Pages 57–58; cf. also **121–22**). It has become a commonplace to speak of the "crisis" of Qoheleth (as well as the author of Job). This crisis is located for many scholars (e.g., H. Preuss) in the failure of the religion of traditional wisdom. This religion was governed by faith in an *Urhebergott*, a God of origins or creator God, whose mechanical order of retribution, according to which good is a reward for a good act and evil is the punishment for an evil act, broke down, plunging Qoheleth into a crisis. Not only are there many assumptions behind this scenario, but one must surely ask if this view is not too simplistic (cf. Murphy, 1992: 140–43, and see my further remarks below in this Supplement concerning Chapter 8, "Wisdom Literature and Theology"). Had the subtlety of sages left them without any response to the troublesome questions of everyday life? Did they wait centuries until these two books came along to correct this alleged view? This understanding of "crisis" has not disappeared, and it is represented by the study of A. Lange (1991). In Lange's view, Qoheleth, seeking a way out of his perilous situation, embraced the "wisdom nomism" (identification of Torah and wisdom) proposed by Sirach, only to finally reject it (no matter that Sirach is to be dated at least a hundred years *after* Qoheleth!). In desperation, Qoheleth considered folly, in the form of enjoyment of life, as an alternative, even though this meant breaking the Law (pp. 174–78). The term "crisis" has certainly been overworked here! One must instead affirm that Qoheleth was a sage. He certainly questioned the wisdom tradition, and he succeeded in purifying it by his extreme "sic et non" style. Perhaps he was more skilled in his methodology and questioning than he was in arriving at results, but he never ceased pursuing what was best in the wisdom enterprise: where is wisdom to be found? Even if he confessed to failure (7:23–24), this was due to his high regard for wisdom. In contrast to the frenetic judgment on crisis, K. Dell (1994) takes a more relaxed approach by looking at the reception that was soon given to the work of Qoheleth. In view of the traditional "Solomonic authorship," and also the views expressed in the epilogue, the authority of the book was affirmed by the time of canonization, when it was accepted as wisdom even though it challenged traditional teaching. This is indicated by the harmonization of the book with the Torah — evident in the tone of the epilogue that reflects the attitude of Ben Sira, as pointed out by G. Sheppard back in 1980 (see **p. 55** at **n. 19** above). It is important to recall here that Qoheleth and Ben Sira are separated perhaps by only a few generations.

SUPPLEMENT

References

Backhaus, F. J.
1993   *"Denn Zeit und Zufall trifft sie alle." Studien zur Komposition und Gottesbild im Buch Qohelet* (BBB 83; Frankfurt: Hein).

Bonora, A.
1992   *Il Libro di Qoèlet* (Rome: Citta Nuova).

D'Alario, V.
1992   *Il Libro del Qohelet* (RivBibSup 27; Bologna: Dehoniane).

Dell, K.
1994   "Ecclesiastes as Wisdom: Consulting Early Interpreters," VT 44: 301–29.

Fischer, A.
1991   "Beobachtungen zur Komposition von Kohelet 1,2–3,15," ZAW 103: 72–86.

Kaiser, O.
1995a   "Qoheleth," in *Wisdom in Ancient Israel* (Emerton Festschrift; ed. J. Day et al.; Cambridge: Cambridge University Press). Pp. 83–93.
1995b   "Beiträge zur Kohelet-Forschung," *ThRu* 60: 1–31.
1995c   "Die Botschaft des Buches Kohelet," *ETL* 76: 48–70.

Klein, C.
1994   *Kohelet und die Weisheit Israels* (BWANT 12; Stuttgart: Kohlhammer).

Lange, A.
1991   *Weisheit und Torheit bei Kohelet und in seiner Umwelt* (Frankfurt: P. Lang).

Lohfink, N.
1990   "Qoheleth 5:17–19 — Revelation by Joy," *CBQ* 52: 625–35.

Michel, D.
1989   *Untersuchungen zur Eigenart des Buches Qohelet* (BZAW 183; Berlin: de Gruyter).

Murphy, R. E.
1991   "On Translating Ecclesiastes," *CBQ* 53: 571–79.
1992   *Ecclesiastes* (WBC 19a; Dallas: Word).

Perry, T. A.
1993   *Dialogues with Kohelet* (University Park, PA: Pennsylvania State University Press).

Schoors, A.
1993   "Bitterder dan de Dood is de Vrouw (Koh 7,26)," *Bij* 54: 121–40.

Schubert, M.
1989   *Schöpfungstheologie bei Kohelet* (Frankfurt: P. Lang).

213

Schwienhorst-Schönberger, L.
1994 *"Nicht im Menschen Gründet das Glück" (Koh 2,24)* (HBS 2; Freiburg: Herder).
Vilchez Lindez, J.
1994 *Eclesiastés o Qohélet* (Navarra: Verbo Divino).
Whybray, R. N.
1989 *Ecclesiastes* (OTG; Sheffield: JSOT).
Wright, A. G.
1990 "Ecclesiastes (Qoheleth)," in *NJBC* (ed. R. E. Brown, et al.; Englewood Cliffs: Prentice Hall). Pp. 489–95.

CHAPTER FIVE:
BEN SIRA — WISDOM'S TRADITIONALIST

Pp. 88–89. Text. The description of the textual situation of this book remains about the same. We have recovered about two-thirds of the Hebrew, and, together with Ziegler's 1965 critical edition of the Greek texts, we have the basis for modern translations and also for correct chapter and verse references. If one compares the NRSV version of Sirach with the old RSV, one can appreciate the progress that has been made. The discovery of the psalms scroll from Cave 11 at Qumran has shown that 51:13–30 was originally an acrostic poem, but the recovered Hebrew text in vv 13–20a is difficult to interpret.

In general, Ben Sira's work has not attracted many recent commentaries. The reason lies principally in the difficulties involved in establishing a critical text on which to base a study or comment. There has been no scholarly commentary since 1987, when P. Skehan and A. Di Lella (see **p. 79, n. 2** above) combined to produce one, and it remains the best so far.

Recent studies have yielded a mixed bag. The scholarly study of H. V. Kieweler (1992) rightly takes issue with the rather extreme position of Th. Middendorp (1973), who gave too much weight to hellenistic influence. As a child of his time, Ben Sira was surely aware of hellenistic style and literature, but he remained a loyal follower of the Oniads and Judaism. His grandson had it right when he wrote in the prologue to his Greek translation of Sirach: "my grandfather Jesus [Ben Sira] . . . had devoted himself especially to the reading of the Law and the Prophets and the other books of our ancestors, and had acquired considerable proficiency in them" (NRSV). Moreover, there are many indications of his Jewishness in the text: the primacy of the Torah; the frequent reference to fear of the Lord, and the catalogue of Israelite heroes in chaps. 44–50. The survey of Greek authors and hellenistic writers by

Kieweler (pp. 69–262) provides the average reader with a solid introduction to these works. An essay by J. Snaith calls Ecclesiasticus "a tract for the times," suggesting that Sirach showed a positive attitude toward hellenistic culture: "to show pious Jews how to live with Greek culture positively, not rejecting it altogether" (1995: 172). But it is not easy to situate Ben Sira within Hellenism, because Hellenism still remains a rather malleable quantity. One can easily judge from Sirach's tirade against the nations in 36:1–22 that he feels deeply the grinding heel of political domination. Moreover, it is fair to say that his work is so traditional that it constitutes a call to fidelity to any and all who might be tempted by Greek ideas. Did he himself absorb some of these ideas?

In his study of Sirach's theology of suffering and justice, L. Schrader claims that Ben Sira was marked by the *Lebensgefühl* ("the sense of life") that characterized the Hellenism of his day (1994: 303–4), and hence he placed no special value on strict observance of the Torah. This does not seem to do justice to Sirach's identification of Wisdom with Torah (Sir 24:23; cf. 19:20), and it fails to reckon with variations in Torah observance. It is true that Sirach approaches the traditions of the Law from the point of view of wisdom (see **pp. 76–77** above), but this seems like an inner-Jewish development and does not owe anything substantial to Hellenism. Schrader's interpretation of death according to Sirach, especially in Sir 41, is challenging but doubtful (pp. 233–301). He sees a new view emerging from the Greek culture: death is preferable to a troubled life (41:2). He admits that this view is not foreign to Eccl 6:1–6; 7:1, and he rightly claims that it is contrary to the usual biblical view. I do not think that this is a development that can be ascribed to a hellenistic "fear of death." The power of Sir 41:1–13 (and also perhaps 40:1–10) comes from the contrasting meanings that death can hold for the fortunate and the unfortunate. It is not easy to see why the immortality of the name or reputation (41:11–13) should be considered as due to Greek or even Egyptian influence. It certainly did not solve the problem of human transience and mortality, and it is quite contrary to Eccl 9:10. No more than any others did Sirach unravel the mystery of suffering. But he strove mightily to defend the justice of God in dealing with an individual person. The remedies come up very short: postponement of reckoning to the end of life (e.g., Sir 1:13) or the supposed immortality of the name. Suffering is explained in traditional biblical style: as a punishment for sin or as testing (p. 305). Schrader points to several passages that betray a deep sense of the understanding of suffering (e.g., 7:11, 17; 8:7; 11:4), but death remained the great leveller. The astonishing fact is that his general tolerance of death and adversity could coexist with the very different feelings of an "almost" contemporary, Qoheleth. A more balanced view on death in Ben Sira is given by F. Reiterer (1990), who succeeds in developing the several attitudes that the author had about this formidable adversary of humanity.

We owe to O. Wischmeyer (1995) an intensive study of the "culture" of the Book of Sirach. Despite the difficulty in defining this elusive concept, the areas covered in the study fit the common notion of "culture" and fill in a gap in the study of the background to the book. Thus one is introduced to contemporary notions of family, society, politics, and law. Even though in many cases Sirach's own interests lay elsewhere (rather, say, than in politics), it is helpful to understand the realities of his day. In addition, Wischmeyer studies both the material and the higher culture (literature, education). As might be expected from his sympathetic evaluation of various trades (38:24–39:11), Sirach reflects the background of a higher class that had the opportunity for such studies as he pursued. But education for Ben Sira was not of a public kind permeating various classes of society. Rather, Ben Sira belonged to a "private" wisdom school that was *sui generis* (p. 176); it was an elite class that followed him (p. 181). They learned orally rather than by script, and the time-honored ideal of "listening" was foremost. The *cultura animi* of the Greco-Latin world was not neglected in Sirach. Indeed, the formation of character had always been a concern of Israelite wisdom. The author sums up the spiritual direction of Sirach: "the depths of the soul were filled out from a religious, intellectual/erotic and esthetic point of view: with the love of God through wisdom and with the love of Wisdom herself" (p. 247). The union of religion and culture is seen particularly in Sirach's view of the Temple and liturgy (apparently he was not a priest). But there are even deeper evidences of the tie in Sirach's emphasis upon prayer, the Law, fear of God, Wisdom herself — and even history (the "patrology" in Sir 44:16–50:21). We have referred above to the personification of Wisdom (**pp. 133–49**). Wischmeyer agrees with J. Marböck that Woman Wisdom is a "poetic personification," and she emphasizes the elevated linguistic expression of this achievement (p. 285).

On **p. 73** above I provided an "informal table of contents" as a way into the somewhat formless mass of material in Sirach. Wischmeyer gives a helpful outline (pp. 151–53) of themes in chaps. 1–43, based upon reflective and parenetical units and mixed forms and inserts. On p. 187 she presents a theological outline of the book, consisting of creation, humanity (cf. 18:8), history, and wisdom — four fundamentals of Sirach's theology.

It has long been known that Sirach 24 and the Book of Enoch reflect a descent of Wisdom into this world. A more intimate contact between Sirach and apocalyptic literature is a relatively new field, and it is explored by R. A. Argall (1995). He considers the author of 1 Enoch to be contemporary with Ben Sira (cf. p. 7, n. 15), and he investigates three major themes — revelation, creation, and judgment — along with literary features that both share. Ben Sira refers to Enoch in 49:14 and perhaps 44:16 (uncertain evidence). As for the works, there are certain similarities. Enoch brings a revealed Wisdom from heaven (1:1–3; 82:1–2), and Wisdom comes down from heaven in Sirach

24. Despite the similarities that Argall is able to point out (e.g., a tree of wisdom, the important connection between wisdom and life, etc.), he thinks that the two traditions were actually opposed to each other (pp. 98, 250). A study such as this prompts one to read Ecclesiasticus differently, in a much more open manner.

References

Argall, R. A.
1995   *1 Enoch and Sirach* (SBLEJL 8; Atlanta: Scholars Press).

Kieweler, H. V.
1992   *Ben Sira zwischen Judentum und Hellenismus* (BEATAJ 30; Frankfurt: P. Lang).

Reiterer, F.
1990   "Deutung und Wertung des Todes durch Ben Sira," in *Die alttestamentliche Botschaft als Wegweisung* (H. Reinelt Festschrift; ed. J. Zmijewski; Stuttgart: Katholisches Bibelwerk). Pp. 203–36.

Schrader, L.
1994   *Leiden und Gerechtigkeit. Studien zu Theologie und Textgeschichte des Sirachbuches* (BET 27; Frankfurt: P. Lang).

Snaith, J.
1995   "Ecclesiasticus: A Tract for the Times," in *Wisdom in Ancient Israel* (Emerton Festschrift; ed. J. Day et al.; Cambridge: Cambridge University Press). Pp. 170–81.

Wischmeyer, O.
1995   *Die Kultur des Buches Jesus Sirach* (BZNW 77; Berlin: de Gruyter).

CHAPTER SIX:
THE WISDOM OF SOLOMON — A VIEW
FROM THE DIASPORA

Pp. 86–89. Contents. The analysis of the Wisdom of Solomon has been furthered since 1990. Five commentaries have appeared. A. G. Wright completed his study, spanning several decades, with the compact comment in the *NJBC* (1990). It is trimmed down to essentials, yet it gets to the depths of this book. J. Ramon Busto Saiz (1992) published a lengthier commentary in a popular vein. He regards the phrase "justice is immortal" (cf. Wis 1:15), which he uses as his title, as the thesis of the entire book, especially the first part. His view of chaps. 10–19 is more venturesome; he regards these chapters as written either by the author at an advanced age when he had lost his creative ability, or by one of his students who wanted to effect a closure (pp. 9–10). Busto Saiz further regards chaps. 10–19 as displaying the work of wisdom in history, especially in the midrashic interpretation of the Exodus events. The most formidable Spanish commentary is by J. Vilchez (1990). The Italian commentary by A. Sisti (1992) is largely a reflection of previous work. In the German DNEB series is the imposing work of A. Schmitt (1989). Although the text commented upon is the "Einheitsübersetzung," the ecumenical version, the author is not bound by it, and the comment is necessarily compact, but no less competent.

Readers of the Book of Wisdom are usually stirred by the doctrine of immortality developed in chaps. 1–6 and by Solomon's description of his relationship to Woman Wisdom in chaps. 7–9. There is no doubt that the main thesis of Wisdom 1–6 is immortality, the gift given to the just (cf. Wis 1:15). M. Kolarcik (1991) has investigated the meanings of death, which serves as a foil to (eternal) life in these chapters. The term is ambiguous. It designates the limitation of human existence, or mortality. This meaning is apparent in the way the wicked of chap. 2 use it as a motive for their *carpe diem* mentality (Wis 2:5–6). Physical death is also interpreted by the author as punishment for wickedness (Wis 1:12, 13, 16). Finally, there is the ultimate death that separates mortals definitively and forever from God. But this death does not deny physical mortality, as the prayer of Solomon in 7:1–10 makes clear. Mortal as he is, he looks forward to the gift of wisdom that will be with him and work with him so that he knows what pleases God (7:10). In 5:1–14, the wicked understand what ultimate death is; they are separated from the holy ones, with whom the just live forever, as members of God's family (5:5, 15). Kolarcik remarks with reference to 1:13 and 1:24: "The death that God did not make and the death which entered the cosmos through the devil's enmity does not refer to the human condition of mortality. Rather this antithesis to the divine refers to the ultimate death which separates humans from God" (p. 180)

The section dealing with history is elusive unless one knows the text of Genesis and Exodus fairly well. Chapter 10 portrays Wisdom as a savior from the days of Adam, through the patriarchal period, and down to the Exodus — a welcome role, surely, but without giving a proper name to the parties concerned. Instead, there is a constant reference to the "just" who were protected (Adam, Noah, etc.). There follows a detailed presentation of the Exodus plagues. Although it is clear that the author depends upon Exod 1–15, he exhibits a great deal of freedom in the treatment of his sources. Some events from the wandering in the desert are chosen, but nothing from the laws. The operating principle is a contrast between the plagues inflicted upon the Egyptians and the gifts bestowed upon the Israelites. This principle is further specified: the Israelites are benefited through the very things that punish the Egyptians (11:5, 16). Examples are provided from the Exodus narrative: e.g., Israel receives water from the rock, but the water of the Nile is turned into blood. These contrasts take liberty with the Exodus text. That is to say, they are a type of midrash, utilizing the biblical record to make points that are worthy of meditation. U. Schwenk-Bressler (1993) describes chaps. 10–19 as an example of how "early Judaism" explains a text. He points out the "tricks," as it were, that the author uses in his interpretation of the early history: the deliberate avoidance of proper names in chap. 10; mere allusions to the events in Exodus; the actualization of these events for the readers of the book (this reference to the current reader is always to be kept in mind). The Exodus text is referred to, but in words and in a view shaped by the author. The historical traditions have become didactic — a development to be seen also in Pss 105 and 106. For the wisdom movement this is a totally unexpected turn of events; the early history has been turned into a wisdom story; the events of salvation history are the work of Wisdom. The biblical text receives two layers of understanding: a superficial one for those who are not really acquainted with the early history, and a deeper one for those who know the events to which the author is referring. Schwenk-Bressler sees these later chapters as an "existential" interpretation, softening the murmuring of Israel, and expanding the witness against the impotence of other deities, and against hellenistic mysteries (Isis; p. 63). He prefers to leave open the question of midrash as the literary genre for chaps. 11–19 (p. 55).

Pierre Dumoulin's study (1994) focuses on one specific event in chaps. 11–19: the gift of manna in Wis 16:15–17:1a. The gift of the manna is seen to be a gift of life, the preservation of the lives of the Israelites. While water and fire in storm afflicted Egypt, the Israelites were kept alive by a food that resisted fire and moreover responded to the various tastes of humans (Wis 16:20–21: "the food of angels," revealing the divine "sweetness"; cf. Ps 34:9[8], "taste and see . . ."). This was a gift made possible by the power of the One who created the world, because "the universe fights on behalf of the just" (Wis 16:17; cf. 16:24). It was a gift that tested the obedience of the people (Exod 16:4; cf. Deut 8:2–3), while it also symbolized the Law, the "word that preserves those who believe in you" (Wis 16:16). Moreover, the peculiar characteristic of the manna, its melting at a sunbeam, becomes a reminder to pray early (Wis 16:27–28). Finally, the manna is "ambrosial food" (NRSV "heavenly food"). Behind this phrase lies the idea that ambrosia is the food of the gods, and whoever eats of it shares in their immortality (perhaps a subtle allusion to the immortality of the just affirmed in Wis 1–6?).

Page 94. Conclusion. Unfortunately the Book of Wisdom remains largely unread today. Yet its portrayal of the "righteous" person in chap. 2 seems to have become a pattern for the passion narrative of the Gospels (L. Ruppert,

1993: 1–54). It displays the greatest amount of Greek influence among the deuterocanonical books (H. Hubner, 1993: 56–81), yet it also remains faithfully Jewish. For example, we may look at the way immortality is conceived. If average Christians were asked today concerning immortality, they would probably reply that immortality means that although they will die, they will live forever. Is that immortality for the author of the Book of Wisdom — is immortality explained by means of time? According to the Book of Wisdom, immortality is to be explained in relational terms (not ontological, say, in terms of an undying soul). Wis 1:15 proclaims that righteousness is undying or immortal. The relationship that is forged with God in the here and now will go on, unless humans themselves destroy it. Thus immortality depends upon the One with whom one expects to be immortal.

References

Busto Saiz, J. Ramon
1992   *La justicia es inmortal* (Santander: Sal Terrae).

Dumoulin, P.
1994   *Entre la manne et Eucharistie. Etude de Sg 16,15–17,1a* (AnBib 132; Rome: Istituto Biblico).

Hübner, H.
1993   "Sapientia Salomonis und die antike Philosophie," in *Die Weisheit Salomos im Horizont biblischer Theologie* (ed. H. Hübner; Neukirchen-Vluyn: Neukirchen).

Kolarcik, M.
1991   *The Ambiguity of Death in the Book of Wisdom 1–6* (AnBib 127; Rome: Istituto Biblico).

Ruppert, L.
1993   "Gerechte und Frevler (Gottlose) in Sap 1,1–6,21," in *Die Weisheit Salomos im Horizont Biblischer Theologie* (ed. H. Hübner; Neukirchen-Vluyn: Neukirchener).

Schmitt, A.
1989   *Weisheit* (DNEB; Würzburg: Echter).

Schwenk-Bressler, U.
1993   *Sapientia Salomonis als ein Beispiel frühjüdischer Textauslegung* (BEATAJ 32; Frankfurt: Lang).

Sisti, A.
1992   *Il libro della Sapienza* (Assisi: Porziuncola).

Vilchez Lindez, Jose
1990   *Sabiduria* (Navarra: Verloo Divino).

Wright, A. G.
1990   "Wisdom," in *NJBC*. Pp. 510–22.

CHAPTER SEVEN:
WISDOM'S ECHOES

Pages 97–110. The uncertainty of the conclusions that have been proposed concerning wisdom influence on the rest of the Old Testament has been discussed above, especially **pp. 98–102.** Methodology remains the problem. As pointed out above, the discussion of this topic is beset with the danger of arguing in a circle. On the basis of the traditional wisdom books (vocabulary, forms, content, etc.), one proceeds to the judgment that other books reflecting at least some of these characteristics are to be considered as wisdom compositions. This is an oversimplification produced by abstract classification. Perhaps the question has not been framed correctly. The point is not the discovery of wisdom elements in other books. Rather, it is a question of recognizing that the wisdom tradition formed part of the general cultural mix of Israel. Hence it found expression, even unconsciously, in many works — but this does not mean that they are necessarily wisdom compositions. From this point of view, I think the choice of the word "echoes" is a happy one, even if it is indefinite.

The most frequent target of such studies in recent times has been the Psalter. S. Terrien (1993: 51–72) has summarized results and taken a strong position on a rather wide extent of wisdom influence. This is too sanguine. The fact remains that no list of psalms has achieved a consensus. Perhaps all would agree that Ps 37 deserves to be so classified. Reading this psalm, one gets the impression that any one of the verses could fit very well into the Book of Proverbs. The study of Ps 34 by A. Ceresko (1985) is a careful analysis of the wisdom style that easily wins our assent. But not much more can be said in view of the variety of opinions. One can only be surprised at the very frequent reference to wisdom in the latest, but unfinished, commentary on the Psalms by F. L. Hossfeld and E. Zenger (1993). The presence of wisdom passages in several psalms is more or less taken for granted. However, their approach to this question is more by way of content than by way of traditional literary traits. They detect very often the influence of the "piety of the poor" — "poor" is seen as a religious term. The main concern is to interpret the psalms according to their immediate context (the psalms that surround them). While Ps 37 is entitled "teaching about life (written by) a wise person for the poor," the real emphasis of the psalm lies in the personal piety. It is suggested that the psalm was integrated in Pss 35–41 by a postexilic "redaction of the poor" (so Zenger, the commentator, p. 231).

Several of the essays written in honor of J. A. Emerton deal with wisdom in various books, e.g., Amos, Hosea, Jeremiah. Among them, R. N. Whybray (1995: 152–60) considers the Psalter; he rejects the use of "wisdom psalms" as a blanket term but affirms that it "may be useful if it extends the corpus of wisdom literature by identifying those few psalms and parts of psalms which have marked affinities with the acknowledged wisdom books" (p. 160). H. G. M. Williamson (1995: 133–41) forges a subtle approach to the association of Isaiah and the wise. He recognizes that the conventional distinctions between wisdom and prophecy are inadequate for solving the problem. Instead, he proposes epistemology: Isaiah condemns Israel on the basis of wisdom standards of behavior (e.g., 1:2–3, 21–23; 3:13–15, etc.) without having recourse to Mosaic Torah. Moreover, his split with the advisers to the king (29:14) comes about on the issue of their reliance on Egyptian military force (31:1), and the reaction of the prophet is not unlike Prov 21:31.

I think that my treatment of the Song of Songs on **pp. 106–7** above is adequate and carefully nuanced. The issue in this case does not concern the basic form of the poetry. They are love poems. True, they have been collected, and the intention of the collector may have gone beyond the purpose of the original compositions, but this is a delicate judgment to make. Do love poems cease to be that simply because they come to be collected? The redactor/collector may have had other purposes, but we do not know them. The importance of Mesopotamian and especially Egyptian love poetry as background to the Song of Songs was not indicated in the Appendix. See now R. E. Murphy (1990: 41–57). M. V. Fox (1985) provides a translation of both Egyptian love poetry and the Song, and O. Keel (1994) gives a translation and comment that bring to bear the fruit of ancient Near Eastern iconography.

References

Ceresko, A.
1985   "The ABCs of Wisdom in Psalm XXXIV," VT 35: 99–104.

Fox, M. V.
1985   *The Song of Songs and the Ancient Egyptian Love Songs* (Madison: University of Wisconsin).

Hossfeld, F. L., and Zenger, E.
1993   *Die Psalmen I: Psalm 1–50* (DNEB; Würzburg: Echter).

Keel, O.
1994   *The Song of Songs* (Minneapolis: Fortress).

Murphy, R. E.
1990   *The Song of Songs* (Hermeneia; Minneapolis: Fortress).

Terrien, S.
1993   "Wisdom in the Psalter," in *In Search of Wisdom* (J. G. Gammie memorial volume; ed. L. G. Perdue et al.; Louisville: Westminster/John Knox). Pp. 51–72.

Whybray, R. N.
1995   "The Wisdom Psalms," in *Wisdom in Ancient Israel* (Emerton Fest-

schrift; ed. J. Day et al.; Cambridge: Cambridge University Press). Pp. 152–60.

Williamson, H. G. M.

1995   "Isaiah and the Wise," in *Wisdom in Ancient Israel*, pp. 133–41. See R. Whybray entry above.

CHAPTER EIGHT:
WISDOM LITERATURE AND THEOLOGY

Biblical scholars still have difficulty in recognizing a proper role for wisdom in their presentation of Old Testament theology. J. Scharbert has written a large work on Old Testament theology (1995), with ten conspicuous section titles in each of which the Lord's name, *yhwh*, appears, but the treatment of wisdom is meagre. The two volumes of R. Albertz (1994) are geared to the history of religion more than to strict theology. Wisdom plays only a small role and is understood mainly in the light of social classification: the upper class cultivated the "theologized wisdom" found in Prov 1–9 and in the views of Job's friends; the lower class (the "piety of the poor") is particularly manifest in the Psalms (vol. 2, 507–22). Earlier wisdom has ended up merging with Torah piety (vol. 2, pp. 556–63). Despite the fact that the late H. D. Preuss marginalized biblical wisdom entirely (revelation takes place only through history; 1991–92: vol. 1, p. 238), his study of Old Testament theology devotes more attention to wisdom than those of Scharbert or Albertz. Unfortunately it is practically all negative in tone. In a convivial "conversation" with Preuss, W. H. Schmidt (1992) has urged the recognition of wisdom literature within the Bible.

L. G. Perdue (1994) has studied the wisdom literature directly, sympathetically, and creatively. After summarizing the positions of several theologians, he proposes a theology of creation at the heart of wisdom (see my comments above on **pp. 118–21**). He urges the use of metaphorical imagination, rhetoric, and social location (family, court) in the interpretation of the wisdom books. He also sums up the key metaphors that are to be found, such as fertility, artistry, word, and battle. He emphasizes that creation and providence, or in other words cosmology and anthropology, cannot be marginalized: "Wisdom theology, with its emphasis on creation and providence, should be a valued resource, not only for reconstructing ancient Israelite and early Jewish faith, but also for contributing to the contemporary articulation of believing communities seeking to describe their faith in coherent and meaningful ways" (p. 342).

On **pp. 115–18** above I pointed out two views that cripple the correct evaluation of Old Testament wisdom: overemphasis on the role of order

as the "goal" of the sage, and also the concept of retribution when interpreted in a mechanical, ordered way, as in the deed/consequence theory of
K. Koch. A few observations may be added here. A typical example of
deed/consequence interpretation involves the well-known saying about falling into a pit that one has dug (for another), expressed in Prov 26:27 and
in many other places. This is not the wooden, dogmatic saying that some
make it out to be. The point is that the digger can be caught by surprise;
one can fall into the pit oneself! The deed/consequence theory has been
used to depreciate the thought of the sages, especially by German scholars
(e.g., H. D. Preuss). Perhaps a change in attitude is occurring, as can be
seen in the study of J. Hausmann (1995: 231–47, especially 243–47). She
accepts the *Tat-Ergehen Zusammenhang*, as it is called, but she also expresses some reservations; it is not "uniformly" present, for example, in
the Book of Proverbs. R. E. Clements (1995: 279) instances Prov 26:27 as
"the celebrated application by the wise of the laws of motion to the moral
realm." Presumably he means by this the boomerang effect of deed/con-
sequence. But he betrays uncertainty about its working: "it is usually left
unclear how this desirable state of affairs in the preservation of a just order
is to be brought about. Sometimes God is said to intervene directly . . . at
other times it is made to appear as though wickedness unleashes destructive
forces which inevitably bring retribution on the wrongdoer" (p. 279).
B. Janowski (1994: 247–71) has also expressed serious reservations as to the
understanding of the deed/consequence mentality.

In many studies there is reference to "natural law" and, somewhat inter-
changeably, to "natural theology" (see **pp. 123–24** above). In a recent study
James Barr (1993) points out, in vigorous confrontation with Barth and
Barthianism, that there *is* a natural theology operating in both Testaments,
and he offers many texts that illustrate its growth: e.g., Pss 19 and 104, and
of course the wisdom literature and Paul's Areopagus speech. He describes
this natural theology within the Bible as "not a foreign body intruded, but
an interpretative stage through which the revelatory material passes" (p. 131).
But his most interesting statement comes in the form of questions: "If one
believes that God has revealed himself in his creation and continues to do
so, why is that 'natural' theology and not 'revealed'? . . . If one believes that
God was revealing himself in ancient Israel, why is this not 'natural'? Perhaps
all theology is both 'natural' and 'revealed'" (p. 115). I agree with the thrust
of these questions. I would allow a technical, conceptual distinction between
natural theology and supernatural theology. What is proper to each can be
distinguished, as one might distinguish the Christ-event from the teaching
that Christ offers in many parables and sayings (that could be classified as
"natural revelation"). But in the concrete order of things this distinction is
merely theoretical. On **p. 124** above I wrote that "biblical wisdom is a thematic expression of God's revelation as mediated through creation. Humans

live in a de facto supernatural order." This claim is that of the late theologian Karl Rahner, and I think it is a necessary basis for a total understanding of Israelite wisdom.

At the outset of this section I remarked on the difficulty that wisdom has in gaining a recognized place within biblical theology. One reason has been the erroneous path that has led scholarship to postulate the theories of world order and deed/consequence that have just been discussed. When wisdom is seen as "bankrupt," who wants to recognize it? When it is also viewed in an exaggerated way as an offshoot of Egyptian wisdom, it finds difficulty in maintaining itself as genuinely biblical. I think that this reasoning is mistaken and inadequate. But a positive argument that wisdom belongs to Old Testament theology on an equal footing with anything else is not easy to compose. It was not without good reason that F.-J. Steiert (1990) entitled his study: *Die Weisheit Israels — ein Fremdkörper im Alten Testament?* (Israel's wisdom — a foreign body in the Old Testament?). He showed more than adequately that we are not simply dealing with Egyptian wisdom. This is Israelite wisdom (in Proverbs and elsewhere). But how is one to *prove* this? What kind of argument is proper to the subject matter? If one assumes a "doctrine" of Yahwism, one inevitably makes history the axis of thought, and the ultimate arbiter of what constitutes theology becomes the covenant, Torah, etc. Then wisdom seems to be off the beaten path. The use of the sacred name, *yhwh*, in the wisdom books is not probative per se. Perhaps a negative argument is possible: Israel's wisdom literature would have looked different without the revelation of God to the chosen people. But, of course, we do not know what Israel's wisdom literature without God's revelation would be like, and in addition this argument assumes some sort of "Yahwism" as a standard of judgment — a vicious circle.

Perhaps it is enough to say that the Israelites never had two heads, one for Torah and the "sacred" traditions, and another for the wisdom experience. Inevitably the one influences the other. There is only faith in *yhwh*. Inevitably history and experience meld together. Religious faith and daily encounter merge. The data of their historical legacy doubtless molded the Israelites as they confronted the world and tried to understand it. They did this without any explicit reference to "revealed" Mosaic law, but they also did not come to their experience as a *tabula rasa*. One may point to the identity of wisdom and Torah that characterizes the Book of Sirach, but this identification came at the end of a historical process. What went on in the previous centuries? When one compares Israel's wisdom with that of her neighbors (see the sources for foreign works listed in the Appendix, **pp. 151–79** above), I think Israel comes off as unique in her achievement. But I am not interested in raising apologetic arguments to make this point.

From a canonical point of view, one cannot act as if the five (three) wisdom books were not present in the canon of the Old Testament. True, these

"Writings" were among the last to be approved, as was also the Book of Psalms. But they did become "Scripture," and thereby part of Israel's legacy to the church. Perhaps an analogy with the Book of Psalms might help to see these books in a proper light. The psalms in general contain explicit references to the traditional sacred beliefs concerning law and covenant, etc. But many are reflections of raw experience, especially the laments. Were one to read some psalms with the customary prejudice that accompanies the study of wisdom, they could also stand "outside" of the assumed standard of "Yahwism." The use of the sacred name proves nothing on this score, as the existence of the so-called "Elohistic" psalter would indicate. Another factor needs to be kept in mind: the wisdom literature is basically postexilic. Only the major portion of Prov 10–31 is an exception to this. Does this not suggest that the tradents of wisdom did not make the distinction that modern scholarship has insisted upon so strongly between "orthodox" Yahwism and wisdom? One must recognize that standards different from our own were operative in the post-exilic period. There is no need to deny that the written Torah was well on its way to ascendancy within the Tanakh, but it remains true that the wisdom movement was not seen as a rival or deviant expression of faith.

References

Albertz, R.
1994 A History of Israelite Religion in the Old Testament Period, 2 vols. (OTL; Louisville: Westminster/John Knox).

Barr, J.
1993 Biblical Faith and Natural Theology (The Gifford Lectures for 1991; Oxford: Clarendon).

Clements, R. E.
1995 "Wisdom and Old Testament Theology," in Wisdom in Ancient Israel (Emerton Festschrift; ed. J. Day et al.; Cambridge: Cambridge University Press). Pp. 269–86.

Hausmann, J.
1995 Studien zum Menschenbild der älteren Weisheit (FAT 7; Tübingen: Mohr [Siebeck]).

Janowski, B.
1994 "Die Tat kehrt zum Täter zurück. Offene Fragen im Umkreis des 'Tun-Ergehen Zusammenhangs,'" ZTK 91: 247–71.

Perdue, L. G.
1994 Wisdom and Creation: The Theology of Wisdom Literature (Nashville: Abingdon).

Preuss, H. D.
1991–92 Theologie des Alten Testaments, 2 vols. (Stuttgart: Kohlhammer; English translation: Westminster/Knox).

Scharbert, J.
1995   *Theologie des Alten Testaments* (DNEB; Wurzburg: Echter).
Schmidt, W. H.
1992   " 'Wie kann der Mensch seinen Weg verstehen?' Weisheitliche Le-
        benserfahrung — ein Gespräch mit H. D. Preuss," in *Alttestament-
        licher Glaube und Biblische Theologie* (ed. J. Hausmann et al.; Stutt-
        gart: Kohlhammer).
Steiert, F.-J.
1990   *Die Weisheit Israels — ein Fremdkörper im Alten Testament? Eine
        Untersuchung zum Buch der Sprüche auf dem Hintergrund der ägyp-
        tischen Weisheitslehren* (Freiburg: Herder).

CHAPTER NINE:
LADY WISDOM

For reasons that may be apparent now (from the feminist view of personified wisdom), we might better speak of Woman Wisdom. The point of Chapter 9 was to put everything out on the table: to set out succinctly the pertinent biblical data on Wisdom in as objective a form as possible, and I think it succeeded in that goal. I also tried to differentiate between the various texts that were examined. Thus the Wisdom of Prov 8 differs from the Wisdom of Sir 24, despite some similarities. Sirach clearly identifies Wisdom with the Law, whereas the text concerning Wisdom in Proverbs leaves her identity open and is to be viewed in the light of the "strange woman," who serves as some kind of foil. I doubt whether one can draw a consistent portrait of Wisdom in her journey through these books. From a hermeneutical point of view, I indicated that the earlier levels of the identity of Wisdom (say, in Proverbs, as opposed to Sirach) retain their validity. They need not be lumped together, nor is the final stage in the development of Wisdom the only valid view. I have attempted (Murphy, 1994) to extract from these texts some conclusions about God, but rather unsuccessfully, I think. A 1995 essay deliberately set apart a theological discussion (Murphy, 1995: 233).

Much has been written about the background of the personification of Woman Wisdom (see **pp. 137–38** above), but uncertainty reigns. M. V. Fox (1995) has definitely shown that the parallel of Wisdom with Egyptian Ma'at will not stand, and neither will the association between the alleged world order in Israelite wisdom and Ma'at.

Judith Hadley (1995: 234–43) has reviewed various identifications of Wisdom with a goddess. She analyzes the data of Prov 8 and Job 28 to "examine whether or not this personification of Lady Wisdom refers to an actual person (divinity or hypostasis) or is merely a literary device" (p. 234). She seems to favor the latter theory, for she gives as her opinion that "the apparent apotheosis of Lady Wisdom in the biblical literature is not a legitimization of the worship of 'established' goddesses, but rather is a literary compensation for the eradication of these goddesses" (p. 236). Her dissertation on the cult of Asherah is announced as "forthcoming." The discoveries of the drawings and inscriptions at Kuntillet Ajrud and Khirbet el-Qom have caused much discussion over the last few decades, especially the interpretation of what seems to be a reference to *yhwh*'s Ashera. O. Keel and C. Uehlinger (1992: 237–82) take a firm stand that these discoveries have produced no compelling arguments against the thesis of a Yahwistic monotheism in this period (roughly 8th century), and that in fact they militate against the recognition of a *paredros* or consort for the Lord (p. 282).

Not unlike the "literary compensation" of J. Hadley is the hypothesis of J. Blenkinsopp (1995: 43–44; cf. also 1991: 457–73) that Woman Wisdom was created in reaction to the "strange woman": "A more promising line of inquiry, I believe, begins with the assumption that the Woman Wisdom of Proverbs 1–9 was conceived as a counter to the baleful influence of the Outsider Woman, who therefore is the primary symbolic persona in these chapters. The Outsider Woman represents alien cults, especially those with a strong sexual component" (1995: 43). Behind this symbol are the goddess cults, especially those of Asherah. There is, as we have indicated already, no reason to deny levels of meaning in these figures in Prov 1–9, but there is no real evidence to show the direction of the influence, how one affected the development of the other. Certainly the development of the figure of Wisdom in the latest books is dependent on the figure of Woman Wisdom, and not upon the "Outsider Woman." The figure of the woman who is a "stranger" is still much debated, but the study of C. Maier (1995) will prove to be basic to the solution of the problem. She analyzes all the pertinent texts, and situates this woman against the postexilic background in which she belongs.

References

Blenkinsopp, J.
1991   "The Social Context of the 'Outsider Woman' in Proverbs 1–9," *BibInt* 42: 457–73.
1995   *Sage, Priest, and Prophet* (Library of Ancient Israel; Louisville: Westminster/John Knox).

Fox, M. V.
1995   "World Order and Ma'at: A Crooked Parallel," *JANES* 23: 37–48.

Hadley, J.
1995   "Wisdom and the Goddess," in *Wisdom in Ancient Israel* (Emerton

Festschrift; ed. J. Day et al.; Cambridge: Cambridge University Press). Pp. 234–43.

Keel O., and C. Uehlinger
1992   *Göttinen, Götter und Gottessymbole* (QD 134; Freiburg: Herder). Pp. 237–82.

Maier, C.
1995   *Die "fremde Frau" in Proverbien 1–9* (OBO 144; Universitätsverlag Freiberg Schweiz).

Murphy, R. E.
1994   "Wisdom Literature and Biblical Theology," *BTB* 24: 4–7.
1995   "The Personification of Wisdom," in *Wisdom in Ancient Israel* (Emerton festschrift, ed. J. Day et al.; Cambridge: Cambridge University Press). Pp. 222–33.

INDEX

◆

INDEX

Fontaine, Carole R., 13 n. 6, 30 n. 3
Fox, Michael V., 51, 152, 163, 170, 177
n. 20
Freedman, D. N., 31 n. 32, 45–46, 48 n. 17
Frost, Robert, 45, 47 n. 16

Gese, H., 176
Gilbert, M., 95 nn. 8, 12, 179 n. 43, 185,
190
Gilgamesh, 155–56
Ginsberg, H. L., 159
God
    Qoheleth's view of, 58–59, 62 n. 23
    See also Fear of God/Lord; Mystery of
    God; *Urheberreligion*
Gordon, E. I., 154–55
Gorssen, L., 62 n. 23
Greek wisdom. *See* Hellenism

Hardedef, 163
Hebel. See vanity
Hellenism, 85, 95 n. 4, 171–75
Hengel, Martin, 125, 172–73
Hertzberg, H., 59
Historical methodology, 111
History of interpretation, 59–60
Home and origins of wisdom, 3–4
Hori, *Satirical Letter* of, 171
Hurwitz, A., 98
Huwiler, Elizabeth, 14 n. 21, 129 n. 30

Idolatry, 92
Imhotep, 163
Imitation of Christ, 60
Immortality, 86–88, 94, 155, 168
Instructions, 10, 160–61
Irony, 44, 63 n. 33
Isaiah and wisdom, 99–100
Isis, 147 n. 5, 162
I Will Praise the Lord of Wisdom, 156–57

Jacobsen, Thorkild, 92, 96 n. 16, 176 n. 6
Janzen, J. G., 46 n. 3
Jerome, 49, 60, 68
Job,
    and the arts, 47 n. 16
    depiction of God, 36–37, 42–45, 48 n. 17
    existence of the man, 35
    structure of, 34–35
    and the three friends, 37–40

and wisdom personified, 41, 134–35
and wisdom traits, 33–34

Kaiser, O., 173
Kayatz, Christa, 161–62, 177 n. 18
Kearns, C., 69
Keel, O., 177 n. 18
Khety, 165
Kierkegaard, Søren, 38–39, 47 n. 5
Knowledge, 11, 58–59, 70–71, 124–25
Koch, K., 116–17, 129 n. 21
Kuntz, J. K., 109 n. 20

Lady Wisdom, 27, 79, 133–49
    in Baruch, 140–41
    in the Book of Wisdom, 142–45
    identity of, 137–39
    in Prov 8, 135–39
    in Sir 24, 139–40
    where to be found, 134–35, 140–42
Lambert, W. G., 156, 158, 176
Lang, B., 19, 147 n. 5
Larcher, C., 95 nn. 2, 4, 10, 11; 96 n. 15
Law and wisdom, 79
Lemuel, words of, 26–27
Levenson, J. D., 130 n. 24
Lichtheim, Miriam, 24, 164–65, 167, 174,
177 n. 24, 178 n. 40
Life, ix, 28, 87, 104, 120
Lindenberger, J. M., 159
Lists, 153–54, 171
Literary forms (wisdom), 5–13
Loader, J. A., 178 n. 36
Lohfink, N., 61 n. 3, 129 n. 22, 173, 188
Loretz, O., 61 n. 3, 172, 189
Luyten, J., 103

Ma'at, 115–16, 161–62, 177 nn. 12 and 18
McCarthy, D. J., 128 n. 17, 130 n. 25
McCreesh, T., 27
Mack, Burton, 77, 149 n. 22
McKenzie, J. L., 97
MacKenzie, R. A. F., 47 n. 10
Marböck, J., 125
Māšāl, 7
    See also Proverb
Melanchthon, 28
Menander, 171
Merikare, 26, 164
Mesopotamia, 1, 153–59

Sinai revelation, 1, 123
Sirach, 45–51
  character of, 66–67
  compared with Book of Proverbs, 70–72
  date of, 45
  hymns in, 71–72
  opposites, doctrine of, 75
  table of contents, 73
  themes of retribution, sacred traditions
    and fear of the Lord, 74–79
  views on determinism and free will, 75
  wisdom and law, 139–40
Skehan, P., 25, 27, 30 n. 5, 148 n. 13
Skepticism, 52
Smalley, Beryl, 2–3
Solomon, 2–4, 15, 21–22, 49, 83, 106
  association with the "wisdom books," 1–3
  in the Greek "Wisdom of Solomon," 88–
    90
  Solomonic collections in Proverbs, 19–23
Song of Songs and wisdom, 106–7, 170
Songs of the Harper, 169–70
Speech, 22
Steck, Odil Hannes, 119–20
"Strange woman," 17–18, 135
Sumer. See Mesopotamia
Synkrisis (comparison), 85, 90

Tanakh, 79 n. 1
Taylor, Archer, 14
Tenach, 79 n. 1
Tensions, 11–12, 20, 29, 53
Theognis, 174
Theology. See Biblical theology; Wisdom
  theology
Thomas à Kempis, 60
Traditionalism (in Sirach), 70–71

Understanding of reality, 112–14, 128 n. 9
Urheberreligion, 58, 62 n. 24, 121, 163

Vanity (hebel), 53–54, 62 n. 14
Van Leeuwen, R., 22
Von Rad, Gerhard, ix
  on the Joseph story, 97
  on "order," 128 n. 16
  on the personification of wisdom, 138
  on reality, 112–15
  on the relationship of Yahwism and
    wisdom, 122
  on the sages' view of reality, 112–14
  on "theological wisdom," 19, 30 n. 13

Way (of life), 17, 30 n. 6
Weinfeld, Moshe, 104, 108 n. 6
Westermann, C., 13 n. 4, 22, 31 n. 20, 122
White, J. B., 170
Whitley, C. F., 172
Whybray, R. N., 97–98, 102, 163
Wife, 27, 106
Williams, J. G., 20–21, 30 n. 14
Williams, R. J., 176 n. 10
Winston, D., 95 n. 2, 189
Wisdom
  and court, 4
  influence within rest of Bible, 97–110
  profile of, 145–56
  See also Lady Wisdom; Personification
Wisdom literature
  as a classification, 1, 151
  the five books, 1
  origins of, 4
Wisdom theology, 118–20
Wright, Addison, 52, 85, 144
Wright, G. E., 121

Yahwism and wisdom, 122–26

Zimmerli, W., 56, 118, 122, 131 n. 38, 188